APR 3 0 1997

Prairie Night

*Black-Footed Ferrets and the Recovery
of Endangered Species*

Brian Miller, Richard P. Reading, and Steve Forrest

Foreword by Mark R. Stanley Price

SMITHSONIAN INSTITUTION PRESS
Washington and London

COPY EDITOR: Ann Goodsell
PRODUCTION EDITOR: Deborah L. Sanders
DESIGNER: Janice Wheeler

Page iv: Excerpt from "Do Not Go Gentle into That Good Night," by Dylan Thomas, is reprinted from *The Poems of Dylan Thomas*, copyright 1952 by Dylan Thomas, by permission of New Directions Publishing Corp.

Page 81: Quotation from "The Cautionary Tale of the Black-Footed Ferret," by R. M. May, in *Nature* 320:13–14, 6 March 1986.

Page 150: Quotation from *The Lost Notebooks of Loren Eiseley* (Boston: Little, Brown & Co., 1987).

Page 163: Quotation as published in *Jackson Hole News* (Wyoming), 22 September 1993.

Library of Congress Cataloging-in-Publication Data

Miller, Brian, 1948–
    Prairie night : black-footed ferrets and the recovery of endangered species /
    Brian Miller, Richard P. Reading, and Steve Forrest.
    p.   cm.
    Includes bibliographical references (p.   ) and index.
    ISBN 1-56098-603-4 (alk. paper)
    1. Black-footed ferret—Wyoming.   2. Wildlife conservation—Wyoming.
3. Endangered species—Wyoming.   I. Reading, Richard P.
II. Forrest, Steve, 1954–   .   III. Title.
QL737.C25M554   1996
599.74'447—dc20   96-26594

British Library Cataloguing-in-Publication Data available

Manufactured in the United States of America
03 02 01 00 99 98 97 96   5 4 3 2 1

⊗ The paper used in this publication meets the minimum requirements of the American National Standard for Permanence of Paper for Printed Library Materials Z39.48-1984.

For permission to reproduce illustrations appearing in this book, please correspond directly with the owners of the works, as listed in the individual captions. The Smithsonian Institution Press does not retain reproduction rights for these illustrations individually or maintain a file of addresses for photo sources.

Cover photo by Dean Biggins

♺ Printed on recycled paper

To our parents

Do not go gentle into that good night.
Rage, rage against the dying of the light.

From "Do Not Go Gentle into That Good Night," by Dylan Thomas

CONTENTS

FOREWORD

This is a most important book, and it should be read by anyone interested in the conservation issues and interventions of the late twentieth century.

The three authors have been deeply involved in the long-running saga of the black-footed ferret, and they have succeeded in writing a book that is both popular and scientific. While the accounts of the ferret's biology read like a novel, the chapters on the recovery effort, which form the bulk of the book, are highly analytical and resemble a thriller. There is also a good measure of gentle and occasionally self-deprecating humor.

This approach does full justice to the black-footed ferret, which, until captive-propagation efforts began in 1985–86, hung on only as a small population in the wild, subject to chance extinction events. Pressures on the species were many, and largely human in origin: exotic disease and land-use policies and practices have directly caused huge reductions in the numbers and range of the ferret's sole food source, the various species of prairie dog.

As the recovery effort illustrates, human fallibility and foibles often guide what individuals and institutions do. Even so, this book is not a polemic. The authors identify individuals and provide a detailed chronology in order to make the case, but their analysis of what it takes to allow endangered species to recover is objective and impersonal. There are lessons at every level. Individuals involved in endangered-species recovery must learn to be flexible problem-solvers and collaborative team workers, and to see their own work in a broader social, economic, and political context.

The black-footed ferret case also argues for the involvement of diverse types of organization, each with particular roles and skills to contribute. Federal and state authorities have statutory obligations toward endangered species in the United

States, but university and technical groups are also needed to provide independent scientific research. Private or nongovernment organizations can help by putting the recovery in a broader conservation context and by acting as advocates.

The fate of the black-footed ferret is bound up with the larger issue of conservation of the grasslands of the western United States. Prairie dogs—the ferret's sole prey—are keystone species in this once-extensive but now much-modified ecosystem. This book is able to demonstrate the paradox of using federal money to restore the ferret while at the same time ranchers are encouraged to eliminate the prairie dog through poisoning. The authors' integrated solution shows how the productivity and wildlife of the prairies can be restored through a revised approach to conservation and human activities in this habitat. The ferret's timely story shows how species and their habitat, as parts of ecosystems, cannot be approached separately in functional conservation, a point relevant to the debate on the reauthorization of the Endangered Species Act.

The black-footed ferret saga takes place in the United States, with the world's most complex institutional and legal basis for conservation. Does the ferret experience offer help for developing countries, in which many reintroductions are now being planned or carried out? Many such countries do not even have legislation defining an endangered species. The International Union for the Conservation of Nature has promulgated guidelines for use when a reintroduction is proposed. Every aspect of the guidelines was addressed in the black-footed ferret recovery effort, and yet the multiplicity of competing interests complicated the relatively simple biological objective. Perhaps the lessons for developing countries are clear: identify the parties who are legitimately involved, build them into a team with a single purpose, and get on with the job. But it is likely that, even when the biological aspects of species recovery are relatively straightforward, complex institutional and political components are as real and as complex all over the world. Any reintroduction will almost certainly fail if adequate thought is not given to them during design and implementation.

This book is a treasure trove of lessons. Above all, it indicates why conservation—including its practitioners—needs to examine itself; why the continuing case of the black-footed ferret already demonstrates the absolute necessity for conservation theory to be combined with the appropriate institutions, policies, and human behavior if we are to reverse the world's accelerating loss of biological diversity as we approach a new millennium. That is why this book is important.

Mark R. Stanley Price

Director of African Operations, African Wildlife Foundation, Nairobi, Kenya
Chair of the Reintroduction Specialist Group, International Union for the Conservation of Nature

PREFACE

"Evolution," in the words of the physicist Joseph Ford, "is chaos with feedback." In a similar vein, without feedback the processes of science too would be permanently mired in primordial ooze. It is in this light that we have written our book, not only to review the status of the black-footed ferret, *Mustela nigripes,* but also to weave the various threads of our knowledge of the ferret into the fabric of future recovery for the species. We hope that by braiding our experiences and perceptions into a conceptual framework, we will not only facilitate ferret recovery but also give others struggling to save imperiled species and ecosystems a leg up when facing similar challenges.

We have taken what we hope is the broadest possible approach to assessing the past and future directions of black-footed ferret conservation; thus the book is intended to be semiscientific and semipopular. The acquisition of knowledge never ceases, but the book necessarily represents events and observations specific to the time of writing (all but Chapter 13 and the epilogue was completed by October 1994).

Scientists have known since the early 1950s that the black-footed ferret was in serious trouble. Between then and the present, the species was twice feared extinct. Only two small colonies have been studied in the wild, with a handful of survivors rescued from the last population. Over the past ten years, we have seen that handful increase to several hundred captive individuals, which are now being reintroduced into natural habitat. Over the years, much has been learned about the black-footed ferret, but very little of that knowledge was translated into timely conservation action. Arguably, there is still too little appreciation of this secretive mammal or understanding of the human processes that led to its near-demise. By these measures alone, the ferret recovery program has not evolved into a highly developed organism.

The normal working environment for any biologist focused on endangered species is charged with emotion, but the hair's-breadth escapes that characterize black-footed ferret recovery efforts sometimes raise the level of intensity to almost pure adrenaline. For much of the recovery program's life, policies and documents about ferret conservation have been relegated to the twilight world of "gray literature" such as press releases or agency reports, and they often reflect strained efforts on the part of the powers-that-be to put a positive light on historical events. Although platitudes have probably reassured the public, to some degree, and also lulled agency representatives into a false sense of security, they are not likely to provide the kind of critical assessment needed to improve and advance the program. Nor is it likely, because of the constraints of agency review processes, that the agencies themselves will perform the kind of critical self-assessment that is so important for the evolution of more efficient and effective programs. Thus the reason for this book.

The first half of this book is a more traditional discussion of the biology and ecology of black-footed ferrets. We have devoted the entire second half to examining those factors critical to ferret recovery efforts, including values, organizational structures, policies, laws, and technical aspects of conservation biology. In the critical light of these latter chapters, the ferret recovery effort does not always present a pretty face, but we feel that a careful look in the mirror of reality is necessary if we are to see this marvelous creature flourish again.

Part I of this book discusses the basis for ferret endangerment. An understanding of the evolutionary and historical events that led to the current endangered status of the black-footed ferret is essential to restoring the processes and ecosystems on which ferrets depend. This necessarily means that the reader must gain some appreciation for the predicament of the prairie dog, a nearly obligate associate of the black-footed ferret.

In Part II, we discuss the biology and ecology of black-footed ferrets. Much of this information was gleaned from our personal observations of black-footed ferrets in the wild and in captivity. The biological material presented in Part II provides the basis for assumptions driving our conservation recommendations in Part III.

In Part III, we discuss black-footed ferret conservation. Biologists and conservationists are increasingly aware that the biological problems of species endangerment and extinction are rooted in social and political processes. A meaningful approach to understanding ferret conservation thus requires an interdisciplinary approach. So not only do we discuss some of the biological, ecological, and technical considerations of reintroduction, particularly those that have proven problematic or controversial in the black-footed ferret program but, more importantly, we investigate policy, organizational, educational, and legal dimensions of recovery, as well as avenues for conservation of the prairie dog. We believe that all of these dimensions are critical to successful implementation of a recovery program. As we hope to make clear in this section, our view of successful conservation is not limited to narrow definitions over short time frames.

Our independent status and day-to-day participation offer an important perspective on the project. Black-footed ferrets may have been located in Wyoming, but taxpayers from Hawaii to Maine are paying for efforts to conserve them. As such, the public has a right to an independent account of the biology and conservation of this fascinating endangered mammal. Although our perspective has its own bias, as all interpretations do, our independent status frees us to reach our own conclusions without the restraint of bureaucratic entanglements or agency review processes.

Although the following pages draw primarily on our own experiences and interpretations, many people and organizations have been instrumental in the black-footed ferret recovery program. Indeed, the achievements of the ferret recovery program are a direct result of the effort and commitment of these individuals and groups, and they deserve special recognition. Funding for our various research projects came from the Audubon Society, the Centro de Ecologia of the Universidad Nacional Autónoma de México, the Charles A. Lindberg Fund, Chevron USA, the Chicago Zoological Society, the Conservation and Research Center of the National Zoological Park, Defenders of Wildlife, Friends of the National Zoological Park, Humane Society of the United States, the Izaak Walton League, Louden Area Ferret Fanciers, the Montana Department of Fish, Wildlife, and Parks, the National Fish and Wildlife Foundation, the National Geographic Society, the National Wildlife Federation, the National Zoological Park, The Nature Conservancy, the New York Zoological Society, the Northern Rockies Conservation Cooperative, Sigma Xi, the Smithsonian Institution, the University of Wyoming Cooperative Research Unit, the U.S. Agency for International Development, the U.S. Army, the U.S. Bureau of Land Management, the U.S. Fish and Wildlife Service National Ecology Research Center, U.S. Fish and Wildlife Service Region 6, the U.S. National Academy of Sciences, Wildlife Conservation International, Wildlife Preservation Trust International, the World Society for the Protection of Animals, World Wildlife Fund–U.S., Wyoming Game and Fish Department, and Yale University.

We extend special thanks to Stan Anderson, Jon Ballou, Dean Biggins, Tom Campbell, John Carlson, Denise Casey, Denny Christopherson, Tim Clark, Ron Crete, Mike DonCarlos, Arnold Dood, Kathy Fagerstone, Louise Forrest (some of whose ferret work is published under the name L. Richardson), Jerry Godby,

John Grensten, Bill Haglan, Denny Hammer, Lou Hanebury, Harry Harju, Dan Hinckley, Pat Hnilicka, Brent Houston, Don Kwiatkowski, Bob Luce, Randy Matchett, Rodney Mead, Ron Naten, Ray Paunovich, Max Schroeder, Ulie Seal, Larry Shanks, Steve Torbit, Astrid Vargas, David Wildt, and Beth Williams for their work on black-footed ferrets and their discussions about conservation of the species. Ben Beck, Joel Berger, Harold Bergman, Cibele Carvalho, Gerardo Ceballos, Courtney Conway, Scott Derrickson, Jack Frazier, Marty Fujita, Hank Harlow, Mike Hutchins, Jerome Jackson, Steve Kellert, Devra Kleiman, Fritz Knopf, Jim Krause, Rurik List, Steve and Sharon Leathery, George Menkens, Steve Minta, Steve Monfort, Lyndsay Phillips, Noel Snyder, Joan Trent, John Wargo, Chris Wemmer, and Lynwood Williamson discussed issues of reintroduction and conservation in general.

Many friends at the Conservation and Research Center of the National Zoological Park, the University of Wyoming, the U.S. Army Pueblo Depot, and the U.S. Fish and Wildlife Service aided our behavioral work associated with captive breeding and reintroduction. In particular, Junior Allison, Barbara Atwood, Dennis Biller, Angela Brummond, Stuart Burke, Maxie Cameron, Larry Collins, Art Cooper, Gary Holder, Kati Hoover, Lowane Johnson, Sharon Leathery, Mary McComas, Joe Montoya, Becky Russell, Laura Walker, and Jerry Williams contributed to physical facilities and administration. Paul Rhymer of the National Museum of Natural History, Smithsonian Institution, helped our behavioral research by using his taxidermy skills to create predator models. Mitch Bush, Steve Monfort, Lyndsay Phillips, and Jackie Zoziarski, all of the National Zoological Park, carried out vasectomies and tubal ligations on Siberian ferrets before experimental release. Wild-caught Siberian ferrets were imported from China as a result of extensive efforts by Steve Kohl of U.S. Fish and Wildlife Service International Affairs. Judith Block of the National Zoological Park provided advice on interstate transportation of Siberian ferrets. For the field work at Meeteetse, Wyoming, the captive work at the Wyoming Game and Fish Department Research Facility, and the reintroduction research, we are indebted to many people who contributed to the collection of data and care of animals. We thank the ranchers from Meeteetse, Shirley Basin, and Wheatland, Wyoming, from Hasty, Colorado, and from south Phillips County, Montana, for allowing us access to their land during different aspects of research.

We also recognize the work of the zoos in captive breeding black-footed ferrets, and the time and effort of biologists from the Wyoming Game and Fish Department (Dave Belitsky, Jon Hanna, Pat Hnilicka, Don Kwiatkowski, Bob Luce, Bob Oakleaf, and Tom Thorne).

Courtney Conway composed Table 14.1, Brent Houston donated his collection of news clippings about black-footed ferrets, and Ray Paunovich allowed use of his film on the natural history of ferrets (part of the Audubon Society series on endangered species) for behavioral analysis. Steve Beissinger, Dean Biggins, Tim Clark, Courtney Conway, Ron Crete, Scott Derrickson, Louise Forrest, Jack Frazier, John Grensten, Lou Hanebury, Mike Hutchins, Jerome Jackson, Steve Kellert, Sharon Leathery, Randy Matchett, Noel Snyder, John Wargo, Chris Wemmer, and Ron Westrum provided reviews and suggestions on various parts of this book. We extend a warm thanks to the science acquisitions editor of Smithsonian Institution Press, Peter Cannell.

Steve Forrest is especially grateful to William Rodgers at the University of Washington for critical review of an earlier version of Chapter 13, to the Gruter Institute for discussions on game theory, and to Louise Richardson Forrest, ferret advocate and manuscript reviewer. Brian Miller is grateful for the patience of Karina Bringas during completion of this book. The support and companionship provided by our friends and families were critical throughout the entire writing process.

Finally, 25% of the authors' profit from this book will go toward the purchase of land to create a reserve for black-tailed prairie dogs. Reserves hold tremendous promise for black-footed ferrets and the many other species that depend on prairie dogs. We hope that this gesture can help turn some of our words about conservation into action.

Brian Miller, Richard P. Reading, and Steve Forrest

INTRODUCTION

The following chapters recount the saga of one of our planet's rarest animals, the black-footed ferret *(Mustela nigripes).* The first two parts introduce the lives of black-footed ferrets and prairie dogs *(Cynomys* spp.)—one cannot be discussed without considering the other. Admirably, the book then goes well beyond a discussion of ferret and prairie dog biology to address nonbiological aspects that are critical to conservation. These points are driven home with specific examples.

The three authors' academic credentials and considerable scientific expertise, accumulated from research involvement (note their repeated appearance in the References Cited section) and familiarity with related work, make them well qualified to discuss the biology of ferrets and prairie dogs, as well as the social and legal aspects of conservation. When the discussion transcends scientific or biological data, the reader may wonder whether the authors' opinions and interpretations are influenced by their own immediate interests—an agency career, journalistic attention, or the like. It is comforting to note the lack of current agency affiliation; this critically important independence allows the authors to speak freely. Their diverse past affiliations broaden their perspectives. Brian Miller was a field biologist on the ferret project for the Wyoming Game and Fish Department from 1984 to 1986 before earning a doctorate in black-footed ferret behavior and conservation at the University of Wyoming. Much of his doctoral work was undertaken with the captive ferret population under the auspices of the U.S. Fish and Wildlife Service Cooperative Research Unit in Wyoming. After completing his doctorate, Miller was awarded a Smithsonian postdoctoral fellowship to study the effects of different captive environments on behaviors necessary for survival and differential release techniques for captive-raised ferrets. He then participated in the first black-footed ferret reintroduction for the U.S.

Fish and Wildlife Service National Ecology Research Center. Miller is currently involved in the preparation of an ecological reserve and black-footed ferret reintroduction site in Chihuahua, Mexico, for the Universidad Nacional Autónoma de México.

Rich Reading has worked with the Northern Rockies Conservation Cooperative, Yale University, the U.S. Bureau of Land Management, and the U.S. Fish and Wildlife Service since 1988 to prepare a black-footed ferret reintroduction site in Montana. He has also participated in studies of ferret release techniques and in the first ferret reintroduction in Wyoming. Reading earned a doctorate in wildlife ecology from Yale University in 1993. Using the proposed black-footed ferret reintroduction in Montana as a case study, he developed an interdisciplinary approach to endangered-species reintroductions that incorporates human values, organizational structures, and biological aspects. He is now working for the United Nations on conservation issues in the steppes of Mongolia.

Steve Forrest earned a master's degree in environmental studies from Yale University and from 1981 to 1985 worked jointly as a field biologist for Idaho State University and Biota Research and Consulting, Inc., a nonprofit group that led an independent study of black-footed ferrets. Forrest has published numerous articles on ferret biology and ecology and coauthored the current U.S. Fish and Wildlife Service black-footed ferret recovery plan. He subsequently earned his law degree at the University of Washington, concentrating on legal aspects of biodiversity conservation. Forrest is currently an attorney in Montana.

The team effort to produce this book reflects the general philosophy of its authors. The team approach has been highly successful in the research portion of the black-footed ferret recovery program, which avoided the *sapo grande* (big toad) phenomenon described in Chapter 14. Finally, a pivotal element in Brian Miller's capability to interpret the political idiosyncrasies of the ferret program was his employment by several of the key organizations involved, including two U.S. Fish and Wildlife Service research entities, the Wyoming Game and Fish Department, and a private research establishment. Miller thus had a multifaceted insider's view of the functioning of the ferret program. In addition, the close ties of all three authors with nongovernmental conservation organizations has helped them stay in tune with conservation issues from a national viewpoint.

This book makes repeated references to the idea that science is a human endeavor. This statement can have various connotations, among them that any interpretation of scientific data involves some degree of anthropomorphism. A supervisor once admonished me to maintain "dispassionate objectivity" when conducting research. This is a virtuous goal, but, even if attainable, it is also productive to allow the human side of the scientist to manifest itself at times. We thus acknowledge that our experiences with ferrets have stimulated a variety of intense feelings. We shared a sense of elation when black-footed ferrets were "re-discovered" at Meeteetse, Wyoming, in 1981, followed by apprehension when we sensed that the species had been given a final chance and that we had better make the most of it. We suffered despair and dejection when standing on the West Core colony of the Meeteetse prairie dog complex after the plague epizootic of 1985. The vitality of a colony full of chattering prairie dogs, over which hawks hunted and numerous other associated organisms (including ferrets) flourished, had been replaced by near-total silence and an overwhelming feeling of death on a monumental scale. The same silence throughout the vast expanses of prairie dog colonies destroyed by rodenticides has elicited anger in each of us. For those of us (Brian Miller and Steve Forrest included) who practically lived with the Meeteetse ferrets for several years and watched the splendid animals only in their native habitat, the emotional low was when we realized that distemper (and possibly plague) reduced the ferret population to a precariously low level and that we had to remove the last animals to captivity. The ferret removal operation culminated with a gathering of biologists at Forrest's house in Meeteetse. On arrival, several of us noted that the abode was severely tilted, but by the end of the night the slope of the floor was inconsequential—everything became tilted in our minds. Spirits washed away what we all knew was the end of an era. We were despondent over the lack of other options for the species and apprehensive about the prospects for captive breeding. Whether we liked it or not, a new era had been forced upon us suddenly by a near-disaster. Chapters 7 and 8 will take you through this frustrating time.

Academic curiosity and scientific questions may stimulate our desire to continue to conduct research on the many questions surrounding prairie dogs and ferrets, but I know I speak for the authors and many others in suggesting that the emotional experiences related above contribute a great deal toward making us driven (obsessed, according to my wife) to try to do something. I do not believe that we disqualify ourselves as scientists by exhibiting human emotions. Furthermore, as we become more knowledgeable about our particular specialty, we are in a better position to advocate a course of action. Some of the actions that can be taken are outlined in Part III of this book. Take a close look. There are lessons in this case history that, if learned, will help keep your favorite species or environment from becoming the next one in peril.

Dean Biggins

National Ecology Research Center, National Biological Service
Fort Collins, Colorado

Part I

The Road
to Extinction

1

THE BLACK-FOOTED FERRET

One moonlit fall night, a young weasellike male animal bounded across the chiaroscuro short-grass prairie of Wyoming's Bighorn Basin. Leaving the territory he had traveled with his mother for the last two months, he was now making his way into an unfamiliar region. This animal appeared eager to move on; he was disturbed by the territorial scent marks of an older male, which he seemed to encounter at every turn. The marks signaled that the ground the young male had been crossing was occupied, and therefore dangerous. So he moved onward, following an almost imperceptible smell wafting across the cooling surface of the prairie. This aroma originated from burrows excavated by large rodents known as prairie dogs (*Cynomys* spp.), and the relatively warm air of the burrows was being drawn from the holes like heated air from a flue. The prairie dog scent hovered like a blanket a few centimeters above the ground, spread by the turbulence of the cooling night air. The young male, whose diminutive legs kept him in constant olfactory contact with the aromas, was making his way across the short grasses to the safety of these burrows.

He had a keen sense of hearing. Occasionally he would stop at the mouth of one of the burrows and cock his head as if listening. Rustling and squeaking noises were important cues to the presence of prey, and he could detect them at some distance.[1] But it was his sense of smell that was most highly developed. Not only could he detect the presence of prairie dogs, but when necessary he could bore through deep snow directly to a burrow entrance.[2]

This animal's vision, like that of most carnivores, was more responsive to movement than to form, not necessarily an indication of poor eyesight.[3] Typical of nocturnal carnivores, he possessed a tapetum lucidum, a reflective layer at the back of the eye that increases visual acuity in the dark (Ewer 1973). Because of

3

this reflective layer, bright light shining in the animal's eyes would reflect back toward the observer like emerald-green coals. His eyes were set wide in the head, giving him a broad arc of vision. This wide angle was no help in dark tunnels, but it provided him the field of vision necessary to avoid predators on the surface.

The animal was a black-footed ferret, *Mustela nigripes* (Figure 1.1). He did not know that he was one of the rarest mammals in North America, a member of a species perilously close to extinction. He was only following his instincts, which were adapted to life in the tunnels of the prairie dogs he sought on this night. His pelage (coat) was sleek, with guard hairs much shorter than those of surface-dwelling creatures of similar body mass. The hairs on his back were only about a centimeter long. Thermal efficiency was not so critical in the temperature-neutral confines of the burrow, and a short coat was advantageous for movement and cleanliness in subterranean quarters. Unlike that of other northern weasels, this species' fur did not change color in winter. Because he spent so little of his life above ground, there was no need for protective coloration in the snow.

Figure 1.1. One of the last wild black-footed ferrets alive in 1986. This adult female was found in Meeteetse, Wyoming, and she produced one of the two litters born there that year. She was taken into the captive breeding program shortly thereafter. Photo by Dean Biggins.

His legs, shorter than those of other animals of similar body mass, allowed him to run through cramped tunnels. The long thin body, short legs, and flexible articulation of the vertebrae equipped him with rapid turning ability in tight quarters; like the weasel he could simply roll and walk back over his own hindquarters as if made of rubber (C. M. King 1989). Any aggressor would encounter a mouthful of teeth at the opening of a burrow even before the tail had vanished from view, and extreme flexibility was also advantageous when killing prairie dogs in subterranean tunnels.

His mouselike ears, rounded and flattened to the side of his head, were similarly adapted to life underground (Figure 1.2). Attached to a blunt-nosed head, they gave the black-footed ferret a perpetually juvenile and endearing look. Closer inspection would reveal, however, that his short and broad skull was adapted for the attachment of large muscles to work the jaw and neck. His sagit-

Figure 1.2. A young black-footed ferret facing the camera in 1983. Photo by Dean Biggins.

tal crest, a bony ridge atop the skull, would be well defined by one year of age, anchoring temporal muscles that gave him a crushing bite. The dental formula behind that bite read incisors, 3/3; canines, 1/1; premolars, 3/3; and molars, 1/2 (E. Anderson et al. 1986). In other words, he had eight pairs of teeth in the upper jaw and nine pairs in the lower jaw. His mouth was adapted for cutting meat and bone with a carnassial pair of teeth on both sides of the jaw, each comprised of the last upper premolar and the first lower molar on that side. The location of the carnassial pair of teeth at the rear of the jaw, in conjunction with the massive temporal muscles, provided enormous shearing leverage. The four canines, long and sharp, could be used to seize prey and then dispatch it quickly with a bite to the throat, neck, or skull. Though the young ferret appeared no more tnreatening than a child's stuffed toy, he was a consummate and efficient killer.

Black-footed ferrets once thrived as specialists in the short-grass prairie ecosystem (Figure 1.3) that covered nearly a fifth of North America from Canada to Mexico (E. Anderson et al. 1986). Ferrets were dominant predators in the subterranean world of prairie dogs, a hidden third dimension in the otherwise two-dimensional landscape of the plains. Prairie dogs provided an abundant and stable food resource, as well as a safe home in their burrows, and black-footed ferrets exploited this resource until Europeans appeared in North America. Then, in less than 100 years, human development of the prairies reduced prairie dog numbers and virtually erased the black-footed ferret from the fauna of the New World.

Black-footed ferrets were not described and named in the scientific literature until 1851, when John James Audubon, the naturalist painter, and John Bachman, then curator at the National Museum of Natural History, published a joint paper and a painting of the black-footed ferret (Audubon and Bachman 1851). They based their description on a skin provided by a British fur trader and mountain man named Alexander Culbertson, who located the specimen near Fort Laramie in Goshen County, Wyoming.[4] Audubon's and Bachman's description closed a chapter in the conversion of the West—the black-footed ferret was one of the last mammal species to be described in the continental United States (Gilbert 1980).

Black-footed ferrets are similar in size and weight to mink *(M. vison)*, Siberian ferrets *(M. eversmanni)*, and the domesticated form of the European ferret *(M. putorius)*. Measurements taken from wild black-footed ferrets indicate an adult male body length (including tail) of around 567 millimeters, compared to 532 millimeters for adult females. On average, females are about 93% as long as males, but the tails of both sexes are about 135 millimeters (E. Anderson et al. 1986). Similarly, skull length for females is 93% that of males. Adult males weigh about 1,040 grams, whereas adult females average 710 grams, or about 68% of the average male body weight (E. Anderson et al. 1986; Miller, Anderson, et al. 1988).

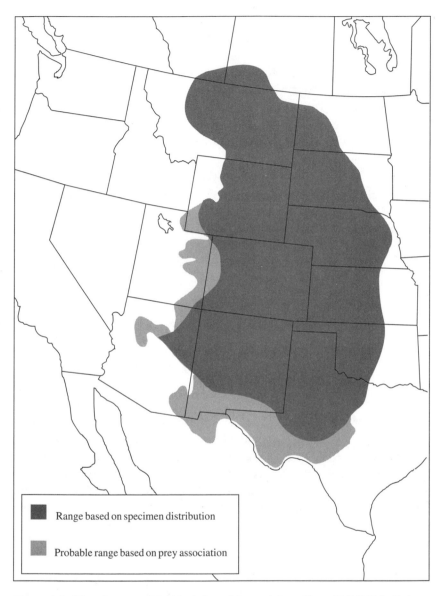

Range based on specimen distribution

Probable range based on prey association

Figure 1.3. Historic range of the black-footed ferret. Adapted from Hall (1981), E. Anderson et al. (1986), and Ceballos et al. (1993).

Black-footed ferrets are buckskin in color, with a darker saddle in the middle of the back. The underside is lighter than the sides or back, as is the fur on the muzzle and throat. In males a longitudinal black stripe in the pubic region may be visible when the animal sits upright on its haunches, which it typically does when approached or when investigating its surroundings. The stripe is usually absent (or faint) in females. The most noticeable color markings are the dark-tipped tail, the dark bandit's mask across the eyes, and the dark legs, from which the North American ferret derives its name (the dark coloration actually extends from the feet to the ferret's shoulders).

Although Audubon and Bachman received credit for introducing black-footed ferrets to science, the species was interwoven into the life of the earliest inhabitants of North America. Skeletal remains of black-footed ferrets have been found in several caves occupied by ancient North American peoples, some showing signs of burning or other manipulation. Later, the Cheyenne (F. R. Henderson et al. 1974) and Blackfeet nations (Homulka 1964) adorned chiefs' headdresses with ferret and ermine *(M. erminea)* hides. The Crow made ceremonial objects from stuffed ferrets decorated with beads, ribbons, and bells (Peterson and Berg 1954). Sioux legends closely associated ferrets (called *pispiza etopa sapa,* "black-faced prairie dog") with the spirit world, and the Sioux used ferrets as ceremonial objects and tobacco pouches (Calahane 1954; F. R. Henderson et al. 1974). Navajo holy men used the long, thin hide as a medicine pouch (C. Sherman pers. com.). The black-footed ferret was known by both the Hidatsas (who called the ferret *tahu akukahak napish*) and the Mandan (who called the ferret *nazi*), and various tribes captured and ate ferrets (F. R. Henderson et al. 1974).

The 1851 description by Audubon and Bachman was not even the earliest written record of black-footed ferrets. Don Juan de Oñate, who marched north into New Mexico in 1599 with 400 men, 130 families, 83 carts, and 7,000 head of livestock, in search of a strait linking the Atlantic and Pacific oceans, listed ferrets among the wildlife he observed (Bolton 1908). Several centuries later, American Fur Company records noted receipt of 169 weasels and 86 ferrets between 1835 and 1839 (Johnson 1969).

Various accounts suggest that the habitat of black-footed ferrets once approximated between 40 million and 100 million hectares of prairie dogs. The number of black-footed ferret specimens in museums is considerable, particularly for a specialized and secretive nocturnal carnivore. Black-footed ferrets have been cataloged from 120 of the 500 counties in their potential U.S. range (Forrest, Clark, et al. 1985a), correlating with Summers and Linder's (1978) estimate that prairie dogs originally covered about 20% of the western grasslands. The fossil record also indicates a wide temporal distribution, from the Pleistocene to the present (E. Anderson et al. 1986; E. Anderson 1989). For a while, some thought that the ceremonial or decorative use of black-footed ferrets by Native Americans indicated rarity. But long-tailed weasels *(M. frenata)* and ermine, both common species, were used by Native Americans in a similar way (Homulka 1964). Weasels and ferrets probably adorned headdresses simply because they were attractive. Their use may have connoted rank, just as weasel fur was reserved for the nobility in medieval Europe and English justices traditionally wore ermine (C. M. King 1989).

Thriving black-footed ferret populations were, therefore, coterminous with prairie dogs throughout the prairie dog's range, which includes the short-grass and midgrass prairies of the Great Plains and the intermontane basins of the eastern Rocky Mountains from Saskatchewan to Chihuahua, Mexico (Figure 1.3). Because prairie dogs were highly successful and widely distributed, they would seem to have provided a remarkably fortunate niche for a species adapted to killing in tight quarters. However, as we shall see, no association could have linked the black-footed ferret to a more certain doom. Since the turn of this century, the prairie dog has succumbed to an eradication campaign that leaves the ferret gazing into the chasm of extinction. The story of the black-footed ferret calls for an understanding of the plight of prairie dogs as well. Indeed, ferrets are only one of many organisms dependent on these keystone species, which provide habitat complexity and potential prey to support an enormous number of other species. The black-footed ferret is thus a lens through which we can examine the galaxy of problems facing an entire ecosystem.

The story of the black-footed ferret and the obstacles imposed upon its recovery are larger than the species itself. Because the plight of the black-footed ferret is unfortunately not without precedent, we hope the achievements and setbacks that we recount here will help conservationists improve the management not only of black-footed ferrets but of other threatened species and their ecosystems as well.

2

THE RISE AND DECLINE
OF BLACK-FOOTED FERRETS

EVOLUTION OF A FOSSORIAL PREDATOR

Mammals originated from mammallike reptiles, called therapsids, in the early
Triassic period of the Mesozoic era, and thus their history spans more than 200
million years (Table 2.1). The first representatives of modern mammals appeared
early in the Paleocene epoch (Tertiary period of the Cenozoic era), and the order
Carnivora descended from an insectivorous mammal of the family Miacidae
about 60 million years ago, during the middle Paleocene (Ewer 1973; E. Anderson 1989).

Approximately 40 million years ago, in the late Eocene and early Oligocene
epochs, the forests that blanketed much of the existing continental land masses
began to give way to grasses. Carnivore families rapidly diversified in response
to these vegetation changes (Ewer 1973). New plants meant new habitats for
herbivorous mammals to occupy, and herbivores expanded accordingly. New
groups of herbivores represented new prey for carnivores, and the carnivores diversified, exploiting this opportunity.

Carnivores of the family Mustelidae, to which ferrets and other weasels belong, remained in ancestral forest habitats throughout the Miocene epoch, which
began 25 million years ago. The early stages of their evolution are difficult to
trace because forest habitats are notoriously poor providers of fossils and because mustelid bones are small. By the Pliocene epoch, however, extensive
grasslands and savannas were more common, and mustelids were preying upon
the rodents that colonized these habitats (C. M. King 1989). Because they
evolved to hunt the ground-dwelling rodents of the grasslands, the early ancestors of the modern ferret were no doubt adapted to living in underground tunnels

10

TABLE 2.1. GEOLOGIC CHRONOLOGY

Era and period	Epoch	Years before present
Mesozoic		
Triassic	—	230,000,000
Jurassic	—	180,000,000
Cretaceous	—	135,000,000
Cenozoic		
Tertiary	Paleocene	63,000,000
	Eocene	58,000,000
	Oligocene	36,000,000
	Miocene	25,000,000
	Pliocene	13,000,000
Quaternary	Pleistocene	3,000,000
	Recent	11,000

Source: Ricklefs (1979).

(a fossorial existence) and were therefore able to survive the harsh cold of the Pleistocene-epoch ice ages, which began 2 million years ago (C. M. King 1989).

If current theories are correct, modern ferrets descended from these weasellike ancestors in Europe. The present family Mustelidae comprises 63 species of 23 genera (Honacki et al. 1982). All mustelids have long, thin bodies and short legs, at least to some degree. The taxon names Mustelidae and *Mustela,* combinations of the Latin words *mus* (mouse) and *telum* (spear), are in reference to that shape (C. M. King 1989).

The Move into North America
The earliest known ferret, Stromer's polecat *(M. stromeri),* arose during the middle Pleistocene epoch (E. Anderson 1989). Modern European ferrets, currently represented by two or three subspecies, date from the late Pleistocene, indicating that these groups diversified quickly (E. Anderson et al. 1986). From Europe, ferrets spread across Asia at a rate of about 750 kilometers per century, and by 100,000 years ago they had reached the Bering land bridge that connected Asia to North America (E. Anderson 1977).

At that point, an ancestor of the modern black-footed ferret, called *M. eversmanni berengii,* moved across the Bering land bridge onto the North American land mass. The North American ferrets, subsequently cut off from their Eurasian counterparts, rapidly spread southeast through ice-free corridors. By 30,000 years ago, modern black-footed ferrets could be found throughout the Great Plains. They had made the crucial evolutionary step of specializing on a single habitat, one provided by the colonial and highly successful prairie dog (E. Anderson et al. 1986).

Because of their extreme specialization on prairie dogs, black-footed ferrets belong to a single North American species with no recognized subspecies (E. Anderson 1977). By contrast, ferrets in Asia exploited various types of colonial rodents and developed into 17 subspecies (Stroganov 1962). Electrophoretic investigation of the differences between black-footed ferrets and Siberian ferrets found them to be distinct but closely related species (O'Brien, Martenson, et al. 1989). At the time of that research, however, Siberian ferrets were nearly impossible to obtain, and the findings were based on only 12 black-footed ferrets from a single colony in Wyoming and 3 Siberian ferrets of unknown lineage. In an ongoing study, researchers are comparing DNA from the two Siberian ferret subspecies living closest to the Bering Strait *(M. eversmanni doricus* and *M. e. amurensis)* to DNA from black-footed ferret skins collected from museums throughout North America (D. Biggins pers. com.; Figure 2.1). That research may provide more information on when the Asian and North American ferret species separated and the genetic extent of differentiation.

Specialization: Body Type and Habitat

All ferrets (and weasels), regardless of where they live, have in common a long, thin body conformation. This shape, an adaptation to life in constricted space, has both advantages and disadvantages. Because of its form, the ferret has strength disproportionate to its mass. For example, ferrets can run while carrying in their mouths prey equal to their own weight, a feat of strength few larger carnivores can match.

This extra strength of ferrets is explained by allometry or body scaling—the structural and functional consequences of size differences in similarly organized animals (Schmidt-Nielsen 1979; C. M. King 1989). As size decreases, the mass of an animal decreases proportionately to the third power of its linear dimension, but the cross-sectional area of muscle decreases only to the second power (Schmidt-Nielsen 1979). Furthermore, equal units of cross-sectional muscle area deliver equal force in animals of all sizes, so a long, thin, small animal is disproportionately strong in relation to its body mass (C. M. King 1989).

This strength and body shape are advantageous to ferrets in hunting as well as in predator avoidance. Ferrets are solitary hunters that apply a kill bite to prey often heavier than themselves, so strength is necessary. Ferret's body length allows them to wrap around their prey and brace against a burrow wall, giving them sufficient leverage to hold a prairie dog until the bite takes effect. Avoiding predators is likewise crucial to black-footed ferrets because where they hunt and live, in the prey-rich environment of a prairie dog town, there is a reasonable chance that they themselves will be pursued by larger predators. When a ferret is on the sur-

Figure 2.1. One of the five Siberian ferrets translocated from China for the release experiments of 1990. The collar around its neck holds a 10-gram radio transmitter for tracking the activities, location, and survival of the animal. Photo by Dean Biggins.

face, its role can change from hunter to hunted at any given moment. The long, thin shape allows ferrets to inhabit subterranean burrows comfortably and to transport dead prey rapidly from one burrow to the safety of another, thus reducing the time they must spend at risk on the surface (Figure 2.2).

This body type is, however, not without cost. Being long and thin increases surface area over that of other animals of similar mass by about 15% (J. H. Brown and Lasiewski 1972). In addition, pelage length is apparently restricted by body diameter; long-tailed weasels, who have roughly the same fur quality as the black-footed ferret, possess coats with only half the insulative value of woodrat coats (*Neotoma* spp.). Finally, long thin animals cannot achieve a spherical resting position. Instead they must rest curled into a flat disk, which exposes more surface area to the harsh natural elements than would a ball-shaped posture. The combination of greater surface area, shorter pelage, and a more exposed resting position causes ferrets to experience greater heat loss than do shorter, thicker animals of comparable body mass (J. H. Brown and Lasiewski 1972). Consequently, energetic demands are increased and, to compensate, so is metabolic rate. Eisenberg (1981) estimated that the metabolic rate of a cold-stressed least weasel *(M. nivalis)* rose 50–100% higher than predicted by a regression slope calculated from basal metabolic rates of mammals over a wide size range.

Although in sacrificing thermal efficiency black-footed ferrets do gain the ad-

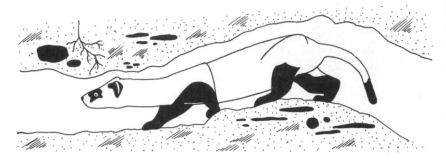

Figure 2.2. A black-footed ferret moving through a prairie dog tunnel. Drawing by Wally Van Sickle.

vantages that burrows provide for predator avoidance and hunting ability, they are unable to store enough fat to compensate for that loss. Huge fat stores would slow the lightning reflexes on which the ferret heavily relies, inhibiting the animal's hunting strategies as well as its ability to avoid predators (Ewer 1973; Eisenberg 1981). Instead of storing fat, ferrets cache (hide) prey for future use (Richardson et al. 1987). These caches are subject, however, to theft and decay (Biggins, Hanebury, et al. 1991).

But compensation for the thermal efficiency sacrificed by the ferret may be gained from the environment of the prairie dog burrow. For example, black-footed ferrets can behaviorally decrease heat loss in winter by reducing above-ground activity (Richardson et al. 1987). Burrow temperatures fluctuate only between 4° and 13°C at a depth of 1–3 meters regardless of the air temperature at the surface (F. R. Henderson et al. 1974). Prairie dog burrows thus provide an environment with far less temperature variation than above ground, reducing the energy required by black-footed ferrets to thermoregulate. Without the burrow, the black-footed ferret would expend a tremendous amount of energy simply to keep warm in winter.

In addition to reducing heat loss, the burrow may help black-footed ferrets retain body water, which would partly explain how they can survive in such arid environments. Captive black-footed ferrets, for example, drink only sparingly and occasionally lap at moisture on meat while eating. Drinking in the wild has never been observed, but this is not unusual. Many animal species living in arid environments control evaporative water loss from lungs and mucous membranes by appropriate microhabitat selection (Eisenberg 1981). Because black-footed ferrets live in dry environments, they may derive most of the water they require from meat. Like many animals living in arid regions, they probably produce high quantities of metabolic water and they concentrate urine to help retain it (Golightly and Ohmart 1984; Joyce 1988). Also, confinement in the burrow may create a semisaturated microclimate that reduces evaporative water loss by limiting convection. Black-footed ferrets may further reduce water loss by leaving the burrows only at night, when surface temperatures are lower and air has a higher moisture content.

Thus, black-footed ferrets are highly specialized to exploit the prairie dog ecosystem, but specialization is an evolutionary gamble. It requires an environment buffered from rapid change. Prairie dogs appear to be worth the wager. The success of prairie dogs resides in their ability to modify a variety of vegetative types occurring in a range of climatic regimes, which permits them a widespread distribution. It may seem that evolving an obligate association with such an environmentally adaptive prey should have provided the black-footed ferret security over evolutionary time. Indeed, until the turn of this century, black-footed ferrets had plenty of prairie dogs to exploit.

THE HOST: THE AMERICAN PRAIRIE DOG

Prairie dogs are colonial, burrowing ground squirrels living on the short-grass prairies of the North American Great Plains (Figure 2.3). There are five species of prairie dog: the black-tailed prairie dog *(Cynomys ludovicianus)*, Mexican prairie dog *(C. mexicanus)*, white-tailed prairie dog *(C. leucurus)*, Gunnison prairie dog *(C. gunnisoni)*, and Utah prairie dog *(C. parvidens)*. The black-tailed prairie dog has the widest distribution, from Saskatchewan to Mexico. Mexican and Utah prairie dogs are both endangered. The Mexican prairie dog is restricted to the states of San Luis Potosi, Coahuila, and Nuevo Leon, and the Utah prairie dog is restricted to southwest Utah (Durrant 1952; Ceballos et al. 1993). White-tailed prairie dogs are found in Colorado, Utah, and Wyoming, and Gunnison prairie dogs are located in Colorado, New Mexico, Arizona, and Utah (Figure 2.4) (Hall 1981).

All prairie dogs belong to the family Sciuridae in the order Rodentia. Sciurids originated in North America in the middle Oligocene epoch (Tertiary period of the Cenozoic era) and spread to the Old World in the late Oligocene (Vaughan 1978). In all likelihood, prairie dogs arose from ground-dwelling savanna rodents that drew the first weasels away from their ancestral forests onto Miocene grasslands.

All prairie dog species are very similar in physical appearance, and all have adaptations for a fossorial (underground) lifestyle. *(Fossor* literally means "digger.")* The total length of these stocky rodents is about 30–40 centimeters, including a short flat tail about 7–10 centimeters long (Tileston and Lechleitner

Figure 2.3. A white-tailed prairie dog barking an alarm call on the prairie dog complex near Meeteetse, Wyoming. Photo by Louise R. Forrest.

1966). Weights can vary from 500 to 1,400 grams, black-tailed and white-tailed prairie dogs being the largest and Gunnison prairie dogs the smallest (Foster and Hygnstrom 1990). Within each of the species, the males are slightly bigger than the females. As is typical for fossorial animals, prairie dog ears are small and do not extend much beyond the pelage of the broad and massive skull. Their coat is a buff-brown or cinnamon color, with a black-tipped tail on Mexican and black-tailed prairie dogs and a white-tipped tail on Gunnison, Utah, and white-tailed prairie dogs. Prairie dogs have short legs, which facilitate running in the cramped confines of a burrow system. Long sharp claws act as shovels for the excavation of burrows.

Though the five species of prairie dogs are physically similar, they differ in behavior and physiology, most notably in ability to hibernate and in social structure (for prairie dog species overall, densities can range from 5 to 45 prairie dogs per hectare [1 hectare = 2.5 acres]). Black-tailed and Mexican prairie dogs are more colonial, live at higher population densities, and do not hibernate, whereas white-tailed, Gunnison, and Utah prairie dogs are less colonial, live at lower population densities, and do hibernate (Longhurst 1944; J. King 1955; Clark 1977; Harlow and Menkens 1986). Less has been published on Utah and Mexican prairie dogs, but their affinities seem to lie, respectively, with white-tailed and black-tailed prairie dogs.

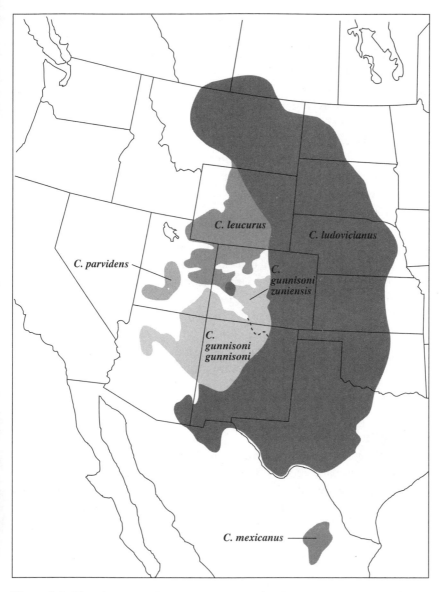

Figure 2.4. Historic range of five *Cynomys* spp. (prairie dogs). Adapted from Pizzimenti and Collier (1973), Hall (1981), E. Anderson et al. (1986), and Ceballos et al. (1993).

The principal foods of prairie dogs are grasses and forbs; about one-fourth of those plant species are not eaten by livestock (Koford 1958). It has been calculated that 300 prairie dogs consume the same amount of forage as one cow with a calf (Uresk and Paulson 1989).

Reproduction and Development

All prairie dog species breed in early spring and produce a single litter annually. Most of the breeding is done by adults that are at least two years old. Yearling males are sexually immature, and yearling females produce fewer pups than do adults; many yearlings fail to breed at all (J. King 1955; Koford 1958; Hoogland 1982; Knowles 1987). The amount of food available affects prairie dog litter size, growth rates, juvenile survivorship, age at first reproduction, and pregnancy rates (Garret, Franklin, and Hoogland 1982).

Prairie dog litters, averaging three to five pups, are born hairless after a gestation of about 30 days (Bakko and Brown 1967; Knowles 1987; Hoogland 1988). Between 14 and 28 days of age the pups develop a coat of hair, and they open their eyes at about 35 days (J. King 1955). Two weeks after their eyes open, the pups emerge above ground and begin to switch their diet from mother's milk to vegetation (J. King 1955). By late spring (June), pups are half of adult size and by the end of summer they are almost full-grown. Both black-tailed and white-tailed prairie dog pups play extensively, but only the more colonial black-tailed prairie dog pups ardently solicit adult attention and grooming (J. King 1955; Tileston and Lechleitner 1966).

Life in a Burrow System

Prairie dogs are active during daylight and live in an extensive aggregation of elaborate underground burrows. These tunnels can be 4 meters deep and can extend 10 meters horizontally. The burrow system includes a guard room just below the surface, where a prairie dog can listen for signs of danger before emerging from the mouth of the tunnel. Nesting chambers and toilet areas are down deeper. Some tunnels are dead ends, and others return to the surface to provide a back door. Prairie dogs dig these tunnels with their front feet and kick the dirt back with their hind legs. Old burrows are continually worked and expanded each year, and some burrow systems are occasionally plugged with a subsoil block. These plugs may extend more than 3 meters through the burrow. A prairie dog burrow system is more than just a home; its distinct spatial pattern defines the social system of the colony (J. King 1955).

Areas covered by burrow aggregations, called colonies or towns, vary greatly in size. Garret, Franklin, and Hoogland (1982), Knowles (1982), and Reading (1993) have shown that colony populations exhibit logistic growth. Initially, colonies expand rapidly in the presence of abundant resources and low competition; but as colonies flourish, competition increases and resource abundance decreases. Expansion is probably limited by a reduction of preferred habitat at the colony edge and by physical barriers such as steep slopes or dense vegetation (Garret and Franklin 1988; Reading 1993).

Burrows of black-tailed prairie dogs are often in hard flat ground, and they are rarely found in areas with more than 10–15% slope (Koford 1958; Tileston and Lechleitner 1966; Reading 1993). A single burrow opening is usually surrounded by a 1- to 2-meter mound of dirt that the prairie dog tamps solid with its front feet and head (J. King 1955). When the entrance at one end of a tunnel has a dome-shaped mound and the exit hole has a volcano-shaped mound, air flow through the tunnel is facilitated (Vogel et al. 1973). Mounds also prevent water from flooding the burrow and serve as a vantage point for detecting predators (J. King 1955; Tileston and Lechleitner 1966).

Although steep slopes generally preclude the presence of prairie dogs, white-tailed and Gunnison prairie dogs can live on grasslands steeper than a 15% slope (Longhurst 1944; Tileston and Lechleitner 1966). White-tailed and Gunnison prairie dog mounds are not dome- or volcano-shaped but instead consist of a large pile of dirt with an average of three entrance holes; each mound can be from 1 to 2 meters wide. In addition, all prairie dog species make burrow entrances with no mound at all. More moundless burrow openings are found on steeper slopes, perhaps because standing water is less of a problem there (Longhurst 1944).

Prairie dogs begin aboveground activity shortly after sunrise. They may feed for several hours on vegetation, bask in the sun while sitting on their mounds, or groom each other. Prairie dogs spend the heat of the day underground and reappear near sunset for another feeding before retiring for the evening (Longhurst 1944; J. King 1955; Clark 1977). On a large colony, at least a few prairie dogs can be seen at virtually any time of day, but most of the activity still occurs during the early and late hours. Inclement weather can affect feeding patterns, as can season of the year. White-tailed, Gunnison, and Utah prairie dogs add an enormous amount of fat in the fall and hibernate over the winter (Tileston and Lechleitner 1966; Clark 1977). Before hibernation, some animals resemble little fat Buddhas when they sit upright on their haunches. Black-tailed prairie dogs, however, are active year-round, unless they are forced to hibernate by food and water deprivation (Harlow and Menkens 1986).

Surface activity is not random. Prairie dogs literally farm their colonies, and a number of species benefit from their work. The burrows shelter numerous vertebrate and invertebrate species. Prairie dogs clip tall grasses and shrubs in favor of short grasses and forbs, which are preferred by wild ungulates and domestic livestock. This farming activity results in plants with less biomass, but those plants have a higher nutrient content and a more succulent texture (Coppock et al. 1983; Krueger 1986). In addition, prairie dogs and associates are a rich prey base for numerous aerial and terrestrial predators. This is particularly true for black-tailed prairie dogs, which are active throughout the winter, when many other prey are dormant. It is not surprising that many early fur trappers concentrated their efforts on prairie dog colonies.

Social Structure, Predator Avoidance, and Communication

Black-tailed prairie dogs seem to exhibit the strongest social structure, with large colonies divided into "wards"; these wards are in turn divided into smaller social groups termed "coteries" (J. King 1955; Tileston and Lechleitner 1966). Each coterie consists of about eight prairie dogs, and members defend their territory against prairie dogs from other coteries (J. King 1955; Hoogland 1983).

During the black-tailed prairie dog's reproductive season, some nonbreeding females may help breeding females raise their litters, a cooperative behavior indicative of a highly developed social system (Hoogland 1983). The two most obvious helping behaviors are grooming and predator defense. There is also evidence that lactating females sometimes competitively kill unweaned offspring of other lactating females in the same coterie, suggesting that breeding females may defend their natal burrow against other breeding females (Hoogland 1983). Once the pups are weaned, however, the social structure of the coterie is re-established. Individuals from the same coterie greet each other with a kiss of identification (they actually touch teeth) followed by mutual grooming. These affectionate behaviors have made the prairie dog a popular attraction in many zoos and several state and national parks.

White-tailed and Gunnison prairie dog colonies lack the infrastructure and visually distinct boundaries of black-tailed colonies. White-tailed prairie dogs are more alert than their black-tailed counterparts, and therefore do not depend as heavily on teamwork to detect predators (Hoogland 1979, 1981). The high level of interdependence in predator detection among black-tailed prairie dogs probably promotes the more complex social system in that species (Hoogland 1981). The need to detect predators and communicate warnings also explains why black-tailed prairie dogs clip shrubs, such as sage or mesquite, more thoroughly than do white-tailed prairie dogs (Hoogland 1981). The scattered distribution of Gunnison and white-tailed prairie dog burrows, and the less intense clipping of vegetation by these species, make it more difficult for humans to see the colony boundaries. This circumstance may partially account for the more sustained eradication of black-tailed prairie dogs by agricultural interests.

Prairie dog colonies are frequented by a number of different predators, all in search of a prairie dog or one of the other animals associated with the prairie dog community. Prairie raptors attack from above, and foxes (family Canidae), coyotes *(Canis latrans),* badgers *(Taxidea taxus),* bobcats *(Lynx rufus),* and black-footed ferrets approach on the ground. Prairie dogs stop eating every 10 seconds or so to scan the horizon for potential danger (Longhurst 1944; J. King 1955). When a prairie dog sees something suspicious, it immediately runs to a mound and sounds the alarm call, a shrill bark. The force of the bark throws the prairie dog's head back. When the prairie dog is down on all four feet, its tail flips excitedly. After the initial warning, all other nearby prairie dogs run to a mound and join the chorus. When the danger has passed, an all-clear "whee-oo" cry signals a resumption of surface activity (J. King 1955).

For a time, researchers believed that an initial warning bark, such as one given by a prairie dog spotting a predator, was an altruistic act—that is, the alarm caller was believed to incur a cost (drawing attention to itself) while bestowing a benefit on its neighbors (alerting them to danger). The cost to the altruistic individual was thought to be tempered somewhat by a mechanism called kin selection: if the act helps one or more of the alarm caller's relatives, the altruistic individual safeguards the chance that at least a portion of its genes will be passed on to the next generation, if only indirectly, via its relatives (W. D. Hamilton 1964).

However, alarm calling may not be as risky to the individual as was once thought. Immediately before the prairie dog gives the alarm call, it runs to a burrow, a "selfish" position of relative safety. The flurry of activity that occurs after the first alert (prairie dogs scrambling to nearby burrows, then all barking from their respective locations) may even draw attention away from the original caller. Thus, the alarm call may benefit that individual as well as its kin.

The auditory communication system of black-tailed prairie dogs consists of about 11 distinct barks, which convey at least 11 different messages that humans can interpret (Foster and Hygnstrom 1990). White-tailed prairie dogs have four different calls, and both white-tailed and black-tailed prairie dogs communicate visually through body posture (Tileston and Lechleitner 1966; Clark 1977).

Susceptibility to Disease

Prairie dogs are extremely susceptible to plague, a disease caused by the bacterium *Yersinia pestis* (Barnes 1993; Culley 1993; J. P. Fitzgerald 1993). Fleas are the vector that transmits the plague bacterium, and the effects of the disease are variable. Some prairie dog towns are completely obliterated by plague, whereas others decline slowly but retain active sections. The spread of plague depends on soils, climate, species of flea, and density and species of rodents. Although there is little empirical evidence of its origin, plague was probably introduced from Asia around the turn of this century (Barnes 1993). It continues to be a profound threat to existing prairie dog colonies.

THE PRAIRIE DOG "PROBLEM"

Before poisoning began, some prairie dog colonies were quite large. One colony in eastern Wyoming exceeded 160 kilometers in length. Another in Texas was 400 kilometers long and 160 kilometers wide; it may have held as many as 4 million prairie dogs. It has been estimated that prairie dogs once numbered 5 billion and inhabited about 20% of the short-grass prairies of the United States (Summers and Linder 1978; E. Anderson et al. 1986).

Almost as soon as the lands west of the 100th meridian were settled, ranchers began to view prairie dogs as pests competing with livestock for forage, and the owners of many large ranches had begun to poison them by the late 1880s. For a decade or so, prairie dog poisoning for purposes of range "improvement" proceeded haphazardly, without organized effort. Strychnine-laced oats were the most readily available and frequently used poison.

In 1902 C. H. Merriam, director of the U.S. Biological Survey (precursor to the U.S. Fish and Wildlife Service), suggested that prairie dogs decrease the productive capacity of land by 50–75% (Merriam 1902). Merriam's estimate was not based on scientific evidence, and recent research indicates that it was a tenfold exaggeration (Uresk and Paulson 1989; see also Koford 1958, Hansen and Gold 1977, O'Meilia et al. 1982, Collins et al. 1984, Krueger 1988). Nevertheless his statement, published in the *U.S. Department of Agriculture Yearbook,* provided official support for prairie dog poisoning, establishing its place among the new "scientific" strategies for farming and ranching.

Many counties and states organized poisoning campaigns, typically involving cooperative arrangements among states, county agricultural agents, and landowners. Initially, ranchers who requested poisoning paid the bulk of its cost. The federal government began paying for prairie dog poisoning in 1915, when the Biological Survey first appropriated money for animal control (Bishop and Culbertson 1976). Ranchers still paid about 25% of the program's costs, however, through a tax on livestock. This sizeable contribution gave members of the livestock industry considerable influence over the poisoning program (Leopold 1964; McNulty 1971; Dunlap 1988). Research on prairie dogs was in turn influenced by poisoning policy. In the early 1900s, such research focused on efficient and cost-effective toxicants and eradication techniques (Lantz 1909, 1917; Bell 1918, 1921). At the time, awareness of ecological relationships was still rudimentary. Even so, a few visionaries, such as the mammalogist E. T. Seton, predicted several catastrophic outcomes of poisoning programs, including the decline of species such as the black-footed ferret (Seton 1926). But policy was set, and critics' voices were largely ignored.

By the 1920s, the Biological Survey was poisoning millions of prairie dogs and ground squirrels each year (Bell 1921; Day and Nelson 1929; Dunlap 1988; see also Figure 2.5). By 1929 animal damage control activities were substantial enough that a new division of the Biological Survey was formed (DiSilvestro 1985). From the beginning, the Division of Predatory Animal and Rodent Control was a service agency whose mandate was to respond to the interests of the livestock industry (Dunlap 1988). Passage of the Animal Damage Control Act two years later provided statutory authority for poisoning, trapping, and shooting on and off of federally owned land, and it remains the primary statute for animal damage control today. The act also indirectly sanctioned the partnership between the Division of Predatory Animal and Rodent Control and private livestock interests (Bean 1983). Renamed Animal Damage Control, the Division was transferred in 1939 to the Bureau of Sport Fisheries and Wildlife of the newly formed U.S. Fish and Wildlife Service (DiSilvestro 1985). Much later, after passage of the Endangered Species Preservation Act in 1966, this bureaucratic placement was to mean that a single federal agency was responsible both for eradicating prairie dogs (Animal Damage Control unit) and for preserving the black-footed ferret (Endangered Species office). This conflict contributed to what McNulty (1971) has called "a bad case of governmental schizophrenia."

Two government reports, the Leopold Report of 1964 and the Cain Report of 1971, characterized the killing of wildlife as far in excess of that justified by available evidence. Both reports noted the longstanding influence of livestock interests and the resistance to change of the Division of Predatory Animal and Rodent Control. Both also called for restructuring of the Division, additional research on ecological effects, and revised funding procedures (Leopold 1964; Cain 1978). In response to the Cain Report, President Nixon promulgated Executive Order 11643, which banned the use of toxicants that caused secondary poisoning. The Environmental Protection Agency then disallowed the use of strychnine, sodium cyanide, and 1080 for predator and rodent extermination. Soon thereafter, however, zinc phosphide products were marketed with a "prairie dog use only" label. Thus far, changes in animal damage control policy have had little impact on prairie dog poisoning.

In 1981, President Reagan reversed Nixon's Executive Order 11643 and sanctioned more extensive animal damage control programs. In 1986, Reagan transferred responsibility for those activities to a division of the U.S. Department of Agriculture, the Animal and Plant Health Inspection Service. This decision elim-

Figure 2.5. A pile of dead prairie dogs collected after the poisoning of a small prairie dog colony in Arizona in the early 1900s. Photo from the U.S. National Archives.

inated the conflicting agendas within the U.S. Fish and Wildlife Service, but also insulated Animal Damage Control from internal change by placing it under the auspices of a department that has traditionally been highly responsive to agricultural interests.

DECLINE OF THE BLACK-FOOTED FERRET

Between 1915 and 1960, the total area covered by prairie dog colonies was reduced from somewhere between 40 million and 100 million hectares to about 600,000 hectares (Marsh 1984; E. Anderson et al. 1986). In 1960, by conservative calculations, prairie dogs occupied only 2% of the area they had covered prior to 1870—a rate of decline surpassing that of North American old-growth forests over a similar period. The few prairie dog colonies that remained were small and geographically isolated.

By midcentury, it was not clear whether prairie dogs would survive. Articles with titles like "Goodbye Little Yek Yek" began appearing in publications such as *Audubon* magazine. Prairie dogs had become numerically insignificant and their former range highly fragmented. As a consequence, E. T. Seton's predictions about the black-footed ferret appeared to be coming true—only about 70 ferrets were seen from 1946 to 1953, and about one-third of those were dead (DeBlieu 1991).

In 1964, as the federal government was about to declare the black-footed ferret extinct, a small population was discovered in Mellette County, South Dakota. A capable team of biologists was assembled, among them Conrad Hillman, the U.S. Fish and Wildlife Service's principal investigator. Ferrets were observed on 20 of the 151 black-tailed prairie dog colonies known to exist in Mellette County between 1964 and 1974; the colonies averaged 8.5 hectares in size (Hillman and Linder 1973). Over those years only 11 known litters of ferrets were produced (R. L. Linder et al. 1972).

The Endangered Species Preservation Act, passed in 1966, initially listed the black-footed ferret as endangered and provided limited funds for management of the species. Protection of habitat, however, was not mandated. Nor was the U.S. Fish and Wildlife Service inclined to discontinue its prairie dog poisoning programs. By 1971, low numbers of black-footed ferrets and deteriorating relationships with landowners had convinced the ferret biologists that a captive population of ferrets was needed to secure the future of the species (R. L. Linder et al. 1972; Hillman and Linder 1973).

The U.S. Fish and Wildlife Service Research Center in Patuxent, Maryland, captured six of the South Dakota black-footed ferrets for captive breeding in 1971 (Erickson 1973; Hillman and Carpenter 1983). All six were given a modified live-virus distemper vaccine to protect them from disease. The vaccine had been tested successfully on Siberian ferrets, but the black-footed ferrets proved more susceptible. Instead of building immunity, the virus in the vaccine killed four of the six (Carpenter, Appel, et al. 1976). It has been speculated that inbreeding had reduced immune-response abilities of the black-footed ferret, or that species differences resulted in differential susceptibility to the distemper virus. Whatever the reason, the damage had been done. Three more black-footed ferrets were captured in South Dakota for the program, but after 1974 no more wild ferrets were seen in South Dakota (Hillman and Carpenter 1983).

Two females and two males from this captive group were monitored over four breeding seasons by Conrad Hillman and Jim Carpenter, a veterinarian with the U.S. Fish and Wildlife Service. One female rejected both males, but the other copulated in three different years and twice produced litters (Carpenter 1985). In each litter, four out of five pups were stillborn and the fifth died shortly after birth (Carpenter and Hillman 1978).

Watching the last of a species dwindle away was painful for the biologists. Jim Carpenter once observed that at Patuxent no species had taken so much of the researchers' souls, and demanded so much of their energy, as the black-footed ferret. Despite their disappointing failure to produce live ferrets, the Patuxent researchers did gain enough knowledge of ferret reproductive physiology to develop a system for determining when a female is in estrus.

When the last captive black-footed ferret died of cancer in January 1979 (Carpenter 1985), the U.S. Fish and Wildlife Service once again debated declaring the animal extinct (DeBlieu 1991). As the Service's ferret biologist, Conrad Hillman continued to search for other populations, but in 1980 the Service "deemphasized"—that is, cut the budget of—the black-footed ferret program. Hillman had worked with black-footed ferrets for 14 years, longer than anyone else, and he still believed that another population existed in the wild (Gilbert 1980). After the budget cut, and discouraged by the general lack of support from Washington, he quit the U.S. Fish and Wildlife Service. Hillman later told an interviewer that he would still be working with black-footed ferrets if he thought the U.S. Fish and Wildlife Service would maintain a bona fide ferret program, but that one person alone could make only a token effort (Gilbert 1980).

The biologist hired to succeed Hillman at the Service was given only part-time responsibilities for ferret management (Gilbert 1980). The 1978 recovery team for black-footed ferrets, created in accordance with the Endangered Species Act, had outlined several alternative scenarios for conservation of ferrets, but money was tight and little was done with those recommendations (Gilbert 1980). The U.S. Fish and Wildlife Service was ready to close the book on ferrets.

Then one cool September night near Meeteetse, Wyoming, a blue-heeler mix ranch dog named Shep provided a second chance for conservation of the species. When he found a masked intruder at his food bowl, Shep followed the western credo of "shoot first," and soon the trespasser was a lifeless corpse. Shep's owners, John and Lucille Hogg, heard the commotion and thought Shep had crossed paths with yet another porcupine, but the body they found the next morning had an unfamiliar and unusual pelt. Lucille wanted to preserve it, but the local taxidermist recognized the animal as a black-footed ferret and called the authorities.

Part II

Behavioral and Population Ecology

3

REPRODUCTION AND DEVELOPMENT OF THE YOUNG

The young male black-footed ferret, now nearly one year old, stirred from his sleep. He lay on his side on a bed of dried grasses in a subterranean prairie dog chamber kept damp and warm by his respiration. His body formed a furry disk, the deep forward curve of his back tucking his head into his lower stomach. Now he straightened his body and rolled to his stomach. Gathering his senses, he stretched, squinted his eyes, and yawned. Then he stood and shook his skin violently from side to side, starting at the head and neck and progressing quickly to the rear. After attacking a bothersome flea by scratching his shoulder with his hind leg, he spent several minutes grooming his sleek coat by licking the fur with his smooth tongue.[1] The black-footed ferret was now fully awake and ready to leave his chamber. He extended his head and neck in a line with his body and entered the burrow that would lead him to the prairie surface 3 meters above.

His nostrils touched the chilly air just as the last bit of purple twilight was fading over the wet March snow. The ferret extended only his head and neck from the burrow, giving him the appearance of a periscope poking above water. From this position, he turned his head from side to side and surveyed his realm.

Last October, he had been a young animal searching for a territory and worried about the scent marks of an older male. He had pressed on and found a region containing prairie dogs but without any indication of a resident male. Despite faint signs that a male had once been present, only two females were using the burrows of the area when he arrived. Instinct told the ferret he had to wander no farther, and he began to mark the area with his own scent. Having secured this piece of land that provided both food and shelter, he was able to survive the winter. Many of his cohorts were not so fortunate. They were forced to move quickly through occupied territories, or to head across open expanses in search of another prairie dog colony. Searching for a home meant spending a great deal of time on the surface, which exposed them to coyotes and owls. Even if they were fortunate enough to escape jaws or talons, these dispersers often found themselves in an area barren of prairie dogs, and many succumbed to hunger. Owning a territory, with guaranteed food and shelter, was the key to survival.

This night, the yearling male crawled onto the surface and bounded toward a burrow on the other side of his territory. That burrow contained a female who was entering estrus, the fertile period of her reproductive cycle. Her presence in the territory marked by the yearling male, however, did not necessarily mean that he would be the one to breed with her. The neighboring male was older and stronger and bore scars attesting to his experience. If the older male chose to trespass, the yearling could lose the opportunity to extend his genes into the next generation. But luck once again favored the yearling: the only ferret in the burrow was the female.

REPRODUCTION

Sexual Maturation

Reproduction is the most important goal in any animal's life. The essence of evolution is not so much Tennyson's "Nature, red in tooth and claw" as which individuals are best adapted to the immediate environment and can thus leave more offspring to propagate the species.

Because of their fragile status, little physiological research has been done on black-footed ferrets. However, a close relative, the domestic ferret *(Mustela putorius furo)*, which is common and available commercially, has been the subject of considerable research. Much of what is known about domestic ferrets can be applied to understanding the black-footed ferret.

In male domestic ferrets, a burst of testosterone courses through the body between 5 and 20 days after birth (Baum and Erskine 1984). If newborn male domestic ferrets do not receive this postpartum testosterone exposure, they will not develop the sexual behavior necessary for reproduction after puberty. When male domestic ferrets reach puberty, hormone receptors in the testicles become more sensitive to luteinizing hormone, a gonadotropin produced in the pituitary. That luteinizing hormone then stimulates the testicles to produce testosterone, the hormonal fuel that powers the male reproductive process.

In domestic ferrets, the annual breeding season lasts from January until sometime between March and July (Hahn and Webster 1969). At the start of that season, triggered by lengthening daylight, males' testicles increase in size. After the breeding season the testicles shrink, and males enter a period of sexual quiescence until the next year.

During fetal development of the female domestic ferret, the hormone estrogen stimulates the brain, laying the groundwork for reproductive behavior after puberty (Ryan 1984; Baum and Tobert 1986). Females of all ferret species reach sexual maturity at one year, although prime breeding age appears to be between two and five years of age for domestic ferrets (C. F. Williams 1976) and under three years of age for black-footed ferrets (E. T. Thorne, as cited in Captive Breeding Specialist Group 1992).

The annual breeding cycle of the female ferret is also neurally keyed by lengthening daylight, with longer days causing the release of a gonadotropin, follicle-stimulating hormone, from the pituitary (Carroll et al. 1985). Follicle-stimulating hormone triggers follicles on the ovary to produce estrogen, a key to the expression of female estrous behavior. Domestic ferrets continue to produce mature eggs from ovarian follicles from March until August if not bred, but the black-footed ferret probably passes out of estrus in about one month (Hahn and Webster 1969; Carpenter 1985). It is possible for a black-footed ferret to attain a second estrus if she does not become pregnant during the first attempt (Miller, Anderson, et al. 1988).

In the female domestic ferret, estrus is readily apparent in the pronounced swelling of the vulva, but that swelling is far less noticeable in the black-footed ferret. So researchers at the U.S. Fish and Wildlife Service Patuxent Research Center developed a technique called vaginal cytology to identify estrus, whereby cells collected in a vaginal wash are examined for changes that typify the estrous state (Carpenter and Hillman 1978; Carpenter 1985). This technique later became a valuable tool in captive breeding.

The breeding season in the wild probably occurs in March and April. Richardson et al. (1987) reported activity shifts among wild black-footed ferrets in March that are comparable to wild weasel activity during the breeding season (Erlinge and Sandell 1986; Sandell 1986), and Siberian ferrets are also reproductively active at this time (Stroganov 1962). In captivity, black-footed ferret copulation attempts have extended into summer, but the main breeding season of the species is also in March and April (Carpenter 1985; Miller, Anderson, et al. 1988).

Copulation

Before copulation, many animals engage in courtship behavior, a form of communication important to mate recognition. Different species have slightly different pre-copulatory behavioral repertoires, and an unfamiliar action, or response to an action, will usually terminate the courting process.

Within the same species, the courting actions of one sex depend on what the other sex does, and in some species male courtship behavior is important material that females use to choose a mate (R. H. Wiley 1973; Cox and LeBoeuf 1977;

Greenspan 1980; Welbergen et al. 1987). In other species, male courtship actually heightens female receptivity (Crews 1975; Silver 1978; Welbergen et al. 1987).

Courtship behavior in black-footed ferrets is difficult to observe. Estrous females do not change their overall activity patterns, and in most cases an experienced and aggressive male simply grabs the female by the neck and mounts, without aggressive female solicitation. When the male is sexually inexperienced or hesitant, however, a female may solicit a male, perhaps as a mechanism to announce her receptivity (DonCarlos et al. 1989; Miller and Anderson 1990a).

Typically, the soliciting female will approach the male in a low crouch, alternately pausing and advancing, with her head and neck extended toward him. One or both animals will emit a chuckling sound. When close to the male, the female will often move beside him and wait. If she needs to intensify her efforts, she might place her head under his chin. If there is still no response, she might move her head and side against him in a catlike motion or crawl beneath his midsection. In one extreme case, an older female, having exhausted all the procedural niceties without response from an inexperienced male, finally seized him by the neck, pulled him into the nest box, and crawled beneath him. Her efforts were finally successful in spurring the young male into action.

Copulation among black-footed ferrets is prolonged and rough (Hillman and Carpenter 1983; Miller and Anderson 1993). If the female is not yet receptive, the male's approaches are met with a flurry of aggression. As her estrous state advances, however, the female becomes more amenable to approach. When the male is allowed to approach, he will grab the female by the scruff of the neck. This neck bite will be maintained throughout copulation, which can last several hours. In some cases of prolonged copulation, male saliva appears to stain the female's neck fur.

The male's penis becomes erect by engorging with blood, an erection supported by a long, thin bone called a baculum. In many animals, the baculum assures sufficient copulatory stimulation to induce ovulation in the female (Ewer 1973). The male black-footed ferret mounts the female with his back arched and tail raised, and his penis penetrates the vagina with a series of rapid pelvic thrusts. Following penetration, there are long periods of little or no motion. The male may then assume one of two postures: he may tuck his hips forward, so that they are even with, or anterior to, the top of the arch in his back (the best indicator of penetration; Figure 3.1); or he might move one hind leg in a circular motion by first raising the leg, extending it forward, then pushing down before drawing it back to the original position (DonCarlos et al. 1989; Miller and Anderson 1989). The domestic ferret experiences multiple ejaculations during a single copulation (Dewsbury 1972).

Ferrets' lengthy copulations—which can last from half an hour to four or five hours—can be costly. Long copulations are energetically expensive and they can increase vulnerability to predatory animals like badgers, even though breeding occurs below ground. Therefore, long copulations must be important for successful pregnancy in the black-footed ferret or the animals would not subject themselves to the increased risk and energy cost. This is true of other mustelids. Domestic ferrets whose coitus was interrupted five minutes after penetration of the penis had sperm present in the vagina and had ovulated, but they did not conceive (Miller and Anderson 1989). In sables *(Martes zibellina),* pregnancy did not occur if copulations lasted less than 20 minutes (Reed 1946).

However, long copulations are not necessary to stimulate ovulation in ferrets. In domestic ferrets, penile intromissions as brief as one minute were sufficient to release an ovulatory burst of luteinizing hormone (Carroll et al. 1985). Precopulatory activity did not cause ovulation, and there was no correlation between length of copulation and the number of eggs released (Carroll et al. 1985).

The more likely explanation for ferrets' lengthy copulations is that the chance of pregnancy is elevated by increasing the number of sperm cells reaching the oviducts, where eggs typically contact sperm (Miller and Anderson 1989). Sperm transport in the female is a function of neurally induced contractions in the female reproductive tract, and a long copulation may provide sufficient neural stimulation for that transport (Chang 1965). Additionally, the vagina of a ferret is

Figure 3.1. Body positions of two black-footed ferrets copulating. Note how the male's rump is pulled under the highest point of the arch of his back; this position is one of the best indicators of penetration. Before penetration, the arch of the male's back is less severe and his rump is behind the back's highest point. Drawing by Wally Van Sickle.

small, and long copulations in which the penis acts as a plug may prevent leakage of sperm. Because ferrets are multiple ejaculators, a short copulation may not deposit enough sperm in the vagina for sufficient numbers to reach the eggs in the oviducts.

In the domestic ferret, eggs are released from ovarian follicles about 30 hours after copulation (Chang 1965), and sperm must spend between 3.5 and 11.5 hours in the female reproductive tract before membrane changes give it the capacity to fertilize an egg (Chang and Yanagamachi 1963). The space vacated on the ovary by each ovulated egg is quickly filled by a corpus luteum. These corpus luteum bodies secrete the hormone progesterone, which is responsible for maintaining pregnancy. Examination of an ovary can indicate whether a female has bred, and counting corpus lutea can reveal reproductive potential, although not every egg ovulated will implant in the uterus and develop into a fetus. If the eggs are ovulated but not fertilized by sperm, the corpus lutea will continue to secrete progesterone in a state that mimics pregnancy. Pregnancy and pseudopregnancy are nearly indistinguishable in ferrets, but it is possible for a black-footed ferret to enter another estrus after a pseudopregnancy (Miller, Anderson, et al. 1988).

Female Sexual Selectivity

As we have seen, female domestic ferrets sometimes solicit male attention by approaching and rubbing. But they also resist copulation during early estrus, becoming more receptive as estrus progresses. Vaginal cytology data show that, despite this behavior, females can be successfully impregnated on the first day of estrus (Miller and Anderson 1990b).

This pattern of female solicitation followed by resistance may be a way of testing male tenacity and maturity. Nearly all carnivores show some correlation between rank and copulatory success (Dewsbury 1982), and lengthy courtship interactions, highlighted by female rejection or fleeing, sometimes test male dominance (Alcock 1984). If the male does not help raise offspring, as is the case with ferret males, the female must measure a male's contribution solely in terms of the fitness bestowed upon her children by the male's genes (Fisher 1930). It thus pays for a female to discriminate based on the male's ability to cope with her aggression.

With weasels, territorial males have higher rank than transient males, but some males are dominant enough to both own a territory and trespass outside its boundaries (Sandell 1986). These dominant males can usually breed any female, whether inside their territory or in the realm of another male. If the dominance system among black-footed ferrets is similar, female resistance during courtship, combined with the lengthy and repeated copulations necessary for pregnancy, may reduce the chances of being bred by a younger male when a more dominant, sexually aggressive male is still available (Miller and Anderson 1993). Of course, this argument assumes that reaching maturity is partially a function of genotype and is a correlate of dominance.

Delayed Implantation

Animals have two basic strategies for energetic partitioning of the reproductive process in a temperate climate with a fixed optimal breeding season. First, the animal can invest a greater amount of energy into gestation and produce a few precocial young, those born in an advanced state of development (Eisenberg 1981). These animals, often herbivores, depend on predictable food resources. The young can flee predators at an early age, and they can be quickly weaned because vegetation requires little skill to harvest. The mother can also replenish her gestational expenditure with easily available food resources.

In contrast, predators like ferrets usually have comparatively short gestations, bear altricial young (those born at a less developed stage), and invest more energy in a long lactation and juvenile development period (Eisenberg 1981). It is difficult for a female carrying a large fetus to hunt. In addition, predators seek an uncertain food resource that requires skill, size, and experience to capture, and post-parturient care and training of young are critical to successful dispersal and survival of offspring.

Thus the altricial strategy has several advantages for predators. First, during winter, when there are fewer prey available and hunting is more demanding, the female can put less energy into gestation. Yet birth can still be early enough in the spring to allow sufficient time for the juveniles to develop the size and skills necessary to survive their first winter (Eisenberg 1981). But putting less energy into gestation means that the energy demands of growing young must be greatly amplified during lactation. The altricial strategy allows the burden of these higher energetic expenses to coincide with the time of greatest prey availability (the spring birth peak). Mustelids, which bear altricial young, increase their energy consumption during lactation 3–16 times over that of the gestation period (East and Lockie 1964; Powell and Leonard 1983; Harlow, Miller, et al. 1985). Lactating black-footed ferrets increase their food intake by a factor of 3–4 (D. Kwiatkowski pers. com., as cited in Miller and Anderson 1993).

A second advantage of the altricial strategy is that bearing precocial young means a longer gestation. In other words, breeding may have to occur in winter to allow sufficient time for juvenile development before dispersal in the fall. Yet mating involves considerable energy, so breeding during the winter may not always be adaptive, particularly for mustelids (Ewer 1973). Their food resources are reduced in winter, and travel in snow is more difficult for short-legged animals (Quick 1951; Sims 1979). In addition, energetic requirements in cold weather are already heightened by the large surface area and short fur of mustelids. The altricial strategy avoids, or reduces, these problems.

Many mustelids also employ a strategy known as delayed implantation. During delayed implantation, mating occurs in the fall and the egg is fertilized, but development is arrested before the egg implants in the wall of the uterus. The egg ceases cell division in the blastocyst stage and simply floats, in a state similar to hibernation, until the next spring. At that time, lengthening days trigger the egg to abandon its "hibernating" state, resume cell division, and implant into the wall of the uterus. The egg then develops normally into a fetus.

Delayed implantation allows a female to give birth early enough in the optimal season for her high energetic demands during lactation and provisioning of young, yet avoids a winter breeding season. For animals that hibernate during cold months, a winter breeding season is not an option. A fall breeding season, combined with delayed implantation over winter, may be an adaptation that allows animals with special circumstances to adjust both mating and parturition to optimal times of the year (Ewer 1973; Powell 1982; Sandell 1984).[2]

Not all mustelids, however, delay implantation. The ferrets (black-footed, Siberian, and European) and least weasels are not delayed implanters although their close relatives the ermine and long-tailed weasels do employ delayed implantation in their reproductive strategy. Sandell (1984) has speculated that because least weasels reach full size in about three months, they can give birth early enough to avoid breeding in winter. But ferrets are larger than weasels and do not delay-implant, so other factors may be involved as well. If fixed gestation is the evolutionarily primitive state, ferrets and least weasels must not have been exposed to the same forces that shaped delayed implantation as a reproductive strategy in species like long-tailed weasels and ermine.

The numerous advantages of the delayed-implantation strategy are clear—the costs of egg storage are minuscule, while the benefits of early breeding are potentially enormous. The strategy would be particularly advantageous where environmental variability is high, as in highly heterogeneous environments with fluctuating food supplies, or where the bioenergetic costs of mating make winter breeding risky.

Ferrets, by contrast, probably evolved to exploit the various species of colonial burrowing rodents that provide a fairly predictable and geographically homogenous food base (at least within the colony). Early ferrets no doubt lived in these creatures' burrows, which were more thermally stable than the surface. In their evolutionary history, therefore, ferrets may not have been exposed to the types of environmental variability that would have favored the development of delayed implantation, and they were optimally sized to exploit the particular prey-abundant niche in which they were found.[3] Similarly, least weasels foraged efficiently in northern clines where the availability of small prey restricted their winter activities to the thermally stable subnivean (under snow) tunnels of deer and white-footed mice (*Peromyscus* spp.) and red-backed voles (*Clethrionomys* spp.). Their small size allowed them to exploit these stable food sources, which were more difficult for the larger ermine and long-tailed weasels to capture (Sims 1979). Sims (1979) cited subnivean maneuverability as a mechanism for resource partitioning that has produced the present pattern of species distribution in North American weasels. During the winter, least weasels and ferrets did not suffer the patchy prey distribution, winter prey reduction, and degree of temperature variation faced by long-tailed weasels and ermine.

In contrast to ferrets and least weasels, long-tailed weasels and ermine have fewer prey available during winter (Quick 1951; Sims 1979), and they often live in shallow dens less than a foot below the surface (Polderboer et al. 1941). These factors increase their energetic requirements and make it difficult to replenish expended energy. Long-tailed weasels and ermine also spend more time in surface travel than do ferrets (utilizing burrows) or least weasels (optimally sized for small rodent tunnels under snow), because their winter prey are distributed more irregularly over the landscape. Exposure to ambient temperature further increases energy expenditure, and snow cover makes travel difficult.

In sum, ferrets and least weasels face different conditions than similarly shaped mustelids that utilize delayed implantation. The factors that resulted in the evolution of delayed implantation (harsh environment, difficulty traveling in snow, and food-resource scarcity during the energetically expensive winter months) simply may not have significantly influenced ferret and least weasel reproductive strategies (Miller and Anderson 1993).

DEVELOPMENT OF THE YOUNG

Birth and Maintenance of Newborn

About six weeks after copulation, the mother ferret gives birth to the young in a prairie dog burrow chamber. No one has excavated black-footed ferret maternal dens, but presumably the birthing chamber is well below the surface to ensure a constant temperature and to remove the kits, as the young are sometimes called, as far as possible from digging predators like badgers. The mother probably collects some kind of lining, such as fur or grass, to cover the nest chamber floor. Alternatively, the mother may usurp a prairie dog's nest chamber.

Unlike the act of sex, the process of birth seems quite serene for black-footed ferrets. The small, thin kits pass from the warm uterus to the cold world very easily. The mother does not seem to experience any contractions. In one case, the mother actually seemed to be resting calmly. Kits were born individually, and the mother licked both the newborn and her own genital area after each birth (Miller and Anderson 1993).

Black-footed ferret kits are born completely helpless, although they can make a cheeping sound almost immediately. Newborns of the three ferret species resemble each other closely. They have a sparse coat of fine white hair, closed eyes, no teeth, flattened ears, and an average birth weight of 7–10 grams (Hillman and Carpenter 1983). Siberian ferrets have pink snouts at birth, while black-footed ferrets have a dark muzzle (Vargas 1994). This feature makes it possible to distinguish the two species when black-footed ferret kits are cross-fostered in captivity to a Siberian ferret mother.

Newborn black-footed ferrets usually huddle together in a small, sleeping, silent ball, but if disturbed they become a small, squirming, "cheeping" ball. Black-footed ferret kits probably cannot maintain their own body temperature very well and depend heavily on their mother for warmth. Newborn weasels and mink will lower their metabolism (and hence their body temperature) whenever their mother leaves the nest, achieving a state similar to hibernation until the mother returns (Segal 1975; C. M. King 1989). This response apparently prevents the young mustelids from using stored energy to maintain a high body temperature when that energy could be channeled into growth. If prey is abundant, the mother can spend more time in the nest, and kits will grow faster (both because of the good food supply and the decreased time spent in a torporous state). Black-footed ferret kits probably use a similar mechanism, balling up to conserve as much energy as possible. A ball of black-footed ferret kits can exchange warmth among individuals as well as reduce heat loss by decreasing the collective surface area of the litter.

The mother nurses her young while lying on her side as the kits crawl to a nipple. The young stimulate milk letdown by pushing against the mammary area with their snouts. Young in large litters do not appear to establish teat ownership, but when litters number only one or two, kits may prefer to nurse exclusively from one nipple. Teats not suckled cease to produce milk. The mother eats the urine and feces of the young until about the 35th day (Miller and Anderson 1993).

By at least 16 days of age black-footed ferret kits have deciduous canines and a few premolars, but they do not eat solid food until roughly 30 days of age (Vargas 1994). The transition from milk to meat is rapid, and most kits are weaned after their 42d day. On occasion, older kits may nurse despite the mother's attempts to discourage it (Vargas 1994).

Pigmentation becomes evident around 16–18 days after birth. Black-footed ferret hair darkens until day 33, when the adult color pattern of dark legs and mask is clearly evident (Vargas 1994). Black-footed ferret kits crack their eyes at

34–37 days of age, and by day 39 both the eyes and ears are open (Vargas 1994). By day 40 the young are mobile, and they are walking by day 41–43. Before this time, and even after the kits begin ambling, the mother will often move her offspring—usually by grasping them on the back of the neck with her mouth and lifting or pulling them along. Kits may also be brought to the surface between the mother's forelegs in a motion that resembles digging (Vargas 1994). By 42 days of age, the kits are nearly one-fifth adult size (Miller and Anderson 1993). In the wild, kits appeared above ground around the age of 60 days. At that time, we counted an average of 3.3 young per litter (Forrest, Biggins, et al. 1988).

Pre-independence Play Behavior

Play behavior was defined by Bekoff (1979) as "motor activity performed postnatally that appeared to be purposeless, in which motor patterns from other contexts may often be used in modified forms and altered temporal sequencing." Bekoff (1979) defined three types of play: social play directed at another individual, object play directed at an inanimate object, and locomotor play characterized by a seemingly frantic flight about the environment.

In ferrets, rough-and-tumble play quickly follows the ability to walk. Such play is accompanied by a great deal of running and jumping with hissing, barking, and screaming vocalizations. In typical social play filmed at six weeks of age, one black-footed ferret kit stood over another (Miller and Anderson 1993). The standing kit bit at the kit below it, while the bottom kit rolled to its back. The bottom kit then used its hind legs to kick at the belly of the top kit as if rapidly pedaling a bicycle. The bottom kit also delivered retaliatory bites. Kits frequently switched positions while engaged in this type of play.

Bites delivered by six-week-old black-footed ferrets were usually but not always aimed at the neck. Poole (1974) reported that the European ferret possesses thick, tough neck skin with a prominent subcutaneous fat layer firmly anchored to muscle by connective tissue. Bites to the neck of a European ferret penetrate the skin, but such wounds do not bleed and they heal quickly. We do not know if black-footed ferret kits have a similar subcutaneous pad, but such a pad would make aiming playful bites at the neck advantageous for three reasons: neck bites would do the least damage to siblings, they are most successful in terms of grip retention, and it is difficult for the animal being bitten to deliver a retaliatory bite.

Approximately 65% (47 of 73) of the bites delivered by six-week-old black-footed ferrets were aimed at the neck (Miller and Anderson 1993). As the kits aged, the frequency of bites aimed at the neck increased. By about 12 weeks of age, approximately 90% of bites during play were delivered to the neck. This figure is roughly equal to the percentage of bites aimed at the neck during adult fights.

Neck biting is an important component in black-footed ferret reproductive, agonistic (competitive), and predatory repertoires. Although inexperienced kits tended to aim bites at the neck, trial-and-error play probably taught them to further concentrate bites toward the front of the body. Thus play fighting seems to offer advantageous experience (Miller and Anderson 1993).

Because biting can be serious business, animals perform species-specific movements to communicate their benign intentions during play (Bekoff 1972). It appears that black-footed ferrets use a play-dance maneuver for this purpose (Miller and Anderson 1993). The play dance, a form of noncontact play, is a series of advance and retreat maneuvers between two or more black-footed ferrets (Figure 3.2). One bounds toward another, but as the gap between them closes they arch their backs, hold their heads erect, and flare their tails. They then dance stiff-legged toward and away from each other and rapidly switch roles from aggressor to defender. Their mouths may be open or closed. With their backs arched high, the young animals leap into the air, often shaking their heads from side to side. When near each other, they then bound forward, backward, and to either side. At greater distances, they walk forward or backward in an exaggerated manner with their backs arched high. As the distance closes, the level of energy expended by each participant usually increases.

Contact occasionally follows the play dance (Miller and Anderson 1993). Sometimes one kit will charge and bump another with its chest, causing the recipient to roll. The aggressive ferret might also lunge by raising its front feet off the ground, pushing off its hind feet, and bumping the defensive ferret with mouth open but without biting. If a bite is delivered, the recipient usually rolls to its back and bicycle-kicks with its hind legs at the belly of the biter. This motion often breaks the neck grip. Both animals may feint or actually bite each other's necks, and attacker and defender roles switch frequently.

A more relaxed form of contact play involves face nibbles. One black-footed ferret nuzzles and nibbles another's neck while the second darts its head from side to side as if sparring. Both animals hold their bodies relatively stationary during this activity.

Locomotor play typically involves frantic acrobatics, such as rolling on the ground, 360-degree spins above the ground, midair somersaults, and stiff-legged leaping (Miller and Anderson 1993). Young black-footed ferrets also chase their tails.

In object play, black-footed ferret kits sometimes bat at rocks, sticks, and brush with one of their front feet (Miller and Anderson 1993). One juvenile was observed bounding toward a stick, pouncing on it with its front feet, and proceeding to bite it. The animal grasped the stick with its mouth, arched its back, and shook its head from side to side violently enough to raise its rear half off the ground.

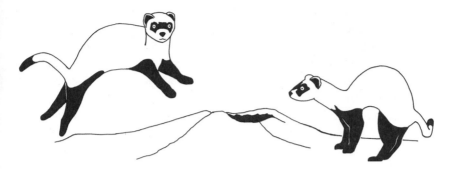

Figure 3.2. Play-dance interaction between two juvenile black-footed ferrets. Drawing by Wally Van Sickle.

Clark, Richardson, et al. (1986) reported that a juvenile black-footed ferret at Meeteetse, Wyoming, repeatedly attacked marker flags, leaping at them with front feet extended and mouth opened, a behavior we also saw in a captive-raised black-footed ferret released to the wild.

Aggressive behavior appears without prior experience, but that does not mean play fighting is not important. Many innate behaviors improve with practice. The animal's level of proficiency may be as important as whether the activity occurs without prior experience. Skills that are well honed by early play may result in an advantage necessary for territory establishment and successful reproduction after the animal reaches adulthood (Symons 1978).

Independence

By late August (about 12 weeks into juvenile ferret development) most black-footed ferrets have reached adult size. Before this point in the young ferrets' lives, the mother has moved the litter repeatedly from one burrow to another, often leading them to a new location where she has killed a prairie dog (Paunovich and Forrest 1987). As the kits verge on independence, the mother begins to take one or more of them on her forays. Some move on their own initiative from the family den to nearby burrows. Males typically leave first. We also observed adult females suddenly leave the area of the family den at this time, forcing their kits toward independence. Later these adult females returned to reclaim their territories.

During this time of dispersal, young ferrets pass safely through adult territories, similar to behavior noted in the feral domestic ferrets of New Zealand (Moors and Lavers 1981). Movements between colonies occur most frequently from early September to early November, with males moving longest distances (Biggins, Schroeder, et al. 1985). Juvenile females typically stay closer to their natal areas; we observed one juvenile female who stayed on her mother's old territory and raised a litter there the following year. That tolerance is seemingly accorded females and not males suggests that male dispersal may be ensuring genetic diversity (and thus, population viability) from place to place, while mothers may be conferring survival advantages to their female offspring by sharing resource-rich territories.

By October, when they are approximately 20 weeks old, the young black-footed ferrets have all gone off on their own, and by November, these animals are solitary and independent, as observed by their tracks in snow (Richardson et al. 1987). This is the most critical time in the life of a young ferret, and most do not survive (Chapter 6). However, those ferrets who secure a territory by winter are likely to survive, as the number of animals tracked in the winter is the same number found the following July. But in order to survive, a young ferret must first establish and maintain a home range.

4

ESTABLISHING A HOME
ON THE RANGE

For two days the male and female black-footed ferrets remained in the depths of the prairie dog chamber, alternately breeding and sleeping for several hours at a stretch. But on this third night, the female was becoming slightly more hostile toward the male's approaches. Ovulation had occurred with the first copulation, and her estrogen levels were now dropping fast. So too was her interest in reproduction. Her rapidly changing internal state meant that further copulation would do little to increase the chance of pregnancy. Her soft chuckling vocalizations of the first night had given way to a threatening hiss.

The male, aware of these changes, took the hint and headed for the surface. In the cold night breezes of late March, he walked a few steps from the tunnel opening and stopped to look for danger, holding his head high and sniffing the air. Pushing off with his front legs, he held his torso upright, like a dachshund begging at a kitchen table. His front legs hung limply in front of him as he turned his head from side to side, scanning the horizon. Convinced that he was safe for now, he dropped back to all four feet.

Tonight, the male undertook a random inspection of his territory. He bounded toward a nearby burrow, his front feet landing side by side and his back arching high as his hindquarters swung through the air toward his anchored front feet. After he pushed off with his front feet, his hind feet landed in the spot the front feet had occupied as he extended forward for another leap (Figure 4.1). Running in this fashion, the ferret was using his spine as an extension of his legs. Swiftness is determined by rate of leg movement and length of stride; by using his spine to elongate his step, he was adding considerable speed to his gait.[1]

Suddenly the male stopped. He had reached one of his scent marks, an invisible signpost announcing that this was his territory. The scent was beginning to

Figure 4.1. Forward-bounding (running) movements of a black-footed ferret. Drawing by Wally Van Sickle.

fade and had to be replaced. Because breeding season is a time of year critical for boundary delineation, the male covered greater distances than usual, and scent-marked more frequently. If his signposts were not maintained, neighboring males would try to move into his realm. The male dropped his genital area to the ground, swayed his back downward, and raised his tail slightly above the plane of his body. He then pulled his torso forward with his front legs while rapidly wiggling his pelvis from side to side. A minute later, satisfied that he had restored an olfactory barrier, the male bounded off toward other checkpoints along the periphery of his home range.

AGGRESSION, CONFLICT, AND THE ROLE OF HOME RANGES

Valuable resources essential for survival and reproduction are often limited, and aggression (whether actual, ritualized, or implied by scent marks) is a means of protecting them. Maynard Smith and Parker (1976) speculated that physical conflict occurs in the animal kingdom when there is no clear asymmetry between contestants. If asymmetry is evident (for example, when one animal is clearly a territory owner and the other is an intruder), natural selection should favor the individuals that modify their behavior according to the chances of winning or losing and the overall effects of conflict on the individual's fitness (Thornhill 1984). Individuals often establish relatively stable alliances precluding agonistic interactions that could be harmful. Black-footed ferrets have tremendous predatory assets that make them extremely dangerous adversaries should conflict escalate to the point of overt hostility. Thus ferrets must have evolved mechanisms to contain aggression.[2]

Among black-footed ferrets, avoidance plays a much greater role than aggression in resolving conflict. Fighting between black-footed ferrets has never been seen in the wild, though it is almost certain that aggressive encounters do occur in nature (fighting has been observed in captivity). Among animals in general, the ferocity of conflict depends on the external situation and the physiological state of the individuals (Tinbergen 1968). For example, two animals meeting at the boundary of their respective territories respond differently than if one were intruding into the heart of the other's residence (Poole 1974). Theoretically, a resident will attack an intruder, but in fact an animal outside its own territory usually retreats. The majority of vicious encounters occur during the breeding season, when hormonal changes and the high stakes of reproduction elevate levels of belligerence. Outside the breeding season, European ferrets, feral domestic ferrets in New Zealand, and Siberian ferrets rarely fight, except in a token or ritual form, whereas breeding-season hostility is real and sometimes even fatal (Volchanetskii 1931; Poole 1966; Moors and Lavers 1981).

Female black-footed ferrets have smaller home ranges than males, with one male's home range often overlapping the ranges of several females (Biggins, Schroeder, et al. 1985; Richardson et al. 1987). Ferrets follow the typical mustelid spacing pattern, whereby individuals occupy territories from which they attempt to exclude members of the same sex (see Powell 1979). Overlap occasionally occurs, but home ranges are usually fairly well defined; there are exceptions, however, to this general rule. Near Meeteetse, Wyoming, we observed two females with litters in very close proximity, and once their offspring occupied the same burrow.

HOW BOUNDARIES ARE ESTABLISHED

Scent
Ferrets recognize other ferrets through either individual contact or detection of scent marks. All mustelids possess anal scent glands. The muscles that control these glands are voluntary, so mustelids can secrete scent a little at a time, or empty the whole gland at once. Skunks are well known for their use of these glands as a specialized defense. With ferrets, the scent is not a weapon but a means to delineate home range boundaries. The deposited scent can also identify the individual depositor and reveal the animal's sexual condition and social status.

The scent is often deposited with an anal drag (described above), which black-

Figure 4.2. Scent-marking behavior of a black-footed ferret. Drawing by Wally Van Sickle.

footed ferrets perform throughout the year (Figure 4.2). Scent marking has been observed several times in the wild. In addition to the anal drag, we saw free-ranging black-footed ferrets straddle and rub their genital areas back and forth over small bushes or rocks. In captivity, black-footed ferrets of both sexes rubbed their anal areas over the edges of ceramic water bowls and concrete blocks. The rubbing motion sometimes left an oily secretion. Marking patterns could also include a body swipe in the snow or a stamped-down patch of snow.

Ermine also perform anal rubs throughout the year, but males increase their frequency during the breeding season; dominant ermine scent-mark three times more frequently than subordinates (Erlinge, Sandell, and Brinck 1982). Data from Meeteetse showed that black-footed ferrets also increased their marking behavior with the approach of the breeding season (Richardson et al. 1987). We suspect that dominant black-footed ferrets, like ermine, probably scent-mark more frequently than subordinates, although this has not been verified in the field.

Defecation and urination patterns may be another form of marking home-range boundaries. When defecating, captive black-footed ferrets make no attempt to cover their feces, and they show a preference for defecating and urinating in the same spots of their cages. In the wild, similarly, urination spots were most often seen near mounded burrows (Richardson et al. 1987). When a species is solitary, olfactory communication is enhanced if droppings are concentrated in a prominent spot (Kleiman 1972). Thus scent-marking generally reduces physical conflict between individuals by defining territories.

Aggression
When two black-footed ferrets do meet, the response is highly variable, depending on location, season of the year, the status and age of the animals, and possibly

their degree of relatedness. If the encounter is not aggressive or territorial, they may sniff each other's anal-genital area or the substrate the other animal has recently occupied. Chuckling vocalization accompanies friendly greetings as well as mating (Miller and Anderson 1993). A similar trilling sound in weasels has been described as a signal of pleasurable excitement (Hartman 1964). We also heard chuckling from a wild weasel after it killed a mouse on a prairie dog colony, and Quick (1951) reported the same sound when a captive weasel killed a mouse. No vocalization has been heard when black-footed ferrets kill prey.

During tense encounters between black-footed ferrets, at least four distinct vocalizations have been identified (Hillman 1968; Hillman and Carpenter 1983; Clark, Richardson, et al. 1986; Miller and Anderson 1993). One is a prolonged hiss, emitted by a threatened ferret. If the threat looms larger, the ferret emits a single explosive bark, often combined with a feigned lunge. When a ferret is cornered, or when contact seems inevitable, the single bark escalates to chattering bursts of barks, often four to seven per second. This chatter-bark is virtually identical to vocalizations made by weasels, other species of ferrets, pine martens *(Martes americana),* and fishers *(M. pennanti),* except that those of the larger animals are relatively lower in pitch. The combination of explosive barks and rapid lunges has been known to startle many larger animals, including biologists. Finally, a shriek or scream (which at lower pitches resembles a snarl) is heard during fights. This shriek, which may be a cry of despair from a dominated animal (the offensive animal is usually silent), is usually accompanied by release of a strong musky smell from the anal scent glands.

When actual aggression occurs, it is quick and decisive. Typically, the attacker starts from an alert or arched position, with head high, and then pushes off with its hind legs and extends its body above and toward the recipient. In response, the opponent sometimes raises its body so that the two animals collide chest to chest (see Miller and Anderson 1993 for a more detailed description of aggressive and defensive actions).

The object of the offensive lunge is to deliver a bite. Most bites are aimed at the neck (e.g., about 90%, or 142 of 161 bites during 19 fights; see Miller and Anderson 1993), but some are aimed at the flank. If the attacker is successful in its attempts to bite the opponent's neck, it often rolls over the other animal to avoid retaliatory bites.

Meanwhile the recipient (while emitting a chattering bark or scream) uses evasive tactics to break the grip of the attacker. The most common evasive move we have seen is a roll that resulted in the attacker standing over the defensive animal. The evading ferret, on its back, bicycle-kicks its hind legs into the attacker's stomach, scratches with its front legs, and bites. If this maneuver breaks the neck grip, the evader twists out from under the attacker and assumes an upright stance on all four feet. It then either counter-attacks or flees. In one instance, a captive ferret's escape was halted when the attacking ferret bit and held the fleeing animal's tail (Miller and Anderson 1993).

One offensive move does not involve biting. A ferret that wants to displace another from a nest box sometimes backs into the box flank first. The advancing animal uses its flank and arched side to bump and push the other animal out of the box.

Threatened ferrets use defensive postures to reduce the chance or success of attacks. In one such posture, the tail is flared and the body is flattened to the floor. The feet are drawn underneath and the erect hair on the back and sides makes the body appear larger than it is. The head is either cocked above the torso or lowered to a position in direct line with the body. The threatened animal often hisses defiantly.

A threatened black-footed ferret may also assume a standing defensive position with the back arched upward, tail flared, and head held erect, either facing the attacker or turned sideways with the head and neck facing the adversary. The mouth can be gaping or closed, a gape indicating a more intense encounter. The ferret frequently hisses.

Black-footed ferrets can make a threatening movement from the standing defensive position. The ferret rears on its hind legs as it whips the upper part of its body (mouth open) from side to side. Descending, the ferret simultaneously stomps both front feet on the surface. Alternatively, the ferret leaps into the air with all four feet off the ground, mouth open, shaking its head. The body reacts to the head-throw with a whiplash effect. This maneuver was also performed by a black-footed ferret whose bottom half and lower legs were positioned in a burrow. Upright with mouth open, the ferret whipped its head from side to side. The force of the motion caused the middle of the body to flex in opposition to the head. As the ferret whipped its head, its front feet were raised parallel to the ground and thrown from side to side by the force of the motion.

From the down defensive position or the arched position, a ferret can lunge forward if an adversary comes too close. The lunge may end in a snap or strike, or the opponent may be bumped with an open mouth but not gripped with the teeth. The snap is defensive and not necessarily an attempt to initiate a prolonged neck grip. The move is usually accompanied by a sharp bark. When the front feet hit the surface, the lunging ferret pushes off and recoils backward to an arched position. The maneuver can be rapidly repeated several times. Two ferrets in an arched position could feint while circling, advancing, or retreating.

Digging

Scent-marking, ritualized threats, and physical contact with an intruder may be methods of protecting critical resources that are common across species. But black-footed ferrets may have one more means of defending those assets. In the process of hunting prairie dogs, black-footed ferrets must often remove loose dirt, or a solid dirt plug, that blocks a tunnel. Earthen plugs were found in 61% (11 of 18) of the excavated black-tailed prairie dog burrows (Sheets et al. 1971) and in 25% (7 of 28) of the excavated white-tailed prairie dog burrows (Hanebury et al. n.d.). Another study found diggings at 38% of 24 burrows where black-footed ferrets preyed on prairie dogs (Richardson et al. 1987). These piles of soil may serve notice that the area is occupied (Figure 4.3).

Figure 4.3. Physical evidence (a digging and ferret tracks with a drag mark to the side) indicating that a black-footed ferret excavated the plug to a prairie dog tunnel, killed a prairie dog, and then carried it to another burrow. Photo by Brian Miller.

Diggings were most commonly observed from December through March at both Meeteetse (Clark, Richardson, et al. 1984) and South Dakota (F. R. Henderson et al. 1974), although the behavior has been noted at all times of the year. When black-footed ferrets dig, they deposit soil on top of the prairie dog mound in a manner distinctive only to ferrets (Hillman 1968; F. R. Henderson et al. 1974; Clark, Campbell, et al. 1984). Because of the characteristic indentation stretching across the top of the dirt pile toward the mouth of the burrow, the ferret digging is often referred to as a trench.

The amount of subsoil in a digging varies. Biggins and Fagerstone (1984) reported an average of 154 grams of soil moved per minute on four observed digs. The largest digging weighed 20.3 kilograms and was produced in 109 minutes, a prodigious feat for a ferret that weighed 1 kilogram and worked without implements. This accomplishment is equivalent to a 90-kilogram person moving a metric ton of soil per hour without a shovel.

For those who search for signs of black-footed ferrets, it is important to note that there is a great deal of variability in ferret diggings (see Clark, Campbell, et al. 1984; Clark, Richardson, et al. 1984). Searching for trenches is often more of an art than a science, subject not only to individual variability but also to age of the digging and weather. If prairie dogs are active, ferret diggings will not last long; if prairie dogs are hibernating, diggings can remain recognizable for a month or more. Prairie dog diggings can be confused with ferret diggings, but generally prairie dogs scatter the dirt more widely. A trench produced by a prairie dog is usually cut into the prairie dog mound itself, whereas a ferret indentation is in the subsoil deposited on top of the mound. Badgers also dig into prairie dog burrows and deposit subsoil on the prairie dog mound, but a badger is too large to fit into a prairie dog burrow without enlarging the opening. A quick check of burrow-opening size helps distinguish between ferret and badger diggings.

Black-footed ferrets also dig in snow, although much less frequently than in soil (Richardson et al. 1987). In these instances, snow is moved to form a trough extending from the mouth of a prairie dog burrow but the soil is not disturbed.

LOCATION AND SIZE OF HOME RANGES

Securing a home range is critical to survival and successful reproduction. The location of home ranges depends on the relative wealth of critical resources. For female black-footed ferrets, the most critical resource is a high and reliable density of prairie dogs. Because prairie dog densities can vary somewhat, it is advantageous for females to stick with a rich area as long as it produces sufficient prey. Indeed, at Meeteetse it was not uncommon to see litters in the same locations from one year to the next, or even the same female raising successive litters in the same location (Forrest, Biggins, et al. 1988). A female with a litter must kill far more prey than a single animal would need, yet her movements are limited by the location of the natal den. She must spend as little time away from the nest as possible: the newborn kits need her body heat to grow rapidly, and she must protect the litter from intruders. Thus females' home ranges must meet elevated energy requirements within a small geographic area. Males typically range farther. Males presumably view females, rather than prey, as the critical resource, and a home range that includes several females increases their probability of successful reproduction (see Powell 1979 for more on mustelid home-range patterns).

Female carnivores, including weasels, typically shrink and expand their home ranges as prey densities increase and decrease (Robina 1960; Erlinge 1974; C. M. King 1975, 1989; B. M. Fitzgerald 1977). Such data are scarce for black-footed ferrets, however, as only two populations have been studied in the wild, one on a black-tailed prairie dog complex in South Dakota and the other on a white-tailed prairie dog complex in Wyoming. The density of black-tailed prairie dogs throughout the area containing ferrets in Mellette County, South Dakota, was estimated at about 28 per hectare (R. L. Linder et al. 1972). The 1984 white-tailed prairie dog density on three colonies inhabited by ferrets west of Meeteetse, Wyoming, was estimated to be 20, 19, and 7 per hectare using mark-recapture techniques (Menkens and Anderson 1991). Black-footed ferrets averaged one litter per 30 hectares on the South Dakota black-tailed prairie dog complex (Hillman, Linder, and Dahlgren 1979) and one litter per 57 hectares on the Wyoming white-tailed prairie dog complex in 1984 (Forrest, Clark, et al. 1985b). In Wyoming, litters were not observed on white-tailed prairie dog colonies smaller than 49 hectares (Forrest, Clark, et al. 1985a). One female that was radio-tracked for 43 days used 53 hectares in the fall (Biggins, Schroeder, et al. 1985), and daily observations revealed that a female with a litter used 41 hectares for 33 days in the summer (Paunovich and Forrest 1987).

Female black-footed ferrets may adjust the size of their home ranges somewhat with changes in prey density, but we caution that behavioral spacing mechanisms (such as the desire to maintain a certain distance from other animals of the same sex) may also influence this process, particularly when ranges shrink below a certain size. The size of male home ranges may be more strongly based on behavioral spacing mechanisms and access to females than on energetic needs. The important aspect of home ranges, however, is still the protection of resources necessary for survival and reproduction.

5

FINDING FOOD WHILE AVOIDING BEING EATEN

Like a tiny periscope, the female black-footed ferret poked her head above ground on a warm July night (Figure 5.1). She watched alertly from the safety of her burrow for nearly a quarter-hour before crawling to the surface. Her four kits lay nestled in a chamber below ground, and watchfulness was the key to their survival and her own.

The female had killed a prairie dog the night before. While nosing around in a burrow, she had encountered a plug of dirt about 2 meters below the ground. The plug was nearly a meter long, but her keen sense of smell told her that food was on the other side.[1] Resolutely, she clawed a chunk of dirt out of the plug. Then, holding it under her chest with her front legs, she began backing up. Her movements resembled those of an inchworm in reverse: she would anchor her rump, pull the dirt underneath her by arching her back, then kick her rump backward and repeat the whole process. Each time she reached the surface, she would drop the subsoil in a pile on top of the prairie dog mound, shake the dirt out of her fur, and reenter the burrow for another load.

After an hour's work, she finally broke through and encountered a wide-awake prairie dog. He was a large male and outweighed her by several hundred grams, but she picked her moment and struck like a cobra. Grabbing the side of his neck with her canines, she wrapped her front legs around the prairie dog's body before he could retaliate. Bracing her back against the burrow wall, she moved her teeth to the prairie dog's throat. The throat-hold closed the windpipe, and soon the prairie dog stopped struggling. She then pulled the prairie dog to the surface and carried him with a neck grip, his hind legs dragging alongside her body as she bounded toward a cache she maintained near the natal burrow (Fig-

52

Figure 5.1. A black-footed ferret poking its head out of a burrow. Photo by Brian Miller.

ure 5.2). Tonight, when the risk of encountering predators would be reduced, she would bring the four kits to the surface and lead them to the cache.

When she sensed that no danger lurked, she allowed the kits, half her size, to pop out of the burrow one by one. Hesitant at first, they were soon barely able to contain their enthusiasm. Their coats were sleek and without blemish; all they had done in life so far was play and show up for meals. In contrast, the mother's coat looked scruffy on her thin body and the energetic demands of raising the litter were taking a physical toll. While the family was assembling near the burrow, two of the kits could contain their high-voltage energy no longer. They suddenly arched their backs and began to hop forward and backward, throwing their heads quickly from side to side in a wild dancing motion. But the mother did not want to dally on the surface, and soon they were all bounding off through the moonlight, the mother in front and the kits single-file close behind her—a little train of ferrets chugging toward the cache.

There was good reason for caution. Although the mother and her litter were relatively safe in the confines of a deep prairie dog chamber, the surface was a dangerous place. The yearling male that had fathered this litter disappeared shortly after leaving her burrow last spring. His good luck had expired, and he paid the price of vigilantly patrolling his territory during the breeding season.

His death rode on wingtips feathered in such a way that not the slightest hiss of

Figure 5.2. A black-footed ferret carrying a dead prairie dog. Photo by Tim Clark.

air displacement was audible during flight. The great horned owl *(Bubo virginianus)* hunts at night with incredible accuracy. Its ears function separately, enabling the owl to measure the difference in time it takes a noise to reach each ear. The slightest sound thus guides it toward the prey no matter how dark the night. The last trace of the male ferret lay in a light March snow. A trail of ferret tracks led to a scuffed area marked with a few drops of blood and the impressions of two wingtips that had brushed the snow as the owl worked to regain altitude.

The yearling male's death left his territory open for another male. In October, the young would be on their own, moving through the colony looking for a home. One newly dispersed male would find the vacant area. He would settle in, scent-mark his boundaries, and with luck survive the winter to reproduce next year. The cycle of life would continue.

PREDATION

Establishing Food Preferences
The food preferences of black-footed ferrets are fairly straightforward: they eat prairie dogs almost exclusively. In South Dakota, black-tailed prairie dogs made up 91% of 82 ferret scats (droppings), with mice representing the remaining 9%

(Sheets et al. 1972). At Meeteetse, Campbell, Clark, et al. (1987) found white-tailed prairie dog remains in 87% of 86 ferret scats they examined. The remainder included deer mouse *(Peromyscus maniculatus),* sage brush vole *(Lagurus curtatus),* montane vole *(Microtus montanus),* and Nuttall's cottontail *(Sylvilagus nuttallii).*[2]

Apfelbach (1978, 1986) concluded that there is a critical period during the juvenile domestic ferret's life in which food preferences are determined. Olfactory imprintation between the ages of 60 and 90 days, a period correlated with neural development, influenced later food choice (Apfelbach 1986). There is a similar imprintation period for black-footed ferrets between the ages of 60 and 90 days when their food preferences are influenced (Vargas 1994). Living in prairie dog burrows and being fed prairie dogs at an early age by the mother permanently solidifies the taste preferences of the young black-footed ferret. Due to early olfactory imprinting on a specific prey species (Vargas 1994), they show immediate preference for prairie dogs when they begin to hunt.

Meeting Bioenergetic Requirements

Estimates of black-footed ferrets' energetic needs have been made from both direct observation and theoretical approaches. One captive ferret ate 50–70 grams of prairie dog meat per day (Joyce 1988), and captive Siberian ferrets ate 62 grams of meat each day (Powell, Clark, et al. 1985). The high energetic costs of gestation increase during lactation and while provisioning weaned but not yet dispersed young.

Biggins, Miller, et al. (1993) estimated annual energetic requirements for female black-footed ferrets by assuming 42 days for gestation, 42 days for lactation, 80 days for postweaning demands on the mother by her litter of 3.3 young, 51 days for replenishing previous demands by the litter, and 150 days of maintenance. Because females must share resources with the males that overlap their ranges, and because one male's range often overlaps several females' ranges, an assumed overlap of 0.5 males per female's home range was taken into account. The model predicted that 66,420 grams of prairie dog were necessary to meet a ferret's annual energetic needs. Biggins, Miller, et al. (1993) assumed that the average prairie dog weighs 760 grams (J. King 1955, Clark 1977), and that 20% of each prairie dog killed is wasted (C. Hillman pers. com., as cited in Stromberg et al. 1983). Grams of meat were, therefore, converted into an estimate of 109 prairie dogs necessary to maintain a female black-footed ferret with an average-sized litter for one year. This estimate was in turn translated into the number of prairie dogs necessary to maintain a stable population undergoing that level of harvest in addition to harvest by other predators. Biggins, Miller, et al. (1993) estimated that 762 prairie dogs were needed per black-footed ferret family each year. Other estimates have ranged as high as 2,000 prairie dogs needed per family annually (Klebanoff et al. 1991).

Eating the Prey

Polsky (1975) postulated that a predator's motivation to kill is separate from its need for food, and that different anatomical sites in the brain govern eating and killing. For that reason satiated mustelids kill and cache prey they cannot eat (Polderboer et al. 1941; Stroganov 1962; Sims 1979; Powell 1982). Richardson et al. (1987) have presented evidence that black-footed ferrets cache prey, and one ferret was seen eating a decaying prairie dog carcass (K. Fagerstone pers. com.). Many small predators, who could only store fat at a cost to mobility (thus sacrificing foraging ability and predator avoidance), are forced to cache prey (Ewer 1973; Eisenberg 1981). In winter, when energy demands are highest, an available cache could ensure the animal's survival.

When eating the kill, black-footed ferrets shear tough pieces of meat with their carnassial pairs. They also tear off pieces of meat by placing their front feet on the food item while gripping it with their incisors and canines; they then jerk their heads back or shake their heads laterally. If a puncture wound on the prey bleeds, they lap the blood before eating the meat. This behavior may be the source of the misconception that mustelids, particularly weasels, suck blood from their prey.

Black-footed ferrets usually begin eating small prey items at the head, and sometimes eat only the head. When eating prairie dogs, however, they begin in the throat area and work down to the organs (Vargas 1994). In some cases, a litter of black-footed ferrets eats an entire prairie dog, including skin, teeth, and claws (Vargas 1994). At other times, they "skin back" a freshly killed prairie dog, much as a trapper removes the pelt from a carcass. Young black-footed ferrets in the wild have been seen dragging around a prairie dog hide like a toddler's security blanket.

The Act of Killing

It is not easy to be a predator. Prey can be difficult to find and dangerous once it is located. Black-footed ferrets are killers of prey that can be the same size as or larger than themselves, a somewhat unusual adaptation seen only in anatomically or behaviorally specialized carnivores (Eisenberg and Leyhausen 1972). Behaviorally, black-footed ferrets greatly reduce risk of injury by hunting at night when prairie dogs are inactive. Anatomically, ferrets possess canines of greater-than-expected length (in relation to body size) which are used to penetrate the head, neck, and throat of their prey. Their long, thin, supple bodies also provide a strength and leverage advantage, particularly when securing prey in the confines of a burrow.

Because prairie dogs can be larger than ferrets, efficient placement of the kill bite at an early age is important to the ferret's survival. There has been debate about the degree of learning involved in the mustelid kill bite. Innate kill bites have been reported for the European ferret (Wustehuße 1960) and ermine (Gossow 1970). East and Lockie (1964), on the other hand, gave live mice to least weasels at regular intervals beginning when the weasels were 39 days old. The initial attempts to capture mice involved random bites, and the weasels seemed frightened if the mice defended themselves, but eventually—between 45 and 56 days of age—they all killed with a neck bite. What East and Lockie observed may have been as much a process of maturation as learning. Some behaviors are innate but only appear at a certain stage of development. Eibl-Eibesfeldt (1956) reported that inexperienced European ferrets initially bit randomly but quickly learned by trial and error to aim at the neck. A 10-month-old male described as "powerful," however, was badly bitten by a rat on his first attempt to kill prey; one month later the same ferret remained wary of rats (Eibl-Eibesfeldt 1956).

Captive research with black-footed ferrets suggests that the neck bite is innate, but proficiency increases with experience and play with siblings helps hone neck-biting skill (Miller and Anderson 1993; Vargas 1994). Both Siberian ferrets (Miller, Biggins, et al. 1992) and black-footed ferrets (Vargas 1994) killed prairie dogs on first opportunity but also killed more efficiently with experience.

Mustelid killing behavior is difficult to see in the wild, and black-footed ferrets may be the most elusive in that they almost always kill prairie dogs underground. Indeed, nearly all documented killing has occurred underground and out of sight of the observer (Hillman 1968; Clark, Richardson, et al. 1986; L. Hanebury pers. com.; R. Paunovich pers. com.). Clark, Richardson, et al. (1986) reported seeing a Uinta ground squirrel *(Spermophilus armatus)* killed above ground with a neck bite, and D. Biggins (pers. com.) found one prairie dog that had been killed by a bite to the thorax. Captive black-footed ferrets killed hamsters with a bite to the back of the neck, top of the head, or thorax (Miller and Anderson 1993; Vargas 1994).

We once observed with Bob Luce, the nongame mammal biologist for the Wyoming Game and Fish Department, a free-ranging male black-footed ferret killing a prairie dog in a burrow. Roughly the first meter of the burrow was visible, and the ferret and prairie dog were just below the surface. The ferret was curled around the prairie dog, holding it with his front legs while gripping the prairie dog around the side of the neck (top canines in the throat). The prairie dog twisted in the ferret's grip so that both animals were briefly lying stomach to stomach. Eventually the prairie dog fought loose, screaming all the while, but the ferret leaped on it from behind and secured another neck grip. This time, the ferret successfully restrained the prairie dog and wedged his body tightly against the burrow wall for leverage. The death grip was difficult to observe, but it appeared to be on the side and front of the prairie dog's throat. The screaming soon ended. The ferret held the prairie dog for a short time, then backed down the burrow dragging the prairie dog out of sight. The total elapsed time of the kill was about five minutes.

Astrid Vargas, who earned a doctorate in black-footed ferret behavior at the University of Wyoming, has more experience than anyone else at evaluating this species' predatory behavior. She found that the kill bite is not delivered to the back of the prairie dog's neck but to the throat. The prairie dog is suffocated by the strength of the ferret's bite. Although ferrets may initially grab the neck in the most convenient location, they move the bite around to the front of the throat for final dispatch (Figure 5.3). Experienced ferrets kill prairie dogs with a single bite to the throat (Vargas 1994).

Developing Predatory Ability

Killing is only part of the predatory sequence. An animal must first be able to locate prey. Indeed, two captive-raised fishers that killed prey on first exposure in captivity later starved to death after release into the wild, presumably because they were unable to search for food successfully (Kelly 1977).

Ewer (1973) characterized most mustelids as solitary, opportunistic hunters. This is certainly an accurate description of the black-footed ferret. A typical mustelid hunting pattern is highly nonlinear; mustelids investigate places where prey is likely to be found (Powell 1978) and probably alter direction to increase probability of contact with prey (Krebs 1973). Black-footed ferrets and Siberian ferrets move in a similar nonlinear manner from burrow to burrow (Hillman 1968).

In addition to locating prey, it is also important for a predator to time the attack properly. Prairie dogs and wild black-footed ferrets often act unconcerned if both are above ground. In one instance several hours after sunrise, we saw a prairie dog enter a burrow occupied by a ferret, exit quickly, then sit motionless less than 1 meter from the entrance. The ferret partially emerged from the burrow and looked alternately toward and away from the prairie dog for several minutes but did not attack.

When we did see black-footed ferrets (all juveniles) attack prairie dogs on the surface, the prairie dogs resisted or even chased the ferrets. This unusual behavior probably reflects the fact that wild ferrets are more efficient killers when in the burrow, and thus less of a threat on the surface. Experienced ferrets probably kill only underground and at night when prairie dogs are inactive.

Figure 5.3. A black-footed ferret killing a prairie dog as prey. Drawing by Wally Van Sickle.

Verbeek (1985) has described many instances of immature raptors pursuing inappropriate prey, including prey too large to handle. Siford (1982) saw a mink unsuccessfully attack a young trumpeter swan *(Cygnus buccinator)* that was two-thirds adult size. Perhaps most graphically, Barrow (1953, as cited in C. M. King 1989) saw a waterhen flying overhead with a weasel gripping its throat. These cases probably exemplify Griffiths's (1975) hypothesis that juvenile predators attack prey opportunistically, whereas adults select their victims. Juvenile black-footed ferrets that attack prairie dogs above ground may be learning by trial and error when it is appropriate to attack prey.

In the sequence of juvenile development, kits first appear above ground during July when they are about two months old and still occupy the same burrow as their mother (F. R. Henderson et al. 1974). At this time, kits are probably all weaned. Tan and Counsilman (1985) reported that, in kittens, weaning influences acquisition of prey-catching abilities. They suggested that physiological changes associated with weaning could alter the behavior of kittens, through either diet-induced hormonal changes or altered neural centers. This may also be the case with black-footed ferret kits, although such research has not been conducted.

Black-footed ferret kits are probably fed prey by their mother after they wean. We do not know whether she presents them with live immobilized prey or whether dead prairie dogs are sufficient stimulus to initiate predator behaviors. But because even juvenile prairie dogs are large and unmanageable for a kit, it seems likely that dead prey are the primary exposure for young ferrets. In other animal species, the mother appears to assist predatory experience in her young with exposure to prey. Experience with prey during infancy in the presence of a mother cat improved the predatory abilities of kittens when they reached adulthood (Caro 1979, 1980a). Heidt et al. (1968) reported a mother least weasel presenting an immobilized (but live) mouse to her 40-day-old young.

Caro (1979, 1980b) showed that, in kittens, some measures of social play with siblings correlated with later prey-catching ability. Play among black-footed ferret siblings, easily observed during July and August, may promote efficient neck-bite placement.

In August (when kits are about three months old) the mother black-footed ferret often moves her kits into individual burrows near her own; at this time the young are first observed hunting alone. Similarly, domestic ferrets first respond readily to prey odors with searching behavior at three months of age (Apfelbach 1978).

If juvenile predatory efforts are unsuccessful, they may still rely on their mother, who resides in the immediate area. They probably learn gradually, through trial and error, to differentiate between inappropriate and appropriate prey opportunities. Dispersal occurs during September and October, coincidental with this increase in predatory skill, completing the kits' transition to solitary, self-sufficient adulthood.

AVOIDANCE OF PREDATORS

Behavioral traits do not exist in isolation, and the constant threat of predation is one of the prime forces of directional selection in many species. Examples of affected behavior include time of breeding, herding, and feeding strategies (Altmann 1958; Morton 1971; Bertram 1980; Caraco et al. 1980; Faneslow and Lester 1988). Other studies indicate that predation is an important selection agent influencing adaptations in a variety of potential prey (Rosenweig 1973; Vermeij 1982). Even in moderately large carnivores, hunting behavior, socialization, and predator-avoidance behaviors influence each other (Caro 1989).

As Powell (1973) showed with weasel populations, black-footed ferret population sizes may be controlled by predation. Whenever a ferret is hunting, the arrival of a larger predator can transform the ferret from hunter to hunted. Dean Biggins of the National Biological Service is currently investigating the role of predation in the evolution of ferret morphology and behavior for a doctoral dissertation. Most studies to date have discussed the evolution of these characteristics as adaptation to hunting rodents in tunnels. Underground hunting has undoubtedly influenced the morphology and behavior of black-footed ferrets, but Dean's central idea is that living below ground likewise ensures safety from surface predators, which may also have played a large role in defining these traits.

In South Dakota, F. R. Henderson et al. (1974) reported predation or pursuit of black-footed ferrets by badgers, great horned owls, domestic dogs *(Canis familiaris)*, domestic cats *(Felis cattus)*, and coyotes. In Wyoming, Forrest, Biggins, et al. (1988) reported predation or pursuit of ferrets by badgers, great horned owls, golden eagles *(Aquila chrysaetos)*, prairie falcons *(Falco mexicanus)*, ferruginous hawks *(Buteo regalis)*, coyotes, and a domestic dog. Great horned owls accounted for three of five known instances of predation on black-footed ferrets at Meeteetse, Wyoming, and were probably their most dangerous avian predator. When ferrets confronted an avian predator, they quickly dove into a nearby burrow (Forrest, Biggins, et al. 1988). During reintroduction of black-footed ferrets into Shirley Basin, Wyoming, coyotes were by far the most common predator (Biggins, Miller, and Hanebury 1992).

Great horned owls and badgers would eat black-footed ferrets, starting at the rump and working their way toward the head. (We usually recovered the front half of the ferret, or at least the head and shoulders, deep in the badger's burrow or below the owl's perch site.) Coyotes, by contrast, would rarely eat a black-footed ferret. Instead, they would typically carry the dead ferret to a nearby hillside and bury it intact a few centimeters below the ground. They would manicure the surface of the grave to blend in with the surroundings, and the burial site would be nearly impossible to see even when radiotelemetry revealed its exact location. We once waited a week for a coyote to return to the carcass, but it did not.

Successful predator-avoidance behavior calls for both recognition of a potential predator and efficient performance of the correct escape response. In wild animals, Bolles (1970) has speculated, innate species-specific defense reactions (such as fleeing, freezing, and fighting) occur rapidly whenever animals encounter certain stimuli. Bolles hypothesized that avoiding predation in the wild has little to do with learning, and it makes sense evolutionarily that a trait as urgent as escaping predation be developmentally fixed (Alcock 1984; Coss and Owings 1985; Magurran 1989).

A number of studies (reviewed by Shalter 1984) indicate that prey recognize a few key characteristics of broad classes of predators. According to Shalter, the general rule may be that young prey possess the ability to respond to a wide variety of stimuli, and through a process of habituation narrow their responses to only those stimuli presenting a real and immediate threat. Through this habituation process, the prey animal not only determines which species represent a threat but also makes the more fine-tuned determination of whether an individual predator is hunting or satiated. The mother probably plays an important early role in the differentiation of novel and familiar experiences (Bronson 1968). In our experience, wild-raised black-footed ferrets are particularly wary and difficult to trap shortly after they began to appear above ground at about two months of age. They gradually became more tolerant of people, cattle, and pronghorn antelope, none of which presented a threat.

Whether predator avoidance is innate or partially learned through habituation is not necessarily an either-or question. Unequivocal statements that predator-avoidance behavior exists innately do not give sufficient weight to the importance of efficient performance. Predator avoidance is certainly a behavior that must be performed well on the initial attempt, but when predator pressures are reduced, some wild populations of animals respond correctly but less efficiently to predator threat (Curio 1969, as cited in Shalter 1984; Morse 1980; Coss and Owings 1985; Loughry 1988).

The development of predator-avoidance skills is certainly genetically determined, but in many species it probably involves a little polish as well. And opportunities arise to develop skills. Vermeij (1982) reviewed the success rates of a number of predators. The highest rate of achievement for predation by raptors was 85%, but eight raptor species had less than a 20% success rate. Predatory mammals usually have postdetection predation efficiencies of less than 50%. So every attempted predation does not result in a fatality, or even an injury to the prey; a bad scare may be enough to increase efficiency in a fixed trait. Through this process, as well as habituation to nonthreatening stimuli, a young black-footed ferret probably increases its chances of living long enough to invest its genes in future generations.

6

ASSESSING POPULATION ECOLOGY OF BLACK-FOOTED FERRETS

One fall night a newly dispersed black-footed ferret wandered through a section of vacant territory. The young male did not know that the previous occupant had been carried off by an owl. He knew only that he did not find fresh scent marks, so he claimed the area as his own by establishing new boundaries. Suddenly, a beam of bright light swept across his eyes, and two humans came running toward him. He immediately jumped into a burrow, but the humans blocked the hole's only exit with a long cylindrical wire tube (Figure 6.1). They wrapped the cylinder in burlap and waited about 50 meters from the trap. The burrow was shallow, and the ferret was anxious to leave. As soon as calm returned to the surface, he began climbing up the tube as if it were an extension of the burrow. Halfway up the cylinder he stepped on a treadle, and a door at the base of the trap closed behind him. The biologists quickly began preparing an ear tag to identify this animal for purposes of collecting future life-history information.

For any species, a well-planned conservation strategy calls for knowledge of key population attributes, including population status and trends, reproduction, dispersal, survival, and mortality. The natural historians studying the black-footed ferret initially faced tremendous obstacles in piecing together the animal's life. Nocturnal, secretive, semifossorial, and—by the time the studies were initiated—quite rare, the black-footed ferret was not amenable to standard techniques for enumerating and tracking wildlife (Figure 6.2).

Most of the techniques for studying ferrets were developed in South Dakota in the 1960s. With the addition of radiotelemetry, the same techniques were used at Meeteetse, Wyoming, in the 1980s. However, the black-footed ferret's rediscovery at Meeteetse in 1981 coincided with a revolution in the life sciences that chal-

Figure 6.1. A black-footed ferret captured in a live trap. Photo by Louise R. Forrest.

lenged prevailing notions of deterministic population growth. The new science of conservation biology—an outgrowth of wildlife biology, landscape ecology, genetics, island biogeography, and recently developed modeling techniques—indicated that limited time remained to gather the requisite information for conservation of this species. Unfortunately, the Wyoming population mirrored the fate of the South Dakota ferrets. Both colonies collapsed, leaving only a few captive animals. Despite these setbacks, the two studies are remarkable for the wealth of population data generated on the species' life history and population ecology.

Gathering the information necessary for the conservation of black-footed ferrets (or any other small population) requires an intensive commitment to monitoring. Survival of black-footed ferrets in the wild now depends on the reintroduction of captive-raised animals. The longer it takes to establish wild ferret populations, and thus the more generations spent in captivity, the greater the erosion of survivorship skills. So a full-scale monitoring effort is essential to develop efficient reintroduction techniques as quickly as possible. The tried-and-true monitoring techniques are still the most reliable. Because each has benefits and drawbacks, the most thorough approach uses all methods as part of a complementary strategy.

Figure 6.2. A black-footed ferret posing above ground. Photo by Dean Biggins.

METHODOLOGIES

Snow-Tracking

Winter searches are an inexpensive and nonintrusive method of monitoring free-ranging ferrets (see Clark, Campbell, et al. 1984; Richardson et al. 1987). Such searches have been used to verify or validate population and behavioral attributes of weasel, fisher, pine marten, European ferret, spotted skunk *(Spilogale putorius),* wolverine *(Gulo gulo),* river otter *(Lutra canadensis),* mink, and badger. Snow must remain on the ground for at least one entire night without wind for animals to leave tracks (wind quickly obliterates signs or creates a crust that prevents track impressions). Complete track sequences (origin to terminus) can be used to verify that each individual counted is unique. At Meeteetse, 3–10 consecutive tracking days were used to develop an estimate, because not all ferrets are active every night (Biggins, Schroeder, et al. 1986; Richardson et al. 1987).

The ferret gait produces a single twin-print pattern spaced an average of 47 or 48 centimeters apart (Clark, Campbell, et al. 1984; Miller 1988). Interstride distance during bounds ranges from 6 to 99 centimeters, depending on speed, snow depth, and whether the ferret is running uphill or downhill. This interstride distance completely overlaps that of weasels, so it cannot be used to distinguish the two species (Figure 6.3). The width of the black-footed ferret twin-print track (average 7.5 centimeters) is nearly identical to that of mink, and similar to that of weasel (average 5 centimeters). The width of the twin print also varies with track age and snow depth. Deeper snow will produce a slightly wider and longer print, and a day-old weasel print in snow can expand after exposure to the sun to nearly the same size as a fresh ferret print. Thus other cues, such as the presence of diggings, hole diameter in snow, and marking behavior, should be used to verify any track sequence.

Black-footed ferrets have characteristic diggings (see Chapter 4), and the presence of a trench will distinguish a black-footed ferret trail from that of a weasel or a mink. Black-footed ferrets average 0.6 diggings each night they are active above ground (Richardson et al. 1987). Ferrets and weasels can best be distinguished by hole diameter in snow. When entering prairie dog burrows, black-footed ferrets make holes 8–9 centimeters wide whereas weasels make holes 5–6 centimeters wide. Because black-footed ferrets have reached adult size by the

Figure 6.3. Physical evidence of a black-footed ferret taking over and occupying a prairie dog burrow. The digging shows twin-print tracks leading to the burrow and the distinctive trench in the pile of subsoil removed from the burrow, but there are no tracks leaving this burrow or any of the surrounding burrows. Photo by Brian Miller.

time snow-tracking is an option, they do not create any holes smaller than 8–9 centimeters. The tracker must follow the trail and examine several holes. Occasionally a weasel will knock all the snow out of a prairie dog burrow, but inspection of several burrow entrances should yield an opening equal to the width of the weasel. Furthermore, weasels occasionally tunnel under the snow for a short distance, then reappear at the surface, a behavior we never observed with black-footed ferrets. When ferrets dig through the snow, they are heading directly for a prairie dog burrow. Weasel trails often alternate between long and short strides, whereas black-footed ferret trails are typically more uniform in stride length.

Snow-tracking techniques can produce viable census data quickly, but several caveats are called for: the technique depends on snowfall, and it does not positively identify individual animals or provide reliable information about the fates of missing animals.

Spotlighting

Spotlighting is most effective when conducted during seasons that black-footed ferrets are most active. During the summer months activity is bimodal, concentrated in the hours immediately after sunset and immediately before sunrise (Hillman 1968; Biggins, Schroeder, et al. 1986; Clark, Richardson, et al. 1986). By November, and throughout the winter months, ferrets are less likely to be active; when they are active, it could be at any time of the night (Biggins, Schroeder, et al. 1986). Richardson et al. (1987) found that ferrets remained underground on 34% of all winter nights, and that they could stay below ground for six consecutive nights. It is therefore more efficient to concentrate spotlighting in the summer and early fall.

Spotlights, usually high-intensity aircraft landing lights (candlepower of 100,000–400,000 candelas), are capable of detecting the reflection from a black-footed ferret's eyes at distances up to 200 meters. Spotlighting must be repeated for three to five consecutive nights in the same location, usually an area of about 150 hectares, because ferrets are not active every night (Campbell, Biggins, et al. 1985). In Meeteetse, the cumulative count of ferrets averaged 82% of the total population when each 150-hectare parcel was searched for four nights (Forrest, Biggins, et al. 1988), indicating that additional nights of spotlighting would produce diminishing returns.

Because vegetative cover on prairie dog towns is generally limited to grasses or highly browsed shrubs, spotlighting offers a means to scan an enormous area over a relatively short time. When conducted in the summer, while females with litters are relatively active and therefore relatively visible, the technique provides a means of analyzing birth rates as well as estimating total population size. Spotlighting alone, however, will not identify individual animals (possible when the technique is combined with trapping) nor supply information on missing animals or causes of mortality.

Marking and Tagging

The intent of marking studies is to permanently identify each black-footed ferret, so that in subsequent years a captured animal can be verified and its relationship to the ferrets around it traced. It is critical to know, for example, what the age-specific survivorship is from year to year, as well as how the members of a given litter fare in subsequent years. Tangential concerns include whether population estimates generated by spotlight counts can be verified statistically by mark-recapture modeling.

Black-footed ferrets in the Wyoming study were caught in unbaited live traps after they were located with spotlights. A numbered metal tag was crimped through the ear of each ferret. Despite use of the smallest commercially available tag (developed for marking fingerling fish), ferrets in the wild sometimes removed the tags. In anticipation of such tag loss, ferrets were also tattooed; later, tiny transponders were injected under the skin of the ear. The combination of methods almost always provided positive identification. In 1984 and 1985 a sample of the total population was marked in mid-September and recaptured the first week in October. In 1985, two estimates were produced by recapturing from 3 to 7 October and from 11 October to 1 November.

Radiotelemetry

In Meeteetse between 1981 and 1984, radiotelemetry provided data on ferret dispersal and mortality from August through December (Biggins, Schroeder, et al. 1985, 1986). Data were accumulated for 894 transmitter-days on 19 juvenile ferrets and 341 transmitter-days on 7 adults. Individual radio-tagged ferrets were monitored for periods varying from several days to several months. The technique was later used during the black-footed ferret reintroductions of 1991 and 1992 in Shirley Basin, Wyoming. During those reintroductions, 37 black-footed ferrets were radio-tagged each fall for a total of 693 transmitter-days (Biggins, Miller, and Hanebury 1992; Biggins, Godbey, and Vargas 1993).

The radio tags have evolved over the years, but the package used most recently is a 6-gram transmitter mounted with Teflon heat-shrink tubing to a 1-centimeter-wide wool neckband (Biggins, Godbey, and Vargas 1993; see also Figure 6.4). The Teflon tubing resists mud accumulation, which can cause abrasion,[1] and the wool degrades so the animal can shed its collar after several weeks (Biggins, Miller, and Hanebury 1992; Biggins, Godbey, and Vargas 1993). Because the ferret's neck and cranial width are nearly identical, collar attachment must be fairly precise. If the collar is too loose, the animal will shed the radio, but if it is too tight, abrasions can occur. A 20-centimeter whip antenna enhances reception, and the radio is powered by a 1.5-volt battery.

Radio-tracking was performed primarily from fixed stations using a system developed by Dean Biggins (Figure 6.5). The stations were modified camper trailers with 11-element dual-beam yagi antennae mounted on 6-meter masts. A survey transit was used to locate each fixed station with precision on the map, and the equipment in each station was tested for accuracy by comparing telemetry bearings to survey azimuths. Mobile units were also used to follow dispersing an-

Figure 6.4. A black-footed ferret wearing a wool collar on which a 6-gram radio transmitter is mounted. Photo by Rurik List.

Figure 6.5. A telemetry station with a dual-beam 11-element yagi antenna. Photo by Lou Hanebury.

imals (Figure 6.6). Surface reception varied with the terrain and the position of the station, but ranges of 10 kilometers were not unusual, and one animal was identified 27 kilometers from the nearest station (Biggins, Godbey, and Vargas 1993). An animal's depth underground greatly affected reception and a signal could be completely obliterated when the ferret was more than 2 meters below the surface.

Because black-footed ferrets spend so much time underground, with periodic signal loss, monitoring by radiotelemetry requires an extensive effort. Yet ra-

Figure 6.6. A mobile telemetry station. Photo by Louise R. Forrest.

diotelemetry provides more detailed information than any other ferret monitoring technique, and it is the only reliable way to collect data on ferret dispersal and mortality, the two major sources of loss in any population of animals. It is particularly important to know the fate of animals during early reintroduction attempts. Without identifying the causes of loss, conservation and reintroduction techniques will improve very slowly. There are two drawbacks to telemetry. First, it is more invasive than other techniques and involves higher risk. With proper care, however, the risk is low, particularly when measured against the return of information crucial for successful conservation and reintroduction. Second, establishing a telemetry system can be expensive and labor-intensive, although the return of information per unit of expense is high.

POPULATION ATTRIBUTES OF FERRETS IN WYOMING

Reproduction

The Meeteetse study observed 68 litters from 1982 to 1985, with 224 young (Forrest, Biggins, et al. 1988). The overall mean litter size of 3.3 young per litter (Forrest, Biggins, et al. 1988) closely resembled the mean litter size in South Dakota of 3.4 young per litter (R. L. Linder et al. 1972), despite geographic differences between the two sites and the association of South Dakota ferrets with black-tailed prairie dogs and of Wyoming ferrets with white-tailed prairie dogs. We saw young black-footed ferrets above ground by the first week of July every year, and one year we saw a female carrying four young with unopened eyes on 26 June (Clark, Richardson, et al. 1986). The ratio of juvenile males to juvenile females did not differ significantly from 1:1 (Forrest, Biggins, et al. 1988).

Mustelids in general, whatever their habitat, have high reproductive rates, 5–12 young per litter (Lavers 1973; Erlinge 1974; C. M. King and McMillan 1982; C. M. King 1983; Forrest, Clark, et al. 1985b). However, smaller litter sizes are more bioenergetically adaptive where resources are stable (C. M. King 1983; Calder 1984), because it does not pay to shoulder the high energetic costs of large litters if no advantage to survivorship is gained. Black-footed ferrets tend to have smaller litters (3–5 per litter), possibly reflecting the habitat stability provided by prairie dog colonies.[2] The negative side of this equation is dependence on habitat stability. Other habitat specialists, like European mink *(Mustela lutreola)* and pine martens, have gone extinct locally when their habitats were disrupted or when introduced pressures (like trapping) caused high mortality (Linscombe et al. 1982; M. A. Strickland et al. 1982; Youngman 1982). Thus the minimum population size necessary for survival may be higher for these species, and numerical reductions may not have to be large to trigger an irreparable population decline (Terborgh and Winter 1980; Wilcox 1980; Soulé 1983). This reasoning could help explain the rapid demise of black-footed ferrets.

Dispersal and Movement

Sibling juveniles at Meeteetse remain together until late August, when they go their separate ways. Field teams observed two types of movement following litter breakup: long movement (1–7 kilometers) to adjacent prairie dog colonies, usually with no return; and short movement (less than 300 meters) to a new location near the natal area (Forrest, Biggins, et al. 1988). Long dispersal movements in Wyoming were most often made by juvenile males. More than half of the juvenile females made short movements and remained on their natal prairie dog colonies during the fall monitoring. No radio-tagged juvenile male remained in its natal colony (Biggins, Schroeder, et al. 1985).

The same pattern characterizes other mustelids and is common in solitary mammals (Waser and Jones 1983). Philopatry by one sex and long-distance dispersal by the other is, after all, a method of reducing inbreeding. It was therefore not unusual that two juvenile male ferrets dispersed long distances in October 1985 even though ferret densities were low and prairie dogs were available locally.

Adult ferrets typically exhibit geographic fidelity to their ranges. Eight of 10 marked adults (two males and six females) caught one year after first capture were no more than 200 meters from their original capture locations (Forrest, Biggins, et al. 1988). Two adult females, however, made intercolony movements. One radio-tagged female left the activity area she used from July through September and moved 2.5 kilometers to another colony; she disappeared shortly thereafter. Another female reared a litter on one colony but moved 1.8 kilometers to another colony the next year and did not rear a litter.

Disappearance and Survival

Black-footed ferrets at the Meeteetse site were geographically isolated from any potential source of immigration. Searches of 43 prairie dog colonies (nearly all the known colonies) between 3 and 200 kilometers from the study area found no other black-footed ferrets. Moreover, as the study progressed, it became clear that ferrets were living exclusively within the prairie dog colonies. Thus emigration from the prairie dog complex was akin to a death sentence. Because juveniles were the most likely to move long distances in search of a vacant territory, they were disproportionately exposed to predators and intraspecific strife.[3] We estimated that 60–80% of all juveniles died each year from causes other than disease (Forrest, Biggins, et al. 1988). Similar high mortality among South Dakota ferrets was deduced from the near-constant adult numbers observed from 1964 to 1972 despite consistent production of young (Hillman and Linder 1973). The fact that young males are more likely to emigrate than young females partially explains the skewed adult sex ratio of 1 male to 2.2 females at Meeteetse during the monitoring period (Forrest, Biggins, et al. 1988).

Predation was the dominant source of black-footed ferret mortality prior to the distemper epizootic. In Meeteetse, we confirmed predation three times via radiotelemetry and five times from discovery of remains or carcasses. Raptors were responsible in five cases. Telemetry confirmed that a great horned owl and a golden eagle each killed a ferret. The ear tags and mandibles of one ferret were found in an owl bolus (V. Semonsen pers. com.), and one ferret skull was found at an owl roost. A coyote killed another radio-tagged ferret, and in two cases the predator could not be determined. By contrast, during the 1991 and 1992 reintroductions of captive-raised black-footed ferrets, 12 were killed by coyotes, 2 by badgers, 1 by a diurnal bird of prey, and 1 by an unknown predator; all sources of mortality were confirmed by radiotelemetry. Telemetry also made possible the rescue and rehabilitation of two starving and two injured animals (Biggins, Miller, and Hanebury 1992; Biggins, Godbey, and Vargas 1993).

Black-footed ferrets do not enjoy long life spans in the wild. The oldest animal we observed was at least three years of age and possibly four or five. On average, adults were 20% more likely than juveniles to survive to the following year (Forrest, Biggins, et al. 1988). Nonetheless, on one of the larger colonies that was studied intensively, disappearance rates fluctuated annually. Annual disappearance rates of all ferrets from this colony, estimated by mark-recapture, were 69% (1982–83), 53% (1983–84), and 86% (1984–85). Disappearance rates were highest through autumn and early winter, with few losses between March and July (Forrest, Biggins, et al. 1988).

The average daily survival rate of wild ferrets at Meeteetse, calculated from radiotelemetry data, was 0.998 (the technique is described by Heisey and Fuller 1985). In other words, the population would decline about 17% over a 90-day period and 59% annually, a finding that corresponds with the annual loss rates of 53–86%, cited above, estimated by mark-recapture. By contrast, the average daily survival rate of captive-raised reintroduced black-footed ferrets in 1991 was 0.978, meaning that reintroduced population declined 86% in a 90-day period (Biggins, Miller, and Hanebury 1992). Data were collected on both wild and reintroduced populations during the fall dispersal period. There were obvious differences between the two groups—wild-born animals were dispersing away from a familiar but occupied location, whereas captive-raised animals were released at an unfamiliar but unoccupied site—but, by this measure, survival rates of wild-born black-footed ferrets were superior to those of their captive-born counterparts.

HABITAT USE BY FERRETS IN WYOMING

The Meeteetse prairie dog complex consisted of 37 colonies ranging in size from 2.5 to 740 hectares, and totaled approximately 3,100 hectares of white-tailed prairie dogs over a 200-square-kilometer area. The boundaries of prairie dog colonies typically expand and contract depending on various factors; at Meeteetse, however, colony dimensions remained fairly static from 1981 to 1984. Twenty-five colonies showed evidence of ferret occupancy between 1981 and 1985.

The average density of adult ferrets on the white-tailed prairie dog colonies at Meeteetse was one ferret per 56.6 hectares (Forrest, Clark, et al. 1985a). The average density of adult ferrets on occupied colonies was one ferret per 54.5 hectares, and colony size was highly correlated with the number of ferrets it supported. The ferret density predicted on the basis of colony size alone was approximately one ferret for each 40–60 hectares of white-tailed prairie dogs (Forrest, Clark, et al. 1985a). Thus ferret occupancy of colonies was fairly consistent. Similarly, ferrets with litters were never observed on colonies smaller than 49 hectares, and ferrets averaged one litter per 57 hectares. On South Dakota black-tailed prairie dog colonies, by comparison, 6 of 11 litters were observed on colonies larger than

40 hectares, for an average of one litter per 30 hectares (Hillman, Linder, and Dahlgren 1979).

Interestingly, when the model prediction that 762 prairie dogs are necessary to support each female with a family (derived largely from captive data in Biggins, Miller, et al. 1993) is divided by the average of 15 white-tailed prairie dogs per hectare reported for three colonies at Meeteetse in 1984 (Menkens and Anderson 1991), the result is 50.8 hectares per female ferret with a litter. When the estimate of 762 prairie dogs is divided by the 28 black-tailed prairie dogs per hectare at Mellette County, South Dakota, reported by R. L. Linder et al. (1972), the result is 27.2 hectares per female ferret with a litter. The model and field data correspond, suggesting a correlation between prairie dog density and female home range size, although in South Dakota the habitat was more fragmented and colony size may have been artificially constrained. The Meeteetse data indicating one ferret per 50 hectares of prairie dogs is thus a very useful quick estimate for ferret potential on a white-tailed prairie dog complex, but it may underestimate the potential of a smaller yet more densely populated black-tailed prairie dog complex. Reintroductions to black-tailed prairie dog colonies should clarify this issue.

POPULATION TRENDS IN WYOMING AND THE EPIZOOTIC OF 1985

Summer spotlighting at Meeteetse accounted for 88 individuals in 1983 (60 young, 28 adults), 129 in 1984 (86 young, 43 adults), and 58 in 1985 (38 young, 20 adults) (Forrest, Biggins, et al. 1988). In 1982, 40 young and 21 adults had been observed in an incomplete survey of about 60% of the study area. Extrapolating from the proportion of ferrets per colony comparably spotlighted in 1983 (59 of 88) and 1984 (69 of 129) gives a range of 79–99 ferrets for the total area in 1982.

We captured 135 different ferrets from 1981 to 1985 and calculated mean population estimates (with 90% confidence intervals) for 1983–85. Those estimates are 95 ± 45 in September 1983, 128 ± 25 in September 1984, 31 ± 8 in September 1985, and 16 ± 4 in October 1985. The population estimates were derived directly from mark-recapture studies in 1984 and 1985. Mark-recapture studies were not conducted in 1983, but a population estimate was calculated for that year from a hypergeometric model (Seber 1982) based on animals marked in 1983 that were recaptured in the 1984 cohort. Four ferrets marked in 1983 survived into 1984. Although violations of the model assumptions occurred, including possible recruitment from adjacent nonsampled colonies and variation between sampled age cohorts, the estimate fell within the confidence interval of the 1983 count by spotlight.

In 1985, unlike previous years when ferret numbers had remained constant between the spotlight period in July and the trapping period in September, ferrets disappeared locally from 27 July to 9 September. Three mothers with litters and three other adults (16 ferrets) could not be relocated, and the overall population estimate for September was 47% lower than the spotlight count in July.

On 13 September 1985, two male ferrets were removed from the wild. Another male and two females were removed between 5 and 7 October, and a third female was captured on 12 October. These animals were to form the nucleus of a captive population, whose progeny would be used to start other wild populations (see Chapter 7). On 21 October, two of these animals were diagnosed with canine distemper, which given the incubation period could only have been contracted in the wild. A rescue effort to remove additional animals from the wild between 26 October and 2 November, along with the ferrets caught earlier, provided a second opportunity for mark-recapture estimation. The estimate derived from this effort (16 ± 4, 4–7 October) was again 48% lower than the September estimate. Subtracting the 10 ferrets captured after the 5–7 October estimate, and ignoring other losses after 7 October, we estimated that 6 ferrets remained in the wild as of 2 November 1985.

That winter (1985–86), we saw signs of four unique snow trails representing four adults (Miller 1988). A final effort to capture the remaining black-footed ferrets, initiated in the summer and fall of 1986, resulted in the collection of two adult males and two adult females. Fortunately, the two females were bred by one of the males, and each whelped a litter of 5, bringing the wild population to 14. The capture of the 4 adults and 8 of the juveniles extirpated that colony and raised the captive population to 18.

Canine distemper, a virus that occurs in certain domestic animals and in wild populations of mink, raccoons (Procyon lotor), striped skunks (Mephitis mephitis), badgers, coyotes, and others, is prevalent throughout much of the West (E. S. Williams 1982). It was identified as the primary cause of the population collapse at Meeteetse. Subsequent studies of the carnivore populations at Meeteetse indicated that an active outbreak of distemper was present in coyotes the year the ferret population succumbed (E. S. Williams 1987). Although some ferret decline could have been due to a loss in habitat attributable to sylvatic plague in the prairie dogs between 1984 and 1985 (estimated at no more than 20%), it is more likely that plague disturbed the distribution of ferrets, bringing them into closer proximity to each other and increasing the chances of intraspecific transmission of distemper. The evidence is compelling that distemper, to which ferrets are

100% susceptible (Carpenter, Appel, et al. 1976; Budd 1981), was the primary cause of the population collapse.

The possibility that plague may have contributed more directly to ferret declines was raised in 1985 by the Biota-ISU field team, a group of consultants and researchers associated with Idaho State University (Clark, Forrest, et al. 1985). That possibility was not given much serious consideration until a black-footed ferret in captivity was diagnosed as having died from massive plague infection in 1993 (*Wyoming Wildlife,* June 1993). The discovery of plague susceptibility raises the possibility that a combination of factors was active in the population crash at Meeteetse.

Given the disappearance dates of two litters (27 July and 17 August 1985), the epizootic was apparently well established by the end of July. Population estimates from July through October 1985 suggest 50% mortality every 30 days during that period. Whether and how ferrets at Meeteetse survived historic epizootics can only be matters of conjecture. Extensive habitat would have provided fewer barriers against transmission of disease but ample opportunities for recolonization of locally extinct patches by ferrets from unaffected areas. Severe habitat fragmentation in this century precludes natural recolonization. Habitat fragmentation may also have played a role in reducing genetic diversity in black-footed ferrets. It is known that the loss of key alleles causes lower disease resistance in some wild mammal populations (O'Brien, Roelke, et al. 1985). However, heterozygosity may not be related to declines from distemper: domestic ferrets, which are in all likelihood highly outbred, also exhibit complete susceptibility to the disease (Budd 1981). Whatever the proximate cause of the 1985 population crash, the black-footed ferret was once again gone from the wild, and the species' destiny now more than ever dangled by a slender thread.

Part III

Conservation

7
EXTINCTION IN THE WILD: THE LIGHT DIMS

If such a mess can be made of efforts to save an attractive creature such as the black-footed ferret in a country as well organized and prosperous as the United States, prospects for conservation in other parts of the world are indeed bleak.

R. M. May, March 1986

When John and Lucille Hogg took the animal that their dog Shep had killed to Larry LaFranchie, the local taxidermist, he recognized the animal as a black-footed ferret and called the authorities. They confiscated the rare mammal, then called a town meeting to see if anyone could provide information about the location of ferrets in the wild. During that October meeting, Doug Brown said he had seen the animals while he was tending cattle on the Pitchfork Ranch. That started wheels rolling. After the disappearance of ferrets from South Dakota, Shep had provided a rare second chance to conserve this vanishing piece of the North American prairie.

PROLOGUE

Translating the how and why of an animal's ecology, physiology, and behavior into action for conservation requires integrating biology with a host of social, political, and economic variables. Effective conservation efforts require the cooperation not only of scientists from different biological fields but also of economists, attorneys, public-relations professionals, politicians, social scientists, and the local community. Biological science may be an important part of conserva-

81

tion efforts, but to ignore these nonbiological dimensions at best reduces efficiency, and at worst results in species' extinction. The term *conservationist* is therefore not limited to biologists but includes an array of disciplines.

Conservation biologists must translate scientific data into action. As Orr (1994) has aptly observed, many people confuse scientific objectivity with neutrality, or not taking a stand. To paraphrase what Dean Biggins stated in the introduction to this book, scientists do not disqualify themselves from their profession by exhibiting emotions; indeed, people with more knowledge are in a better position to encourage a course of action. Promoting a course of action can, however, be harmful to a scientific career, which may precipitate some of the professional confusion between neutrality and objectivity.

Perhaps partly as a result of its built-in advocacy, the view that the science of conservation biology is inferior to the "pure sciences" of academia persists despite growing evidence supporting many of the predictions made by conservation biology. The validation of those predictions suggests that conservation biology may be as reliable as traditional science. The results do, however, have political and economic ramifications that go well beyond the walls of established academia.

To adequately introduce scientific findings into a forum where they can benefit society, conservationists must do more than simply treat the biological symptoms. They must go directly to the causes of declining resources. This means employing integrated approaches to the attitudinal, societal, and economic causes of overexploitation.

Practicing conservationists, therefore, have the opportunity to mesh their specialty with those of experts in other fields (e.g., environmental lawyers and natural resource economists). Meetings focusing on black-footed ferrets have included experts in genetics, physiological ecology, reproductive physiology, endocrinology, nutrition, field ecology, behavior, veterinary medicine, population biology, wildlife management, and computer modeling. Including representatives from the nonbiological disciplines would enhance shared knowledge and improve outcomes. Together, diverse groups of professionals can learn from each other and cooperatively excel toward a common goal. Under the right circumstances, such groups can effectively share knowledge and produce a stimulating and productive environment.

Perhaps more importantly, moving toward holistic restoration programs suggests a new paradigm for gauging the success of our actions. It is no longer enough to talk of success solely in terms of technical achievements, such as whether or not our efforts produce a given number of animals. In a world of ever-shrinking resources, we must expand our measures of success to include assessments of how efficiently results are accomplished in terms of time and money, how our results further the goals of species conservation in general, and how much individual and organizational learning occurs both within and outside of the restoration program. These are concerns that will eventually make or break all future species-restoration efforts. Because these measures are often overlooked, we will attempt to assess them when analyzing the ferret recovery program.

In the following chapters, we propose a plan for conservation, reintroduction, and eventual restoration of the black-footed ferret that integrates biological and technical knowledge with the organizational structure of the decision-making body, the social behavior of participants, local interests and human needs, and the legal parameters of reintroduction. The U.S. government is planning to utilize reintroduction more heavily in the future (Booth 1988). Yet to date, most attempts to reintroduce species have met with limited success (J. M. Scott and Carpenter 1987; Griffith et al. 1989). Importantly, few reintroductions of species have adequately addressed the social, economic, organizational, and policy variables that can profoundly affect success (Tear and Forester 1992; Reading 1993).

We have attempted to address the various factors that any recovery program must consider, and to examine how failure to address these factors has caused frustration in program implementation. Where appropriate, we have pointed out the lessons of the ferret recovery effort for this species and others.

REDISCOVERING THE BLACK-FOOTED FERRET AT MEETEETSE

The history of the wild black-footed ferrets near Meeteetse, Wyoming, has been told, at least in part, by several writers over the years, including Nice (1982), May (1986), Weinberg (1986), Clark and Harvey (1988), Clark (1989), DeBlieu (1991), and Thorne and Oakleaf (1991). It is an intriguing tale, and highly relevant to efforts at conservation of other species. The long hours, harsh weather, and nocturnal schedule created camaraderie among the field workers and many delightful stories about the behavior of ferrets (and biologists) on moonlit nights. Many dedicated people, employed both by agencies and by private organizations, have contributed to ferret recovery. They often gave a great deal without material reward. In some cases their work and advocacy for the ferret are no longer officially recognized, but their deeds and persistence have had great influence on the advances of the recovery program. They were the fixers who often improved program effectiveness when more formal channels were not adequately seeking solutions to problems (Yaffee 1982).

Following the collapse of the South Dakota black-footed ferrets in the 1970s, most participants in that effort had drifted off to pursue other interests, but some continued looking for ferrets. Many of the searches were done to fulfill the clearance requirements of Section 7 of the Endangered Species Act: development on federally owned land requires a search to "clear" the area of any potential impact to an endangered species. Others were motivated simply by the desire to find an extant population of ferrets. These searches generated a fair amount of publicity, and the black-footed ferret became a reasonably well-known animal in the western states, especially for such a rare and secretive species.

One of the biologists who searched privately was Tim Clark. He had received a doctorate in prairie dog ecology and had become intrigued with black-footed ferrets in 1965. Clark looked for ferrets in 11 states over the years. In 1976 Clark, who had an adjunct faculty position with Idaho State University (ISU), formed a private consulting firm called Biota Research and Consulting with Tom Campbell. By 1981 Clark and Campbell had had considerable experience looking for black-footed ferrets but had yet to lay eyes on one. Wildlife Preservation Trust supported Biota's searches, and the two organizations jointly offered a $250 reward for information leading to a population of black-footed ferrets.

Meanwhile Max Schroeder, Dennie Hammer, and Steve Martin of the U.S. Fish and Wildlife Service's Denver Wildlife Research Center (later renamed the National Ecology Research Center) were also looking for black-footed ferrets on Section 7 clearances. When Hammer wanted to initiate a master's-degree project on black-footed ferrets, his fellow students kidded him about researching dinosaurs. But when John and Lucille Hogg's dog Shep killed a black-footed ferret on 26 September 1981, Hammer and Martin had the first opportunity since 1974 to see a live black-footed ferret in the wild.

Soon after the dead ferret was reported to federal authorities, a town meeting was called in Meeteetse to ask if any local residents had knowledge of wild ferrets. Doug Brown volunteered that he had seen the animals while tending cattle on the Pitchfork Ranch, one of the largest landholdings in Wyoming. The Pitchfork was owned and managed by Jack Turnell and his family. Most of the black-footed ferrets were eventually found on Pitchfork land, and Turnell was in a position to make or break the recovery of this unique mammal. Turnell and the other affected ranchers (John and Lucille Hogg, Rick and Ricki Westbrook, Betty and Art Thomas, Jack, JoAnn, and David Winniger, and Doc Gould) were tolerant of the research that followed and became active supporters of the recovery program. Turnell publicly took the courageous stance that fears about "losing land to an endangered species" were unfounded, and that ranching and conservation were not in conflict near Meeteetse (Turnell 1985). Rick Westbrook also remarked that he liked having the ferrets around (*Casper Star-Tribune, Wyoming* magazine, Christmas issue, 1985).

After the October 1981 town meeting, Tim Clark and Tom Campbell quickly rented a plane and mapped about 2,000 hectares of prairie dogs in the area. Meanwhile Steve Martin and Dennie Hammer, with Brown's help, headed for the alluvial outwash above the Greybull River on the Pitchfork to search for black-footed ferrets on the ground. On 29 October 1981 at about 6:30 AM, Hammer and Martin saw a black-footed ferret stick its head out of a burrow. One can imagine their elation and nervous energy. Hammer put his hat over the burrow opening until a trap could be set, and the ferret was captured 11 hours later.

The animal was fitted with a radio-transmitter and Martin, Hammer, Dean Biggins, and Lou Hanebury monitored it until mid-November when the radio was removed. Biggins (a telemetry specialist), Hanebury, Kathy Fagerstone, Max Schroeder, and Dave Seery eventually formed the core of the U.S. Fish and Wildlife Service Denver Wildlife Research Center field team. Spotlight searches by the federal biologists during October and November estimated that 10 ferrets lived in the area. Unfortunately, previous program de-emphasis by the Fish and Wildlife Service (the national entity that includes all regional offices is hereafter called "the Service") had left insufficient funds to keep the Denver Wildlife Research Center team in the field any longer, and the federal biologists had to return to their offices.

Tim Clark and Tom Campbell, meanwhile, garnered private support for the Biota-ISU field team, which began searching for black-footed ferrets in December 1981. Early donations covered only expenses, and the Biota-ISU field team initially volunteered their labor. Eventually Wildlife Preservation Trust International, Wildlife Conservation Society of the New York Zoological Society, World Wildlife Fund US, and the National Geographic Society would be major contributors to this effort. Over the years, the Biota-ISU team had numerous volunteers, but the core of the group was Tim Clark, Tom Campbell, Steve Forrest, Louise Richardson, Brent Houston, Jim Hasbrouck, and Denise Casey.

TRANSFERRING CONTROL OF THE RECOVERY PROGRAM TO WYOMING

While the Biota-ISU team collected information on black-footed ferrets in the winter of 1981–82, federal recovery efforts proceeded slowly. The Endangered Species Act had entrusted the welfare of the black-footed ferret to Region 6 of the U.S. Fish and Wildlife Service (hereafter called "Region 6"), headquartered in Denver. But the Service's Black-Footed Ferret Recovery Team, formed in 1978, had virtually disintegrated and, aside from the meagerly funded research arm of the Denver Wildlife Research Center, few strong advocates for the ferret remained at the federal level. In February 1982, Region 6 transferred lead authority for the program to the Wyoming Game and Fish Department (hereafter called "Wyoming"). Region 6 was to maintain oversight. The rationale for this decision is still vigorously debated, and some observers consider it the most critical decision in the entire history of the program (Carr 1986; Clark n.d.).

Wyoming and Region 6 had a long history of interaction and conflict. Like most western states, Wyoming maintains a fierce resolve that it is the sole entity responsible for its wildlife. Over the years, this position had brought the state into conflict with federal agencies and other groups that sought to usurp what Wyoming considered its right to manage wildlife within its borders.[1]

At the time black-footed ferrets were rediscovered, a dispute was brewing between the Service and western states over bobcat harvest.[2] Friction had also arisen between Wyoming and federal agencies over management of the grizzly bear *(Ursus arctos)*. Perhaps more germane was the Wyoming congressional delegation's recent criticism of Region 6 over its role in black-footed ferret clearance searches required by Section 7 of the Endangered Species Act: to fund its searches, Region 6 had been bidding against private consultants for clearance contracts on federal land. In essence, Region 6 was requiring clearance, then bidding to perform the necessary searches. Because Region 6 also ruled on the validity of these searches, the arrangement presented a conflict of interest (T. Campbell pers. com.).

Region 6's decision to cede control to Wyoming may have been a sacrificial move in this ongoing state-federal conflict. Perhaps Region 6 was trying to avoid repetition of its experience with ferrets in South Dakota. The strong states'-rights philosophy of the newly elected President Reagan may have influenced the ruling. Or the appointment of James Watt, possibly the most antienvironment Secretary of Interior in U.S. history and a Wyoming native, may have been decisive. Whatever its reasons, Region 6 conceded control to Wyoming rather than attempting to forge cooperative management schemes. Even though Region 6 was to retain oversight, the proclivity of its officials to avoid conflict made it easier for Wyoming to consolidate control, in spite of the fact that the program was largely funded by federal money channeled through Region 6 to Wyoming.

Designating Wyoming as the program leader meant that national recovery policy would be directed by a single state agency lacking both resources and the authority to coordinate outside its boundaries (the range of black-footed ferrets originally extended from southern Canada to northern Mexico). The state of Wyoming is sparsely populated and very tight-knit. As a lifelong resident once observed, "It's not a state, it's a club." Would parochialism affect its perception of recovery? Would state interests take precedence over national or international goals? Finally, Wyoming's state biologists were schooled in game management, not small-population biology. Would they draw on outside expertise effectively?

Designating a local agency to handle a local population can be practical, but only if the local agency answers to national interests.

When it was granted control, Wyoming was not in a good financial position (Nice 1982). Its meager resources allowed for the assignment of only two staff members, Jim Lawrence (Meeteetse game warden) and Dale Strickland (assistant chief game warden in the state office at Cheyenne), to ferrets on a part-time basis. As the program developed, the federal government rallied its funds for the recovery effort, but early contributions from the Biota-ISU field team and the private conservation community filled the bureaucratic void that first winter.

PHILOSOPHICAL CONFLICT AND
PROGRAM ORGANIZATION

Relations among state, federal, and private groups started cordially, but different philosophies surfaced early. The Biota-ISU field team and the federal biologists from the Denver Wildlife Research Center thought qualified scientists should learn as much as possible to conserve and restore black-footed ferrets. Having seen chance events destroy the small population of South Dakota ferrets a decade earlier, former Service biologist Conrad Hillman agreed (Nice 1982). Additionally, at a 1982 symposium, Tim Clark of Biota-ISU proposed that a captive population be started as a method of restoring animals across the former range (Clark 1984). Private conservation groups also recommended captive breeding or translocation of wild-born juveniles.

Conservation biology suggests that the last remaining populations of rare species have survived not because they are somehow superior to other populations, but by chance alone. Furthermore, small and isolated populations living in fragmented habitats are extremely vulnerable to collapse from stochastic events. Most of the field researchers thus believed that the single Meeteetse population was a time bomb waiting to explode, and that delay in implementing a conservation program to expand numbers and sites could have serious ramifications.

Wyoming, however, saw the situation differently, adopting a less intrusive preservationist philosophy with the primary goal of protecting the Meeteetse ferret population. The basic premise was that ferrets had survived in the area for hundreds of years and would survive for many more if left alone (D. Strickland 1983), a philosophy that placed a great deal of faith in the guiding hand of nature. The two philosophies led to diametrically opposed strategies for the needs of black-footed ferrets, and the two groups were on a collision course.

In March 1982, Wyoming began defining the structure of the program and formed the Black-Footed Ferret Advisory Team (BFAT) to coordinate the various agencies and landowners. Intentionally or not, Wyoming selected a team that mirrored its management and organizational philosophy. The BFAT was originally chaired by Dale Strickland of Wyoming Game and Fish Department; Strickland was soon replaced by Harry Harju, head of Biological Services for the Wyoming Game and Fish Department. Harju was colorful and outspoken, and for some people unfamiliar with his style, those characteristics could have obscured his deep concern for the black-footed ferret. Other members of the BFAT included a Meeteetse rancher and representatives from the Wyoming office of the U.S. Bureau of Land Management, the U.S. Forest Service, the Wyoming State Land Board, Region 6, and the University of Wyoming. In 1983 Dave Belitsky was hired by Wyoming as a coordinator for the BFAT (a nonvoting position), and Dennie Hammer, Brian Miller, and Jon Hanna were hired as field assistants for the state.

The rarity of black-footed ferrets made it unrealistic to expect that all members of the BFAT would have direct experience with the species. But the team was also unfamiliar with the concepts of small-population biology, a sphere in which they would soon be asked to make complex decisions. When the Biota-ISU team requested that a member of the private conservation community be added for purposes of balance and expertise, Wyoming chose a representative of the National Wildlife Federation in Washington, D.C.—whose membership has historically included a large number of state game and fish employees (Tober 1989). His views coincided with the Wyoming philosophy.

Although the BFAT started as an advisory group charged with coordinating the various agencies and landowners, Wyoming soon ran every aspect of ferret conservation and management through the group. Wyoming chaired the meetings, recorded the minutes, and maintained veto power over recommendations. Thus Wyoming was able to cloak program control in the guise of an independent body, which lent credibility to its decisions while providing cover in the event of disaster.

The field workers, in the meantime, were becoming increasingly frustrated as evidence mounted of the need for proactive management in the face of Wyoming's cautious strategy. One member of the BFAT was strongly sympathetic to this proactive approach—Ron Crete of the Region 6 field office in Helena, Montana. Because of his activism, Crete was criticized by Wyoming for being "too close" to the field workers from Biota-ISU and the Denver Wildlife Research Center. Region 6 was unwilling to confront Wyoming, even on positions supported by their own federal biologists. Eventually, Region 6 chose a different representative for the BFAT.

In addition to the BFAT, Wyoming also centralized control through other mechanisms. First, they could grant permits. Second, when the BFAT coordinator was hired, he served as an on-site enforcer for Wyoming as well as facilitating communication. Third, Wyoming eventually required, as a condition for research permits, that the Wyoming Game and Fish Department veterinarian be present for any handling of animals, a condition that the field teams initially welcomed. For example, the BFAT had given permission to the Biota-ISU and Denver Wildlife Research Center teams to census animals by spotlighting and capture-recapture techniques, and to investigate the fates of dispersing juveniles through radiotelemetry (see Chapter 6). But Wyoming's veterinarian was soon telling researchers when they could and could not trap and how many animals could be radio-collared. In some cases, this altered the BFAT-approved study plans after the work had already begun (see the minutes of the BFAT meeting, 22 September 1983). Ironically, Wyoming had been reluctant to embark on captive breeding because data was lacking on juvenile mortality and population stability in the wild. Now Wyoming was also impeding the collection of that information.

DELAYS AND CAPTIVE BREEDING

An incomplete summer count in fall 1982 revealed 61 ferrets (21 adults and 40 juveniles) at Meeteetse. Because there were no prairie dog colonies nearby to house dispersing animals, the field teams believed that dispersing juveniles were probably disappearing into a black hole. In 1983 the count reached 88 (28 adults and 60 juveniles). These data convinced researchers of an annual surplus production with density-dependent juvenile disappearance. In other words, whatever the production rate, mortality would be largely determined by the lack of available habitat. As a result, Louise Richardson of Biota-ISU drafted a strategy paper suggesting that some of the surplus animals be used for captive breeding and reintroduction. Presented to Wyoming in December 1983, it received no immediate response (the paper was later published as Richardson et al. 1986).

Calls from the conservation community to begin captive breeding became more urgent. At the request of the New York Zoological Society and Wildlife Preservation Trust International, Wyoming called a meeting in Cheyenne on 10 April 1984 to discuss the issue. At the gathering, the Wyoming Game and Fish Department veterinarian, Tom Thorne, recommended captive breeding (and acknowledged Louise Richardson's proposal). Thorne said that Wyoming would help initiate wild ferret populations in other states, and the New York Zoological Society offered to assist with captive breeding.

Wyoming replied that captive breeding might be the best strategy for starting other populations, but the state agency insisted that they should be the leader and the facility should be located in Wyoming (minutes of the Black-Footed Ferret Captive Breeding Meeting, Cheyenne, Wyoming, 10 April 1984). Tom Thorne's preference was to establish the breeding center at the Wyoming Game and Fish Department Research Facility in Sybille Canyon, where he headed the veterinary lab (minutes of the same meeting, 10 April 1984). But because that facility was not adequate for the task, the proposed plan would require construction funds from the U.S. Fish and Wildlife Service. A committee was formed to investigate the feasibility of breeding black-footed ferrets in captivity.

Tom Thorne's early support for captive breeding was crucial. He was the first Wyoming official to endorse the concept, albeit on a "yes, but only in Wyoming" basis. Without his internal advocacy, it is likely that Wyoming would have delayed even longer, which—as we shall see—would have had catastrophic results. As it was, the delays attributable to Wyoming's insistence on control brought the ferrets to the very brink of extinction.

The 1984 summer count found 43 adults and 86 juveniles, for a total of 129 ferrets. The captive-breeding committee, formed after the April 1984 meeting, had recommended removing some black-footed ferrets in fall 1984 for captive breeding, and there were clearly excess juveniles available for that project. In September, however, a symposium on black-footed ferrets was held in Laramie, Wyoming (later published as S. H. Anderson and Inkley 1985). At a BFAT meeting on the eve of the symposium, Wyoming announced that it had already rejected the recommendation of the captive-breeding committee to capture some ferrets in 1984 (BFAT meeting minutes, 17 September 1984).

Wyoming's decision generated a great deal of discussion during the symposium, with a large number of people supporting quick action. Mike Bogan of the Denver Wildlife Research Center called for immediately removing a few ferrets from the wild to start a captive propagation program: "Some long-term projects have an immediacy about them and should be started soon . . . we should begin now to remove a few 'test' animals to captive situations" (Bogan 1985). Captive propagation was also supported by Chris Wemmer (1985) of the Conservation and Research Center of the National Zoological Park (part of the Smithsonian Institution) and by Jim Carpenter (1985) of the Service's Patuxent Wildlife Research Center, as well as others. The drumbeat of criticism persuaded Wyoming to direct the BFAT to form a committee that would recommend a site for captive breeding. The committee, not unexpectedly, chose the Wyoming Game and Fish research facility in Sybille Canyon.

Sybille Canyon was chosen for captive breeding despite the interest of several other prominent facilities. During the April 1984 meeting, the New York Zoological Park expressed a desire to cooperate; in summer 1984 the Washington State University Mustelid Center also declared an interest in captive-breeding ferrets, and it formally presented a captive-breeding proposal on 8 May 1985 with all costs to be borne by the nonprofit sector (memo from Jon Jenson, Wildlife Preservation Trust International, 8 May 1985, attached to the proposal). And in 1985 the National Zoological Park said they could breed black-footed ferrets at their Conservation and Research Center in Front Royal, Virginia, and would fully cover the costs (Randall 1986). Later, the director of the Wyoming Game and Fish Department reflected on the decision to reject the Conservation and Research Center's offer, saying, "We did not know whether Front Royal was suitable until our veterinarian visited there some time later" (*Casper Star-Tribune,* 25 November 1985). Yet the National Zoo's Conservation and Research Center was already a world-famous facility that was conducting a number of captive-breeding programs for endangered species.

It is likely that these offers were ignored (and other opportunities not investigated) simply because, as one Wyoming official said, if ferrets left the state, "we'd have no control over them" (Carr 1986; May 1986; Weinberg 1986). When it became clear that ferrets would not leave Wyoming, there were few subsequent offers of facilities or financial support.

A related problem confronting captive breeding was the physical structure to house black-footed ferrets. Even though ferrets had to remain in the state, the Wyoming research facility was inadequate, and black-footed ferrets would not be captured unless Region 6 could secure $235,000 in federal money to construct a new building at the Wyoming research center, plus annual Section 6 funds to hire staff and equip the facility; annual operating costs were estimated at about $155,000 a year in 1991 (Captive Breeding Specialist Group 1992). Although it made sense to breed ferrets in their native range, this action was essentially holding the ferret hostage. Plenty of zoos in or out of the western region of the United States could have been approached to establish the main captive center (with a satellite population at Sybille for local involvement), an arrangement that could have cost far less money.

Without pursuing any alternatives, Region 6 agreed to Wyoming's insistence that the main breeding center be located within the state. One outside observer wryly commented that "whenever Wyoming stomped their cowboy boots, Region 6 rolled over and urinated on its belly." By May 1985, Region 6 representatives were optimistic that they could secure funding for a Wyoming facility via a congressional allocation, and that the money would be available by 1986 or 1987 (Thorne 1987). Consequently, Wyoming agreed to capture six animals after the fall 1985 population census, assuming maintenance of a normal (but unspecified) population of ferrets; similar captures would be made in 1986 and 1987 (Thorne 1987). The animals captured in 1985 would be housed in temporary quarters until the new building was completed. Ulie Seal of the Captive Breeding Specialist Group (a subgroup of the International Union for the Conservation of Nature, or IUCN) emphasized the importance of starting the captive-breeding project immediately and not awaiting completion of the new building. A disaster could occur at any time, he warned, even that summer.

FACING THE THREAT OF DISEASE

A few weeks later, Seal's warning appeared prophetic. Sonya Ubico, a Fish and Wildlife Service biologist, discovered fleas carrying plague (Ubico et al. 1988). Dead prairie dogs began appearing on the surface of the prairie dog colonies, and by mid-June the prairie dog complex was undergoing a full-scale epizootic. The prairie dog population appeared to have declined about 20%. One colony supporting seven ferret litters in 1984 contained only one litter in 1985 (Forrest, Clark, et al. 1985b). Yet there was no evidence that ferrets were starving. A campaign to dust the prairie dog burrows with the insecticide Sevin was advocated by the Denver Wildlife Research Center. Region 6 purchased 5,900 kilograms of powder, and the application was organized by Wyoming.

Because evidence at the time indicated that Siberian ferrets were resistant to plague (Thorne and Williams 1988), Wyoming thought the disease would not harm the black-footed ferrets directly. Yet black-footed ferrets were still disappearing, and Wyoming was criticized by independent biologists and members of the general public. In response, *Wyoming Wildlife,* a Wyoming Game and Fish Department magazine, ran an article titled "Black-Footed Ferrets 'Plagued' by Columnists." The piece remarked on "undue criticism toward the agencies charged with black-footed ferret management" and accused dissenters of "wishing to ride the ferret's coattails to fame, fortune, and escalated professional status" (Skinner 1985). Black-footed ferrets were later found to be susceptible to plague—so disease may have played a role in the population decline—and ferrets were also disappearing from places where prairie dogs were still numerous (Forrest, Clark, et al. 1985b).

By early August 1985 we had counted only 58 animals, 20 adults and 38 juveniles (Forrest, Biggins, et al. 1988). Of the 52 juveniles marked in 1984, not one survived to 1985. The earlier pleas of Mike Bogan, Chris Wemmer, Jim Carpenter, Tim Clark, and Louise Richardson, among others, to capture a few juveniles in 1984 now looked very astute, as did the captive-breeding recommendation of the committee formed after the April 1984 meeting.

Alarmed by the falling numbers, the Biota-ISU team immediately published a list of recommendations, one of which was to "take blood samples from selected animals and test for multiple disease vectors" (Clark, Forrest, et al. 1985). Of course there was no guarantee that blood (or fecal) samples would have revealed the problem, but disease has to be considered when a population is declining rapidly. Wyoming did not act on the recommendation, and Region 6 remained silent.

Wyoming had also decided that information gained from radiotelemetry was not worth the risk to a sample of animals. Mud accumulation under several collars in 1983 had rubbed the skin raw. Although no such problems occurred in 1984, the 1985 radiotelemetry studies of the Denver Wildlife Research Center were canceled. Telemetry was (and still is) the most reliable method of pinpointing causes of mortality in black-footed ferrets. When a ferret dies underground, the body can be located and the cause of death determined. Without telemetry, ferrets were simply disappearing and no one knew why. The resulting speculation only fueled divisiveness. Some Wyoming officials even denied that a problem existed. As a Wyoming biologist told the *Billings Gazette* (13 August 1985), "The people at Wyoming Game and Fish Department disagree pretty strongly with the contention that ferret numbers have fallen dramatically" (see also Weinberg 1986).

By September 1985 there were only 31 ferrets, and by early October the estimate was 16 (Forrest, Biggins, et al. 1988). The population was dropping about 50% a month, and no one knew why. Extinction no longer seemed like a topic for casual academic discourse over coffee; it was suddenly a very real possibility. Yet Wyoming seemed content to ride out the decline (BFAT meeting minutes, 29 August 1985). Relations between the Biota-ISU field team and Wyoming reached new lows. The Biota-ISU team, frustrated at the lack of action during the crisis, became more outspoken to the press. Wyoming, not wanting to be stampeded, became more entrenched in its position.

As agreed in May 1985, ferrets for the captive-breeding program were not trapped until completion of the September 1985 mark-recapture estimates. The cause of ferret mortality came to light after those captures. If the captive-breeding plan had not been established in spring 1985, and ferrets had not been taken into captivity where they could be closely observed, it is very possible that they would now be extinct. The wild population was left at such a low level in 1985 and 1986 that it would have been vulnerable to the slightest perturbation.

When Biota's final report of the mark-recapture population estimates revealed further declines (Forrest, Clark, et al. 1985b), Wyoming called a BFAT meeting for 22 October 1985. At the tense gathering, the Biota-ISU and the Denver Wildlife Research Center field teams were put on the defensive from the start. Some Wyoming officials criticized the census methods of the field workers, suggesting that the population was not as low as the figures indicated. Then Tom Thorne, the Wyoming veterinarian caring for the captive black-footed ferrets, entered the meeting to report that one of the animals had died the night before, and that the autopsy had revealed distemper virus in the feces. This new evidence sent a shock wave through the room. Ulie Seal, present at the meeting, declared that a crisis now existed and that plans should be made to rescue the few remaining ferrets immediately (BFAT meeting minutes, 22 October 1985). Indeed, several days earlier, before distemper was discovered, the Denver Wildlife Research Center had suggested capturing all the ferrets for protection from whatever unknown agents were causing the decline (*Cody Enterprise,* 21 October 1985). At this time, only about a dozen black-footed ferrets remained in the wild.

Of the initial six black-footed ferrets captured between 13 September and 12 October 1985, two had canine distemper (E. S. Williams et al. 1988). The fifth animal caught showed signs of a disease one day after its capture on 7 October. The sixth animal, captured 12 October, also showed symptoms shortly after capture. Because the incubation period for distemper is 7–21 days, both animals had clearly contracted the disease in the wild (BFAT meeting minutes, 22 October 1985). Because all six were housed in the same room at Sybille Canyon, the two with distemper exposed the remaining four. Tom Thorne predicted the others would die, which they eventually did.

To sum up, the field teams had been warning of population drops since July 1985. A recommendation on 6 August to take blood samples from wild ferrets and test for multiple disease vectors (Clark, Forrest, et al. 1985) was ignored. When symptoms of a disease were noticed in the fifth ferret captured, animals were not immediately isolated. Indeed, a sixth ferret, captured several days later, was also placed in the same room. There was no final revelation until 22 October, after one of the animals had already died (BFAT meeting minutes, 22 October 1985). Thus at least one black-footed ferret had exhibited symptoms of a disease for about two weeks in captivity at a time when the wild population was declining 50% a month. Timely information is imperative for officials to address delicate situations. As it stood, the recovery program lacked the flexibility to react adequately and promptly to the population decline, causing a needless loss of ferrets.

CAPTURING THE REMAINING FERRETS AND EXTINCTION IN THE WILD

After the discovery of distemper, Wyoming immediately initiated a second trapping to replace the first six black-footed ferrets. This second group, which was isolated individually at the Wyoming state veterinary lab in Laramie, was free from distemper. It is possible that the disease had run its course during October 1985.

Wyoming was now committed to captive breeding but refused to capture all of the remaining individuals. This philosophy was put succinctly by the Wyoming Game and Fish Department director, Bill Morris, who said, in reference to captive breeding of ferrets, "I have no compunction killing an animal, but I have a hell of a time putting one in a cage" (DeBlieu 1991). Wyoming's intention was to capture all ferrets in the central colonies of the complex, where canine distemper was known to exist; the smaller, geographically dispersed outlying colonies were to be left alone (Thorne and Williams 1988; E. S. Williams et al. 1988). Wyoming hoped that trapping all ferrets in the central colonies would prevent transmission of the disease to the few ferrets living on peripheral colonies, and that the peripheral ferrets would then repopulate the core area after the disease had run its course (Thorne and Williams 1988; E. S. Williams et al. 1988). An adult male and two adult females with litters were known to be living on those outlying colonies. Both the Biota-ISU and Denver Wildlife Research Center field teams opposed this strategy, countering that the peripheral colonies were small, with high extinction rates, and that it was unlikely that ferrets would be safer there.

Even the plan to take animals from the central colonies proceeded slowly. Wyoming only allowed capture of one animal a day, the rate at which their carpenter could construct cages. Suggestions to contract with a lumberyard to build cages quickly were not implemented (B. Miller pers. obs.). On 2 November 1985, Wyoming terminated the trapping effort, announcing that every ferret seen had been trapped (*Billings Gazette,* 6 November 1985). While this was technically true, trapping actually stopped after capture of the sixth animal. It had been decided in May 1985 to capture six ferrets, and once the sixth was in captivity no more spotlight searching was allowed. So, although no more black-footed ferrets were seen, there were still a few individuals left that could have been captured with continued spotlighting. Indeed, Dean Biggins and Brian Miller saw two separate snow trails in the central colonies of the complex on 10 November 1985.

The Region 6 office in Denver continued to support Wyoming over the federal field team from the Denver Wildlife Research Center. On 17 November 1985, the *Casper Star-Tribune* quoted the head of the U.S. Fish and Wildlife Service Endangered Species Office, John Spinks, as saying that he had no reservations about giving Wyoming the lead role in ferret recovery because "the state of Wyoming has demonstrated nothing but the highest degree of professionalism." Later in the interview he admitted being "too far removed from the situation to have a thorough knowledge of the details of the program." On 20 November 1985, the Defenders of Wildlife wrote to the Secretary of Interior to urge that Wyoming be relieved of responsibility for the captive-breeding program (*Casper Star-Tribune,* 9 December 1985).

Calls for capturing the whole ferret population persisted through the winter, but some Wyoming biologists countered that there were more ferrets in the field than the censuses indicated. In fall 1985, field workers estimated a population of about 16 ferrets by mark-recapture before the 12 were removed for captivity (Forrest, Biggins, et al. 1988). In the winter of 1985–86, Dean Biggins and Brian Miller estimated a winter population of four adults by snow-tracking (Miller 1988). These animals, plus the 6 in captivity, meant that only about 10 members of the species remained in existence. Several Wyoming officials, however, continued to assert that the population had not crashed. Ignoring the field work, they estimated that 20–25 adults remained in the wild (*Cody Enterprise,* 23 October 1985; Prendergast 1986). Although winter surveys had accurately predicted the number of adults in the past (42 animals in the winter of 1983–84 compared to 43 adults in the summer of 1984, Richardson et al. 1987; 24 animals in the winter of 1984–85 compared to 20 adults in the summer of 1985, Miller 1988), Wyoming did not accept the estimates. A Wyoming memo stated, "The point is that the winter survey results are not appropriate for developing population estimates. However, we predict, that is exactly what the hand wringers will do" (D. Belitsky and T. Thorne, Wyoming Game and Fish memo, 27 November 1985).

The Captive Breeding Specialist Group of the IUCN, which began advising Wyoming in 1985, also advocated the capture of more animals (Captive Breeding Specialist Group meeting minutes, 12 December 1985). Because there were very few wild black-footed ferrets available at the time of the second capture, the captive population was composed of three adult females, one juvenile female, and two juvenile males. The Captive Breeding Specialist Group stated that the lack of an adult male made for a 90% chance of failure the first year. An adult male had been located on a peripheral colony in the wild, but he was not captured and disappeared over the winter of 1985–86. No captive young were produced in spring 1986.

In 1986, when the fate of the remaining free-ranging ferrets was discussed, Wyoming claimed that the number of ferrets in the Meeteetse population had been underestimated, either because distemper was less severe than it had appeared or because animals had dispersed to the smaller outlying colonies and survived. Bob Oakleaf, who had recently been assigned ferret responsibilities by Wyoming, designed guidelines to test these ideas, and they were accepted (Wyoming Game and Fish Department 1986). If more than four litters were found in the central area, then either canine distemper was less severe than had been presumed or animals had dispersed to outlying colonies, escaped the disease, then migrated back to the central area. Alternatively, if three or more litters were found on outlying colonies, then black-footed ferrets had dispersed to the peripheral colonies, escaped disease, and survived (Wyoming Game and Fish Department 1986). Neither condition was met.

The Wyoming theory about salvation through the outlying colonies, which was never accepted by the field biologists, had proven wrong. Of 58 animals counted in August 1985, 11 were located on outlying colonies; 1 of those animals was captured in the ill-fated first trapping effort for captive breeding. Only one ferret was seen on the outlying colonies in 1986, indicating that the survival rate was 10%. Forty-seven ferrets occupied the central colonies in 1985, and 11 of these animals were captured in the two fall trapping efforts. The 1986 spotlight searches revealed only three ferrets remaining on the central colonies (i.e., 8% survival rate). Clearly, the population drop had been devastating to ferrets both in the center of the complex and in the smaller outlying prairie dog colonies. In fact, the strategy of waiting until the population was very low, then capturing animals only from the central area, may have contributed to narrowing of the genetic base in the captive population. And because only an estimated 4.16 founding animals—a number representing the genetic contributions of unrelated individuals to future generations—had donated their genes to the entire captive population (Captive Breeding Specialist Group 1992), genetics is an important issue.

The summer counts in 1986 revealed only four adult ferrets (two males and two females) left in the wild. This finding was in line with earlier estimates by winter snow-tracking. One of those males was near enough to the two females to breed them, and they produced two litters of five animals each in the central area of the complex. When Wyoming's contentions of high ferret numbers in Meeteetse were disproven by the summer spotlight surveys, no choice remained but to capture the remaining animals (*Casper Star-Tribune*, 29 August 1986), bringing the captive population to 18. The last ferret was captured during the night of 28 February–1 March 1987.

ORGANIZATIONAL LESSONS FROM MEETEETSE

The recovery program for wild black-footed ferrets was crippled from the start by unproductive conflict. The various key organizations, actors, and interest groups involved with ferrets (e.g., federal agencies, state agencies, nongovernmental conservation groups, and ranchers) represented different definitions of the problem, goals, methods of operation, values, perspectives, philosophies, and ideologies. Such diversity is not uncommon in endangered-species programs. Unfortunately, although diverse views can strengthen programs by drawing on multiple problem-solving strategies and superior ideas, such differences can also create power struggles that drain effort and attention from the task of recovery.

Conflict often starts when various entities promote dissimilar paths toward recovery. Typically, the participants are well intentioned, but without an effective method of conflict resolution that can utilize disparate views, key participants begin to struggle for control of the program in an effort to advance the course of action they endorse.

The logical extension of such conflict can be an inversion of goals. In other words, the goal of attaining power can surpass the goal of species recovery if the two come into conflict (goal inversion). This trap is easy to fall into, and those who do may continue to think that they are acting in the interest of the species. The organizational deficiencies often remain undetected because blame is deflected onto "biopolitics" or "personality differences" (Schon 1983). The simple fact that conflict resurfaces when the cast of characters changes demonstrates that the problem is structural and not personal. Thus, a high-quality and efficient recovery program requires a firm grasp of organizational theory to avoid these suffocating pitfalls.

Region 6's failure to exercise appropriate oversight and to spot the organizational weaknesses from the very beginning was more likely attributable to its own structural deficiencies than to the individuals involved. Agencies like the Fish and Wildlife Service tend to rely on conventional means when addressing problems. A typical bureaucratic format—working through a long, narrow chain of command—is adequate for routine and unchanging tasks, but does not allow the creative input and quick responsiveness necessary in the uncertain, complex, and urgent environment surrounding a species in crisis. Yet the top-down bureaucratic response is usually adopted regardless of the situation. Besides providing a method to control participants, it is familiar and easy to implement, thus allowing overburdened administrators to move on to the next problem.

During a crisis, weaknesses in a program's organization become even more evident. When differences of opinion heighten, a rigid organizational structure typically does not use open democratic methods to seek new solutions but instead tries to consolidate more control (Clark n.d.). This approach usually results in the elimination or subordination of dissenters, reduced program flexibility, redefinition of the problem (or denial that a problem exists), information or communication failures, and increased control of publicity in an attempt to legitimize the established doctrine (Clark n.d.). While these events may smooth internal bureaucratic functioning, the narrower orientation usually has disastrous effects on decision-making and program direction, as it did with black-footed ferrets. Chapter 14 will explore these ideas in more detail and offer a solution.

8
CAPTIVE BREEDING

HISTORY OF CAPTIVE BREEDING IN WYOMING

The Biota-ISU team, which had functioned as the main source of nonagency information to the public, left the black-footed ferret program at the end of 1985. Its data indicating a population crash had been timely and correct, but the resulting negative publicity had threatened the legitimacy of Wyoming's program. With the departure of Biota-ISU, the Captive Breeding Specialist Group (CBSG) became the main nongovernmental participant. Because its parent organization, the International Union for the Conservation of Nature, is internationally respected, the CBSG was initially welcomed to help restore credibility to the Wyoming program. Indeed, the CBSG went out of its way to praise Wyoming publicly, which initially made Wyoming more receptive to CBSG advice.

But it was not long before tension developed between the CBSG and Wyoming as well. The CBSG had assembled a team of reproductive physiologists, nutritionists, geneticists, and other researchers to develop a strategy for the breeding program. Acutely aware of the importance of time, they wanted to move quickly. When reproduction is delayed, genetic diversity dwindles. Additionally, each new generation in captivity can further erode behavioral and physiological traits necessary for survival in the wild.

Wyoming, however, maintained its cautious approach. For example, a technique using vaginal cytology to determine when a female black-footed ferret was in estrus had been developed 10 years earlier by Jim Carpenter at the U.S. Fish and Wildlife Service's Patuxent Wildlife Research Center, yet Wyoming did not employ it in 1986. At the start of the 1987 breeding season, the technique was used only once a week. By March, when time was slipping away with little evidence of potential reproduction, Wyoming began using it several times a week. Knowing when females were in estrus was critical to the success of captive breeding. That knowledge, and the arrival of the wild-caught adult male from Meeteetse on 1 March 1987, produced the first living litter of captive black-footed ferrets, a grand event. Nine of the 11 females in captivity bred, and two conceived litters. Seven surviving young were produced that year.

Though Region 6 was paying for the advice of the CBSG, decisions continued to be made by Wyoming, which often made for delays. The advice of the CBSG was not binding, and Region 6 did not attempt to assert its own decision-making authority.

Nevertheless, prospects for reestablishing the species through captive breeding gradually improved. During the 1988 captive-breeding season, 13 of 14 females produced litters totaling 34 young. The dedication of the Sybille staff (coordinated by Don Kwiatowski), and the advice of the CBSG had paid dividends.[1]

The CBSG had pushed hard to split the ferret population among several captive centers so that a local catastrophe in Wyoming would not eliminate the entire species. Criteria for division of the captive population had been established in early 1987. After the 1987 breeding season, there were enough females but one too few males to divide the population, so all the animals remained in Wyoming for one more year. When the success of the 1988 season brought the population of black-footed ferrets well over the desired mark, satellite populations were established at the Conservation and Research Center of the National Zoological Park in Front Royal, Virginia, and at the Henry Doorly Zoo in Omaha, Nebraska.

The CBSG held its last advisory meeting after the 1988 breeding season. For nearly a year, the program had planned to initiate a Species Survival Plan (SSP) under the auspices of the American Association of Zoological Parks and Aquariums (AAZPA) after dissolution of the CBSG. There are SSPs for a number of endangered species bred in captivity; they coordinate the efforts of the various involved institutions. The black-footed ferret SSP would therefore coordinate breeding strategies for the three sites.

Issues of control, however, persisted. As a Wyoming memo (F. Petera, Wyoming Game and Fish Department, 21 August 1987) reviewing an early draft of the new federal recovery plan stated:

We have taken the lead in black-footed ferret management and intend to retain control over the species in the near term future. Since we have all of the ferrets, we believe that someone from this agency should be SSP Coordinator. We would rather prepare a plan similar to a SSP plan, without AAZPA endorsement, and assure cooperation between participating organizations through memoranda of understanding. If this Recovery Plan binds us to a SSP plan with the associated entities, we intend to oppose approval of the Plan. . . . Portions of the Recovery Plan are designed to turn control of this program over to private interests. . . . The Wyoming Game and Fish Department, which has taken the initiative in capture of black-footed ferrets and implementation of the captive breeding program, will continue to maintain responsibility for control of the captive breeding program.

In fact, Wyoming had opposed captive breeding until outside pressure forced it to examine the strategy, and even then had agreed only if federal money would build a facility in Wyoming.

Wyoming reasserted several months later that, if it could not participate in the SSP as Species Coordinator, it could not endorse the recovery plan (D. Crowe, Wyoming Game and Fish Department memo, 1 March 1988). This position had serious implications: it meant that the ferret population would not be divided unless Wyoming maintained control of ferrets that left their state. This was a heavy club to wield, because concentrating all the ferrets in one location put the population at risk of disaster (fire, disease, etc.), and memory of the loss of the single wild population at Meeteetse was still fresh. Adamant about preventing outsiders from dictating its actions, Wyoming wanted to maintain control when the ferret breeding program went elsewhere. Region 6 again took a passive stance, and Tom Thorne, the Wyoming veterinarian, was named to start and head the black-footed ferret SSP. It was also agreed that zoos receiving ferrets could not compete with the Wyoming facility for federal funds.

A few months after the ferrets were moved to Omaha and Front Royal late in 1988, an article on the role of zoos in black-footed ferret recovery appeared in *Zoogoer,* a small regional magazine published by the Friends of the National Zoo. Wyoming felt it did not give them sufficient credit and threatened to delay the start of the SSP. In a memo, Wyoming declared its intention to "reevaluate our relationship with the zoo community and the cooperation we will receive from it," and to again weigh "the pros and cons of establishing a species survival-like plan without the sanctions of the AAZPA" (A. Reese, Wyoming Game and Fish Department memo, 28 March 1989). Wyoming, which had not yet formalized the SSP with a written petition to the AAZPA, was threatening to withdraw from the earlier agreement. Only after the zoo apologized did Wyoming renew efforts to form a black-footed ferret SSP.

So far, the Conservation and Research Center is the only site to breed black-footed ferrets successfully on the first attempt. Captive black-footed ferrets are now housed at the main breeding center in Wyoming and at zoos in Omaha, Front Royal, Toronto, Phoenix, Louisville, and Colorado Springs.

GENERAL CONSIDERATIONS OF CAPTIVE BREEDING

Captive propagation is a tool for maintaining populations of species threatened with immediate extinction. A proactive strategy that prevents degradation of the supporting ecosystem is obviously preferable to expensive last-minute programs undertaken only after a species' numbers have been greatly diminished. All too often, because our legal and economic systems do not promote such proactive management, we are left with the option of salvaging the few remaining animals and plants for zoos and herbaria. Biological brinkmanship has already allowed several species (including the black-footed ferret) to face imminent extinction. In these cases, captive propagation provided a means to maximize individual survival and fecundity in a controlled environment (Carpenter 1985; Wemmer 1985).

Captive propagation, however, is not a panacea. It is expensive in time, space, and money, and decisions to use it should be made carefully. The black-footed ferret program cost more than $1.5 million in 1991 alone (U.S. Fish and Wildlife Service 1992), and the California condor *(Gymnogyps californianus)* program cost approximately $25 million over the years (Nash 1992). Leader-Williams (1990) has estimated that keeping African elephants *(Loxodonta africana)* and black rhinoceros *(Diceros bicornis)* in captivity is 50 times more expensive than protecting an equal number in the wild. Furthermore, the added expense does not protect habitat or associated species in the ecosystem.

According to a survey of reintroductions, successful projects released an average of 726 animals each over 11.8 years (Beck, Rapaport, et al. 1993). To avoid failure, therefore, a captive breeding and reintroduction project must be capable of intensive commitment and support for an extended period of time. Costs can be defrayed somewhat by using existing facilities, and Frankel and Soulé (1981) have listed 26 rare mammals (including 8 carnivores) with self-sustaining populations in zoos. Soulé et al. (1986) have estimated that, if present trends continue for the next 200 years, 800 more mammalian species may require captive maintenance for survival. This is a clear call to alter present trends, as it is highly unlikely that we have funding or space to house viable populations of that many mammalian species.

Alternatively, habitat protection, legal protection, technical assistance, and education can often reverse species decline without resorting to captive propagation and reintroduction (Cade 1986; W. G. Conway 1988; Derrickson and Snyder 1992). It would make very good sense to first identify the cause of the problem in the wild, then use these approaches to neutralize it. After identifying and correcting the problem, conservationists may need to speed population recovery by adding animals through reintroduction or translocation (moving wild-born animals from one site to another). When augmenting a population, translocation has proven more successful than using captive-raised animals (Griffith et al. 1989; Beck, Kleiman, et al. 1991); we observed such differences in daily survival when wild-born black-footed ferrets were compared to captive-raised black-footed ferrets (Chapter 6).

Clearly, solid data from the field are essential to the conservation of declining species. First and foremost, the cause of the decline must be identified and addressed. If captive breeding is proposed to rebuild a given population, we need to determine whether such an effort is necessary (and, if so, when), the potential viability of a captive-breeding program, the likely duration of time in captivity (shorter durations may result in fewer genetic and behavioral changes), and the likelihood of successful reintroduction. For example, decisions about captive propagation and reintroduction require information about culturally transmitted behaviors (parenting routines, migration routes, and the like may be lost during confinement), the number of geographically separate populations remaining in the wild (single populations are ripe for disaster), the degree of predator pressure (the reintroductions listed as successful by Beck, Rapaport, et al. 1993 typically did not have major predator problems), and the causes of population decline.

Captive propagation in a species' native area, combined with habitat protection and education, can play a large role in raising local consciousness of conservation (Kleiman 1989). Captive breeding of the black-footed ferret appears to have raised national awareness about the plight of the species and the destruction of its habitat, the prairie dog ecosystem. Yet that awareness has not translated into real protection for the prairie dog ecosystem because we are not adequately addressing regional misconceptions about, and attitudes toward, the prairie dog (see Chapters 2 and 11). Since the ferret entered captivity, several other species that depend on prairie dogs have continued to decline and have been proposed as candidates for endangered status.

Because captive breeding is expensive and high-profile, it may be showcased by a managing agency as a testament to its commitment and to deflect attention from the politically sensitive issues of habitat protection (in the ferret's case, continued prairie dog poisoning). Some governments and private organizations may even promote unnecessary captive programs in order to secure funding (Schaller 1993). In sum, the captive-breeding option can draw attention to habitat destruction, but it can also be misused to deflect money and attention from that need.

Captive propagation does, however, offer opportunities for managing small-population demographics—opportunities that can be limited in natural systems. In the wild, both disease prevention and predator control can be expensive, and the benefits are often only short-term. In captivity, there is potential to manipulate the reproductive physiology of the animal to increase litter size and frequency of parturition per animal (Carpenter 1985; Wemmer 1985; Wildt and Goodrowe 1989). This has not been the case, however, with black-footed ferrets. Both the proportion of females producing young and the litter size are smaller than in the wild (comparing captive survivorship at the age wild-born ferrets were first seen above ground at Meeteetse). We do not know if the explanation rests in husbandry, genetics, or behavior. For example, not all species breed well when natural behavioral repertoires are altered by the captive environment, and seemingly insignificant husbandry practices can also have detrimental effects (Derrickson and Snyder 1992). Some techniques that enhance survival in captivity, such as hand-rearing and domestication, negatively affect survival after release back to the wild.

Ideally, any conservation plan to breed animals in captivity should have the goal of reintroduction, and it should be an integral part of a comprehensive strategy. It should not replace protection of habitat in the wild, and the structure of the captive environment should be adapted to maximize chances of survival after reintroduction. An initial capture of 20–30 founder animals has been proposed as a minimum to start a captive-propagation project; founders should represent an equal sex ratio, a cross-section of age classes, and maximal genetic diversity (Foose et al. 1986). If the species is restricted to one locale and is vulnerable enough that removal of a few pairs would heighten its chance of extinction, disaster could be imminent. In such cases, managers could consider capturing the entire population, as was done with black-footed ferrets. If ferrets had not been brought into captivity, it is likely that they would now be extinct.

HUSBANDRY

Reproductive physiology, nutrition, pathology, behavior, and the general health and fitness of animals are vital considerations for captive populations. Reproductive specialists can provide important information on the estrous cycle, photoperiod, gestation, parturition, and other aspects of reproduction necessary for successful captive-breeding and reintroduction programs. Nutritionists and physiologists can also make significant contributions to captive well-being. Diet and photoperiod are important aspects of husbandry; indeed, circumstantial evidence indicates that reduced levels of vitamin E and low light may have decreased fertility and sperm quality during the 1987 black-footed ferret breeding season (Captive Breeding Specialist Group meeting minutes, 30 May 1987). Similarly, the introduction of a new dietary plan, the Flushing diet, may have reduced the number of ferret offspring in 1991 (1991 Black-Footed Ferret Interstate Working Group meeting minutes).

Disease must be controlled in captivity and at the reintroduction sites. It is possible that some endangered species are unusually susceptible to disease because of reduced genetic diversity (O'Brien, Roelke, et al. 1985; O'Brien and Evermann 1988; Thorne and Williams 1988). With black-footed ferrets, coccidiosis has been a problem in captivity, and canine distemper decimated the wild population.

Whether distemper is exotic to North America is not clear (Budd 1981); it may have been introduced following European settlement (Gorham 1966). The historical impact of canine distemper on black-footed ferret populations is therefore unknown. Regardless of whether distemper was introduced or native, the recent fragmentation of the prairie dog ecosystem probably increased the disease's ability to destroy small colonies of ferrets. Their increasing isolation made it more difficult for black-footed ferrets to recolonize extirpated sites. Distemper may continue to affect isolated wild populations of reintroduced ferrets, but researchers from the Wyoming state veterinary lab are working to develop a vaccine (1992 Black-Footed Ferret Interstate Working Group meeting minutes).

The specter of epizootics in the captive environment requires establishment of several separate captive populations. Veterinarians obviously play a central role in these decisions. For endangered birds, Derrickson and Snyder (1992) recommend selecting breeding facilities within the species' natural range, using two or three geographically separate facilities that are essentially closed, hiring staff who are not caring for other captive birds, protecting birds from arthropod vectors, and requiring "scrub-downs" before human visitors enter the facility. These precautions also reduce the chance of passing a disease to the wild via reintroduced animals.

Although several facilities are necessary, a caveat about multiple breeding centers is called for. The ferret program consists of one large center (with about two-thirds of the captive black-footed ferrets) and six small satellite centers. In retrospect, three larger sites might have been a better arrangement. The goal of captive breeding is reintroduction as quickly as possible, but each new breeding facility typically requires a learning period before production begins. The resulting delays lengthen the generational time in captivity—which can erode survival skills, making reintroduction less efficient. Care should be taken that the desire to start new facilities does not supersede the goal of reintroduction, deflecting young animals from the latter purpose.

Another crucial question is when the sterile conditions of the captive environment should be abandoned during the reintroduction process. Eventually, captive-raised animals must face the diseases and pathogens of the real world. This is not a trivial concern. The expense of maintaining antiseptic protocols in the field raises the cost of reintroduction considerably. Similarly, maintaining ferrets in sterile conditions before release may increase susceptibility to the host of parasites and pathogens they will encounter immediately after release, making transition to the wild even more difficult.

GENETICS

Understanding genetic considerations is important to conservation biology, which recognizes that the ability to evolve is fundamental to the viability of any species. Small populations may be subject to significant declines in genetic variability through *genetic drift* (a process whereby small populations can lose genes due to chance events), and that loss may in turn reduce adaptability in the face of environmental change, increase susceptibility to disease, and lower reproductive potential (Nei et al. 1975; Lacy and Clark 1989). Extinction is the likely result of these collective impacts if the species is constrained to smaller and smaller populations. Genetic researchers have suggested that an effective population size (see below) of 50 animals is necessary to reduce the consequences of inbreeding in the short term, and that 500 animals are necessary for adaptive evolution in the long term (Frankel and Soulé 1981). Although these numbers have been subject to debate, most geneticists recommend using them as a general guideline, with the caveat that genetic effects vary greatly among species.

Effective population size must not be confused with the actual population size. An effective population assumes random mating, equal genetic representation in future generations, and equal sex ratios (Frankel and Soulé 1981). Effective population sizes (N_e) are always smaller than actual population sizes (N) in the wild, because random mating is hindered by fluctuating populations and sex ratios, reproductive variability, and behavioral factors such as dominance and dispersal (Bertram and Moltu 1986; Lande 1988). For black-footed ferrets in the wild, the ratio $N_e:N$ probably equals 0.3:1 (U.S. Fish and Wildlife Service 1988; Lacy and Clark 1989), a ratio that may be fairly typical of many wild populations (Flesness pers. com., as cited in U.S. Fish and Wildlife Service 1988). In other words, an N_e of 500 requires an N of about 1,500 individuals. Modern models include demographic and behavioral information, such as type of social organization, in estimates of genetically effective population sizes (Lande and Barrowclough 1987).

Opportunities to manage the genetics of small populations can be increased in captivity (Carpenter 1985; Wemmer 1985), whereas genetic lineages of free-ranging animals can be observed but not predicted. If several natural colonies exist, managers can move individuals between those populations, but survival of translocated animals can be problematic (Wemmer 1985). On the other hand, gene flow between captive subpopulations can be managed and monitored to avoid inbreeding and preserve genetic diversity. The genetically effective population size, usually smaller than an actual wild population *(N)* because of unequal genetic contribution by members of a mating population, can in theory reach 2*N* if a captive program is carefully managed to that end (Seal 1978; Frankel and Soulé 1981).

Ballou and Oakleaf (1989) estimated that an effective population of 250 captive black-footed ferrets would maintain 80% of its genetic diversity for 200 years. Although that is an acceptable level, many geneticists recommend 90% retention as an objective. That goal would require an effective population of 1,500 ferrets, which will only be possible if wild populations are established (Ballou and Oakleaf 1989).

The effects of natural selection may be reduced in captive populations. But because the evolution of small wild populations can be driven by stochastic events in addition to natural selection, and given that stochasticity can be reduced in captivity, it may be possible to maintain greater genetic diversity (and thus evolutionary potential) in captive populations than in small wild populations. However, there is more to an animal than genetics, and the effects of captivity on behaviors necessary for survival vary greatly from species to species (Kleiman 1989; Derrickson and Snyder 1992). Additionally, inadvertent artificial selection can make a surprise appearance if procedures are not carefully watched. For example, small exotic cats reproduced more successfully when habituated to friendly keepers (Mellen 1991), yet domestication was reported to be maladaptive when many species were released into the wild (Derrickson and Snyder 1992).

It is also important to analyze genetic variation among different populations or subspecies (Templeton 1990). If animals that exhibit a high degree of local adaptation are moved to a different environment, they may not adjust well. For example, a captive ibex subspecies, *Capra ibex ibex,* was crossed with *C. i. aegagrus* and *C. i. nubiana* before reintroduction. These ibex subspecies were under different selective pressures for the timing of reproduction, with the southern ibex subspecies giving birth earlier in the year. When the hybrids were released in what was then Czechoslovakia, they bore young at a time that was maladaptive to the harsh winter (Grieg 1979). Consequently, there was a high rate of juvenile mortality.

Genetic mixing after reintroduction can also produce problems. If the wild population of a subspecies still exists near the reintroduction site, interbreeding can genetically swamp the reintroduced population or vice versa (Ryder 1988; Kleiman 1989). Alternatively, mixing two locally adapted populations can produce an outbreeding depression (Cade 1988; Stanley Price 1989; Kleiman 1989). Outbreeding depression can reduce fitness (genetic contribution to the next generation) by disrupting coadapted gene complexes, which are combinations of genes that function well together (Templeton 1990). Alternatively, if few genes are involved in coadaptation, fitness may decline temporarily, then return to original levels, or there may be no decline at all (Templeton 1986). Reintroduction programs require careful planning to avoid harming the existing wild population through genetic swamping or outbreeding depression.

Debate has flourished about interbreeding of newly discovered black-footed ferret populations with the existing captive stock, but in reality no other populations have been located. The driving factor in evolution of the black-footed ferret is the environment of the prairie dog burrow, and that environment is similar from Canada to Mexico. For that reason, mixing black-footed ferrets may not pose a problem (should a new population be discovered), although genetic testing should verify that assumption.

Genetic considerations were key to the recovery strategy for black-footed ferrets, and were used to determine the target number of 1,500 individuals (actual population size based on an N_e of 500). We do not recommend, however, targeting wild population numbers by genetics only, because of the tremendous influence exerted by environmental and demographic stochasticity (to be discussed in the next section). Genetic data were also used to pick individual black-footed ferrets for reintroduction: animals used in the first releases had a higher inbreeding coefficient than ferrets remaining in captivity. In other words, because mortality was expected to be high, only genetically surplus animals were released to avoid damaging the captive population (Russell et al. 1994).

Genetic studies were among the first recommendations of the Captive Breeding Specialist Group for management of the captive black-footed ferret population (CBSG meeting minutes, 12 December 1985). Region 6 advanced funding for such studies in 1988, but as of June 1994 Wyoming had not completed genetic sampling. To reduce inbreeding, a stud book maintained by the SSP at the University of Wyoming determines which mating pairs will result in maximization of "founder genome equivalents," the percentage of genetic material from the original founder generation still present in the individual. But black-footed ferret family lines were initially estimated using locations of capture in 1985 and 1986. Those field estimates, which were intended to be temporary, continue to form the basis of the SSP stud book today. Though such measures as founder genome equivalents and inbreeding coefficients offer a powerful tool to manage captive animals, the ferret stud book is based not on genetic data but only on best guesses.

Furthermore, there were three ferrets of disputed parentage in 1988. Those three animals entered the breeding population in 1989 and produced nine offspring, and those lines have continued contributing to the captive population over the years (memo from acting regional director, U.S. Fish and Wildlife Service, 25 February 1992; memo from regional director, U.S. Fish and Wildlife Service, 3 April 1992). The disputed parentage was not enough to spur Wyoming into completing the genetic sampling, which it has characterized as not critical: "The proposed genetic work will not result in significant changes in the way the population is managed" (J. White, Wyoming Game and Fish Department memo, 13 March 1992).

As of 1992, apparent genetic abnormalities, such as short tails, webbed feet, misshapen canines, and internal hemorrhaging began to appear in the captive population (Godbey and Biggins 1994). The 1993 reintroduction in Montana and South Dakota was canceled because of poor captive production, including low fertility and high postnatal loss of young kits. As of 2 August 1993, there were only 127 black-footed ferret kits (Tom Thorne, Wyoming Game and Fish Department memo, 2 August 1993), produced from about 333 adults (Bill Russell, memo to U.S. Fish and Wildlife Service, 14 September 1993). At the 1993 Black-Footed Ferret Interstate Working Group meeting, the final tally was 280 born, 171 died, 61 returned to the captive population, and 48 released. Because the captive population maintains 250 adults under the age of three years, roughly one-third of the 250 must be replaced each year. A 28 May 1994 article in the *Wyoming Tribune-Eagle* stated that although ferret production in 1994 appeared to be better than in 1993, it was still "not as high as hoped for."

The low production in 1993 may be attributable to other causes (the same article mentioned sulfa drugs given to pregnant females), but genetics should certainly be investigated. Having only an estimated 4.16 founding animals is obviously restrictive, but if there are genetic problems, options are still available. First and foremost, however, the problem needs to be defined and understood, and performing the genetics work is essential to that task.

DEMOGRAPHIC CONSIDERATIONS

Colonies of reintroduced animals must be large enough to withstand fluctuations in both the environment and population size, because unpredictable vacillations in either can increase the chances of extinction (Gilpin and Soulé 1986). The larger the population, the better its chances of surviving demographic and environmental variability. Larger populations also facilitate natural biological and evolutionary development.

To understand these population dynamics, biologists must analyze demographic parameters such as fecundity, mortality, population growth rate, age structure, sex ratio, and life expectancy in natural populations (Kleiman, Beck, et al. 1986; Stanley Price 1989). Historically, the viability estimates of some endangered species, like the red-cockaded woodpecker *(Picoides borealis),* were based on genetics alone (U.S. Fish and Wildlife Service 1985). More recently an awareness has surfaced that demography and environmental stochasticity, instead of genetics, were the factors that often drove a species into oblivion (Lande 1988). Thus many current models have been based on demographics. Hurricane Hugo demonstrated the vulnerability of even a large red-cockaded woodpecker population to catastrophic events, indicating the need to consider the spatial distribution of a population and to manage several separate colonies (Walters 1991). Distemper could play the same role for black-footed ferrets as the hurricane did for red-cockaded woodpeckers. Even with the captive population of ferrets as a reserve, it will be important to start several wild populations as soon as possible.

Demographic characteristics are also important for defining habitat quality, which is the foundation of any habitat-management plan (Van Horne 1983). It is all too easy to base habitat qualifications on animal densities alone, because it is faster to do so and the planning process may be battling time. Also, many researchers work for institutions that reward multiple publications, prompting the use of faster analyses. Yet Van Horne (1983) cited several examples of density estimates that prompted misleading conclusions. First, surveys are usually taken in the warmer months, even though winter may be the critical season with respect to mortality. Second, because population dynamics can reflect environmental stochasticity (food or predator changes), densities may mirror conditions of the recent past, or the temporary present, rather than long-term habitat quality. Third, social interactions can prevent subordinate animals from entering higher-quality habitat. Dispersing juvenile animals can lend a misleadingly high density to poorer habitat because dominant animals are defending territories in the good habitat. Even though numbers can be temporarily high in poor habitat, or habitat "sinks," few of those animals will survive and reproduce. The good habitat, or "source," on the other hand, will have a stable adult population that will survive and reproduce. Without attention to demographic factors (such as age structure, mortality, and reproduction) and behavioral information (such as social structure), one cannot truly differentiate the quality of habitat types.

Because of these various factors, current population-viability models are incorporating demographics, genetics, behavior, and environmental components into complex algorithms. These models are tools that can greatly aid reintroduction by predicting desirable captive-population sizes and age structures, the sizes and number of reintroduction sites, and numbers, age structures, and sex ratios of animals to be released. These models depend, however, on solid data from the field, and their assumptions must match the requirements of the species. Without accurate information at the input stage, the output may be more applicable to theoretical than actual populations. Worse yet, when models are fed guesses, the results can be easily guided toward a predetermined management strategy. Like any other scientific prediction, models should always be tested and refined (preferably with field data). If models remain untested—which can occur, given the time constraints that conservation issues always face—a situation can develop wherein future models are based on the unsubstantiated theory of past models. If these untested assumptions are incorrect, the results move farther and farther from reality over time.

Model predictions were used by the Captive Breeding Specialist Group to estimate the probability of survival for black-footed ferrets remaining in the wild after the epizootic of canine distemper (R. B. Harris et al. 1989). Wyoming has used modeling to predict the necessary demographic structure in captivity and the number and genetic makeup of animals to be reintroduced (Ballou and Oakleaf 1989). Reintroductions are thus prevented from adversely affecting the genetics and demographics of the captive population.

EFFECTS OF THE CAPTIVE ENVIRONMENT ON BEHAVIORAL TRAITS

General Objectives of an Enriched Environment

Although reintroduction of captive-raised animals has become an increasingly popular tool in the effort to conserve biodiversity, the effects of captivity on natural behavior are not well defined, and there is a great deal of variability among species (Kleiman 1989; Derrickson and Snyder 1992). Generally speaking, reintroduction is far more difficult than it might seem, and behavioral details should not be taken for granted.

Relaxed selection pressures in captivity may erode morphological, behavioral, or physiological traits necessary for survival if those traits are genetically expensive to maintain (for a review of specific examples, see Derrickson and Snyder 1992). In addition, if the genetically determined range of expression for a particular trait is no longer modified by critical environmental factors (such as during an imprintation period), relaxed selection pressures in captivity may increase behavioral variability of individual animals to the point that adaptive traits are underrepresented in the reintroduced population. Our studies have noted a great deal of behavioral variation within cage-raised Siberian ferrets, even though the entire stock of captive animals originated from only three females and two males (Miller, Biggins, et al. 1997).

Because of the potentially profound effect of the captive environment on development of behavioral traits, integration of plans for captive breeding and reintroduction is imperative. If planned separately, the constraints and objectives of a captive-breeding program can differ from the objectives of reintroduction: captive animals are raised with great care and reduced risk to assure rapid and continued reproduction, but once released into natural habitat, they must cope with hunger, predation, disease, parasites, and inclement weather to survive.

Successful wild animals have developed an array of finely honed behavioral and physiological responses to adapt to these stresses. Effective development of these adaptive responses often requires natural expression of genetically influenced behavioral traits; or, if the trait is learned, it can require the appropriate stimuli at a critical time (Gossow 1970). Indeed, development of any complex behavior pattern is the result of extensive interaction between genetics and the animal's experience (Polsky 1975). Some behaviors may require repeated cues throughout juvenile development if animals are to perform them efficiently as adults (Gossow 1970). The failure of captive-raised reintroduced animals to survive as well as wild-born translocated animals of the same species (e.g., Schladweiler and Tester 1972; Cade et al. 1989; Griffith et al. 1989; Beck, Kleiman, et al. 1991; J. W. Wiley et al. 1992; and Chapter 6 of this book) underlines the importance of the captive environment.

There is always an appropriate behavioral response for the stresses that an animal encounters in nature, and an "enriched environment"—one that subjects the animal to more natural stresses—can allow expression of that behavior. In addition to preparation for reintroduction, these periodic bouts with natural stresses benefit the animal's mental state, and are necessary for normal psychological and behavioral development (Shepherdson 1993). A totally stress-free environment produces abnormal behaviors and an inability to cope when stress does occur. At the other extreme, the chronic stress of caged animals manifests itself in abnormal actions because there is no adaptive behavioral outlet by which the animal can control the situation. This may explain why enriched environments have helped alleviate some reproductive problems in captivity. Nonreproductive gorillas *(Gorilla gorilla)* sometimes reproduced after being moved to a seminatural enclosure, and cheetahs *(Acinonyx jubatus)* bred better when they were allowed to capture and kill live prey (reviewed in Shepherdson 1993).

For these reasons, we recommended that at least a sample of young black-footed ferrets targeted for reintroduction be raised in an environment as close to natural as possible (Miller, Biggins, et al. 1990b, 1992). This preparatory step may be especially important for the "higher" vertebrates. Indeed, pre-release exposure to the enriched environment of an enclosed prairie dog arena has proven behaviorally beneficial for captive-raised Siberian ferrets released into the wild (Biggins, Hanebury, et al. 1991), and pre-release exposure to a similar arena increased survival of captive-raised black-footed ferrets after reintroduction (Biggins, Godbey, and Vargas 1993; Vargas 1994). Similarly, the program for the golden lion tamarin *(Leontopithecus rosalia)* used pre-release conditioning strategies successfully (Kleiman, Beck, et al. 1986; Bronikowski et al. 1989); survival of the masked bobwhite *(Colinus virginianus ridgwayi)* improved with a pre-release conditioning program (Ellis et al. 1977), and large enclosures were used to establish social group structure before reintroduction of the Arabian oryx *(Oryx leucoryx)* in Oman (Stanley Price 1989).

In some cases (e.g., domestic dogs), wild behavioral repertoires can be restored after generations in captivity by re-creating the correct environment during the critical period (J. P. Scott and Fuller 1965). This may not always be true, however, particularly for behaviors that are culturally transmitted. Indeed, learned behaviors can erode much faster than genetic diversity (May 1991; Shepherdson 1993). If captive breeding is augmenting a fragile wild population, the wild animals may be able to transmit some learned knowledge to reintroduced individuals. The same thing may be accomplished by surrogates of a similar subspecies or a similar species. If a species has critical traits that are culturally transmitted and no individuals remain in the wild, an enriched environment that mimics nature may be necessary throughout the entire captive-breeding program. For the transmission of some knowledge (e.g., migration routes), however, even an enriched environment may not be sufficient.

Shepherdson (1993) invokes two interrelated factors that are important to survival of captive-raised animals after release: proficiency gained from earlier experience, and the ability to learn new skills after reintroduction and to adjust those skills as needed in the dynamic natural environment. Both of these factors can be enhanced by enriching the pre-release environment. He cautions, however, that reproducing natural cues in a beneficial manner is not always easily accomplished. Golden lion tamarins that ranged free in a large wooded area of the National Zoological Park demonstrated beneficial behavioral adaptations after reintroduction, but previous attempts to train the animals in enriched cages failed to bestow similar advantages (Bronikowski et al. 1989).

In examining pre-release conditioning and the effects of the captive environment on reintroduction, we will discuss critical periods, recognition of home sites and movement, early neural development, avoidance of predators, locating and securing prey, and interaction of behavioral traits.

Critical Periods

Imprinting is a phase-specific learning process that requires specific stimuli during a sensitive period in an animal's development. The length of the sensitive period varies from species to species and is related to the speed of development (Immelmann 1975). Imprinting during the sensitive period is permanent and ensures that critical information will be available to the individual before its first application. Animals that miss specific stimuli during a sensitive period may still be able to develop particular behavioral traits later in life but will do so less efficiently (Hasler 1966; Gossow 1970; Immelmann 1975; Caro 1979).

Most evidence for a sensitive period exists in the bird literature, but there is information for some carnivores and other mammals. Dogs, gray wolves *(Canis lupus)*, cats, and European ferrets exhibit a sensitive period for socialization early in life (J. P. Scott and Fuller 1965; Poole 1972; Leyhausen 1979). Unless cats, ermine, and European ferrets are exposed to prey during juvenile development, they do not kill efficiently as adults (Gossow 1970; Caro 1979, 1980a). Adult food preferences in European ferrets are developed via olfactory imprinting at two to three months of age, a period correlated with neural development (Apfelbach 1978, 1986). There is a similar imprinting period for black-footed ferrets (Vargas 1994).

Raising a sample of animals in an enriched environment will reduce their risk of missing specific stimuli during a sensitive period. If a sensitive period is missed, the animals may be forced to learn a critical behavioral trait at a time when efficiency cannot be maximized. If the stimuli are first experienced after reintroduction to the wild, the animal will have to learn at a time that may be inefficient and may be overwhelmed by the other variables of a strange environment.

Recognition of Home Sites

One of the ecological implications of sensitive periods can be imprinting on a home site. In one case, captive mallards *(Anas platyrhynchos)* raised in elevated wooden nest boxes chose elevated wooden nest boxes after reintroduction, as did their wild-born offspring; conversely, mallard ducks raised in ground nests chose ground nests after attaining sexual maturity (Hess 1972). Cage-raised golden lion tamarins were released from a familiar nest box fastened to a tree; they typically remained close to the nest box for periods averaging 12–18 months, but eventually moved farther from the site of release (B. Beck pers. com.).

Early Neural Development

In many mammals, division of neurons and formation of synapses continues for weeks or months (or even years, among larger mammals) postpartum (Immelmann 1975). An enriched early environment can beneficially alter brain morphology (and increase brain weight); increase the number, pattern, and quality of synaptic connections; and enhance other cerebral measures that affect behavior later in life (Greenough and Juraska 1979; Rosenzweigh 1979).

Animals that experience environmental complexity early in life employ cues better in problem solving. N. D. Henderson (1970) demonstrated that the genetic potential of food-finding ability was reduced considerably by raising animals in a typical laboratory cage. By contrast, Norway rats *(Rattus norvegicus)* from an enriched environment were more adept at maneuvering through an unfamiliar maze (Greenough and Juraska 1979). Renner (1988) showed that rats raised in an enriched environment could avoid predator models faster than rats raised in an impoverished environment. Enriched captive conditions, therefore, could provide beneficial advantages for animals about to enter a novel and dynamic wild environment.

Avoidance of Predators

Successful predator-avoidance behavior calls for both recognition of a potential predator and the correct escape response performed in an efficient manner (see Chapter 5). Bolles (1970) speculated that, in wild animals, many innate species-specific defense reactions occur when animals encounter certain stimuli. In addition, young prey may possess the ability to respond to a wide variety of stimuli, and through a process of habituation (see Chapter 5) they narrow their responses to those producing a real and present threat (Shalter 1984). The mother probably plays an important early role in helping her young with recognition of novel and familiar experiences (Bronson 1968). This habituation process allows an animal not only to determine which species are a threat but also to discriminate more precisely whether an individual predator is hunting or satiated.

Although some species maintain stereotypic antipredator responses whether in captivity or the wild (S. M. Smith 1975; Shalter 1984; Kleiman, Beck, et al. 1986), a depauperate environment may reduce congenital abilities over time (Derrickson and Snyder 1992). Schaller and Emlen (1962), Price (1972), and Smith (1972) demonstrated the different responses of domesticated animals and their wild counterparts. Captive-raised masked bobwhites showed inefficient antipredator responses until they were exposed to dogs, humans, and a trained Harris' hawk *(Parabuteo unicinctus)* prior to reintroduction. This pre-release exposure resulted in greater mobility, covey coordination, and predator-avoidance skills (Ellis et al. 1977). It may not be a matter of keeping or losing a trait, but of maintaining it at maximum efficiency. When predator pressures were reduced, some wild populations responded correctly but less efficiently (Curio 1969, as cited in Shalter 1984; Morse 1980; Coss and Owings 1985; Loughry 1988).

Reinforcing (punishing) in the captive environment may not always be practical, and the stimulus may have to be presented in such an unnatural context that animals fail to recognize the cue in a natural setting. In some species the value of an enriched environment for predator avoidance may be less the mock experience with a specific predator than the neural stimulation, enhanced problem-solving ability, familiarity with the natural setting, development of natural movement and activity patterns, and increased physical conditioning (see Chapter 9).

Locating and Securing Prey

Black-footed ferrets kill prey that can equal or exceed their own size. This predatory pattern is observed only in carnivores that are highly specialized anatomically and behaviorally (Eisenberg and Leyhausen 1972). Captive-raised mustelids have at least a rudimentary capacity to kill prey: captive-raised ermine (Gossow 1970), European ferrets (Wustehuße 1960), long-tailed weasels, fishers, and mink (Powell 1982), black-footed ferrets (Vargas 1994), and Siberian ferrets (Miller, Biggins, et al. 1992) all killed upon first exposure to prey. Even if the neck bite of the black-footed ferret is innate, however, proficiency increases with experience (Miller and Anderson 1993; Vargas 1994) and with exposure to an enriched environment (Vargas 1994). Similarly, captive Siberian ferrets killed more effectively with experience (Miller, Biggins, et al. 1992), and the only Siberian ferrets verified as having taken prey after release to the wild had had experience with prey and burrow systems in an enclosed prairie dog arena (Biggins, Hanebury, et al. 1991). Killing a prey item outside its natural setting (especially in one as unnatural as a cage) may be easier than killing a prey item in its own territory. In addition, a predator that has gone without food for a time may become weakened, and each tiring and unsuccessful attempt at killing may make subsequent predatory opportunities more difficult.

Killing prey, however, is only one part of the predatory sequence. For example, two 9-month-old captive-raised fishers killed porcupines *(Erithizon dorsatum)* on the first opportunity in captivity, but starved to death after release in the wild because they were unable to search for food successfully (Kelly 1977). Thus, other facets of predation include learning to search in a particular place, altering direction to increase contact with the prey item, developing a search image (so that prey may be more easily spotted), learning the appropriate time to attack, and refining specialized hunting techniques (Krebs 1973; Lawrence and Allen 1983).

Wild black-footed ferrets use a zigzag hunting pattern that is typical of mustelids (Powell 1982; Richardson et al. 1987). They probably alter direction to increase probability of contact with desired prey items (Krebs 1973). Verbeek (1985) cited many instances of immature raptors pursuing inappropriate prey, and Griffiths (1975) hypothesized that immature predators attacked prey as they found it, whereas adults selected their victims.

Both maturation and experience probably play a role in predatory ability, and the enriched environment of an arena provides predators an opportunity to gain valuable experience with prey in a natural system before being released to the wild. It may also allow young predators to familiarize themselves with prey at an appropriate stage of juvenile development that maximizes killing efficiency during adulthood.

Interaction of Behavioral Traits

Behavioral traits do not exist in isolation. An animal must react to an array of stresses, risks, and conditions in its environment, and the strategy necessary to survive and reproduce depends on the circumstances of the moment or the season. In other words, individual behaviors must be performed in the context of a host of other simultaneous behaviors necessary for survival; the expression of an individual behavior may be adjusted to each situation that the animal faces.

For example, predation pressures determine the time of breeding in the tropical clay-colored robin *(Turdus grayi)* (Morton 1971). Solitary hooved mammals ran quicker than individuals in a herd (Altmann 1958). Yellow-eyed juncos *(Junco phaeonotus)*, ostriches *(Struthio camelus)*, and coati (a carnivore, *Nasua narica*) altered feeding and drinking strategies when threatened with predation (Bertram 1980; Caraco et al. 1980; Burger and Gochfeld 1992). Rats at risk of predation decreased their foraging time and adopted a compensatory increase in meal size that maintained their total daily intake and body weight (Faneslow and Lester 1988). Even in moderately large carnivores, hunting behavior, socialization, and predator-avoidance behaviors influenced each other (Caro 1989).

Behavioral traits of wild free-ranging animals must be performed efficiently in a variety of situations. The seminatural pre-release environment allows animals to develop responses (by whatever processes) to a variety of ecologically relevant stimuli. Enrichment seems to be the safest approach when understanding of developmental processes is incomplete, and it also provides the most holistic pre-release preparation for captive-raised animals.

9

BACK TO THE WILD

Traditionally, reintroduction and translocation techniques have employed one of two methods: "hard releases" in which animals were simply transported to an area and liberated, and "soft releases" involving varying amounts of acclimation, provisioning, protection, and training before and after emancipation. After reviewing more than 40 translocations of fishers, pine martens, and otters, Berg (1982) concluded that success correlated with soft-release methods. Stanley Price (1991) also argued for the soft release of rare and endangered animals to reduce stress, acclimatize animals, and establish social groups. However, Griffith et al. (1989) studied several hundred releases (both translocations and reintroductions) of vertebrate species and concluded that success was not correlated with whether animals were held on a site prior to release, provisioned with food and water, or provided shelter after liberation. Nevertheless, most projects have held animals on the release site for several days or more prior to their release.

There seems to be no solid consensus about which point on the continuum provides the best results at the lowest cost. The literature suggests, however, that the outcomes of reintroductions and translocations may be site- and species-specific, and that releases should thus be designed as experiments to find the methods that produce the best results for the lowest cost.

Several reintroduction programs have experimented with closely related surrogate species to determine the best pre-release conditioning regimen and the best release techniques. For example, the Arabian oryx reintroduction project used the fringe-eared oryx *(Oryx gazella callotis)* to determine optimal herd size and composition (Stanley Price 1986). Similarly, the California condor project released Andean condors in South America and California to test release techniques (Wallace and Temple 1987; Wallace 1990), and we used Siberian ferrets to explore pre-release conditioning and reintroduction techniques for black-footed ferrets.

Release programs have typically consisted of six releases over three years (Griffith et al. 1989), but Beck, Rapaport, et al. (1993) reported that successful reintroductions of captive-born animals last an average of 11.8 years. Successful projects also use more animals. Most successful translocations of fisher, pine marten, and river otter involved more than 30 individuals (Berg 1982), for example, and Beck, Rapaport, et al. (1993) found that successful reintroductions of captive stock used 726 animals by contrast to 336 in unsuccessful projects.

REINTRODUCTION TECHNIQUES
FOR BLACK-FOOTED FERRETS

Experiments with Siberian Ferrets

Because of the obvious expense and time commitments, it is imperative that reintroductions be carefully planned and designed. We spent two years working with the closely related Siberian ferret to test ideas on behavioral development, pre-release conditioning, and release techniques for the black-footed ferret (see Miller, Biggins, et al. 1990a, 1990b, 1992, 1993; Biggins, Hanebury, et al. 1990, 1991). This work was a cooperative venture between the Conservation and Research Center of the National Zoological Park, the National Ecology Research Center (formerly the Denver Wildlife Research Center of the U.S. Fish and Wildlife Service), and the University of Wyoming Cooperative Research Unit. The resulting tactics, research, and recommendations are the product of cooperative work between ourselves, Dean Biggins, Astrid Vargas, Lou Hanebury, and Jerry Godbey.

To prevent establishment of an exotic species during the field releases, Siberian ferrets were sterilized, leaving their steroid-producing organs intact, and all released animals were monitored by radiotelemetry so we could analyze their movement and recapture when necessary. Because the stock of Siberian ferrets had been in captivity for more generations than the black-footed ferrets, we expected the results of field tests to be conservative: that is, we assumed that the additional generations in captivity would negatively affect behaviors necessary for survival. The experiments compared the effects of different captive environments on survival skills and the effects of differential release methods on survival rates, and they refined the radiotelemetry monitoring system that would be used on black-footed ferrets. In addition, Astrid Vargas (1994) at the University of Wyoming Cooperative Research Unit was conducting behavioral experiments with black-footed ferrets raised in different captive environments, evaluating their predatory abilities and testing the development of their dietary preferences.

We first analyzed the innate and learned aspects of predator avoidance by using Siberian ferrets that were raised in captivity at the Conservation and Research Center of the National Zoological Park (Miller, Biggins, et al. 1990b). For these experiments we used a terrestrial and an avian model. The terrestrial model was a road-killed badger stuffed and mounted on a remote-control toy-truck frame by Paul Rhymer of the National Museum of Natural History, Smithsonian Institution (Figure 9.1). The mechanical predator was dubbed Robo-badger by the *Washington Post* and later gained more notoriety in a syndicated column by humorist Dave Barry.[1] The avian model was a stuffed great horned owl attached to a cord threaded through a pulley on the ceiling. By pulling the cord, we could fly the owl harmlessly or make it swoop and dive at the Siberian ferrets. Models obviously differ from a real predator, but because we could make them do the same thing each time the treatments were consistent. Besides, the models did not eat any Siberian ferrets.

We tested the avoidance responses to the terrestrial and avian predators with naive two-, three-, and four-month-old Siberian ferrets. Naive Siberian ferrets reacted innately to the stuffed badger and owl at four months of age, and their response was enhanced after a single aversive experience (being shot with a rubber band). But memory of the experience lasted less than one week. We wanted to use a shock collar, similar to those used in dog training, for the aversive experience of predation but were unable to have one developed. The experience needed to be aversive because avoiding predators is not like learning to find food—the response is located in a different part of the brain and is motivated by a negative experience instead of a positive reward. The learning response was heightened when Robo-badger was replaced by a live dog; Siberian ferrets remembered that experience for at least two weeks (Miller, Biggins, et al. 1992).

In addition to avoiding predators, newly released black-footed ferrets must kill prairie dogs, their primary source of food. To see if captive-raised ferrets had sufficient predatory abilities, we presented some of them with live prey. (Concerns about cruelty are best addressed by explaining that black-footed ferrets are carnivores that depend totally on prairie dogs, which are formidable opponents. If ferrets are unable to kill prairie dogs after release, they will experience a slow and painful death from starvation. Predatory ability is therefore essential to success in restoring the native composition of wildlife to the prairie.)

The live prey tests revealed that cage-raised Siberian ferrets killed mice (Miller, Biggins, et al. 1992) and prairie dogs more efficiently when they had had previous predatory experience. Furthermore, black-footed ferrets raised in an enriched cage (the same size as a standard cage, but with more hiding places, etc.)

Figure 9.1. "Robo-badger" chasing a Siberian ferret into the opening of a mock prairie dog burrow. Photo by Lori Price.

killed more effectively than black-footed ferrets raised in standard cages (Vargas 1994). Black-footed ferrets also killed more efficiently when they had experience. It therefore seemed that an enriched environment and experience with live prey could help a captive-raised ferret adjust more successfully to the wild after release. (As an aside, we had hand-raised several litters of Siberian ferrets whose mothers contracted mastitis and were unable to nurse. Those animals were poor predators, even when the prey was a white lab mouse.)

Locating prey is as important a part of the predatory sequence as the ability to kill it. Captive-raised fishers had the ability to kill but still starved after release because they could not find food (Kelly 1977). Cage-raised Siberian ferrets released into an enclosed 200-square-meter mock prairie dog colony located burrows with prairie dog meat progressively faster as they matured (Miller, Biggins, et al. 1990a). They also located food in a burrow plugged with two-thirds of a meter of dirt, which simulates winter conditions when white-tailed prairie dogs are hibernating.

Although cage-raised Siberian ferrets located food in the enclosed prairie dog arena, they spent excessive time on the surface while doing so, which would expose them to predators in the wild. Furthermore, when introduced into an unfamiliar prairie dog arena, the Siberian ferrets that had previous experience with prairie dog burrows settled into burrows more quickly than the cage-raised group without prior experience (Miller, Biggins, et al. 1992). Recognizing and using burrows, instead of wandering around the prairie surface, is adaptive behavior that should help an animal survive after release.

The apparent benefits of minimal pre-release conditioning in small arenas led us to recommend that a sample of black-footed ferrets slated for reintroduction be raised from birth in large enclosed prairie dog arenas (Miller, Biggins, et al. 1990b; U.S. Fish and Wildlife Service 1990). In early 1990 the U.S. Army offered to donate several large warehouses in Pueblo, Colorado, for pre-release conditioning, but Wyoming officials began opposing the research. They proposed instead that all black-footed ferrets be raised in cages without pre-release conditioning, then moved to the release site and housed in elevated cages on the prairie for 10 days; in addition, supplemental feeding should be offered at the release cages for ferrets that chose to return after release (this proposal was later published as Wyoming Game and Fish Department 1991). At a March 1990 meeting in Laramie that various specialists attended to discuss release techniques, Wyoming officials announced that they had already decided on the above method. At this juncture, reintroduction was still a year and a half away. The moderator—Chris Wemmer, director of the Conservation and Research Center at the National Zoological Park—suggested that nothing be "written in stone" until the rest of the Siberian ferret research and the graduate project by Astrid Vargas had contributed more data. Wyoming officials later contended (e.g., at the 1990 and 1991 Black-Footed Ferret Interstate Working Group meetings) that participants at the March meeting had endorsed the release technique they proposed, but no endorsement appears in the meeting minutes, and a Region 6 memo reported that the meeting produced no consensus about methods of release (L. Shanks, U.S. Fish and Wildlife Service memo, 20 May 1991).

In response to Wyoming's reintroduction plan, we volunteered to compare cage-raised Siberian ferrets lacking pre-release conditioning to Siberian ferrets raised in an enriched environment during the fall 1990 field experiments. Because we were already testing release methods—there had been a small test release of neutered Siberian ferrets in 1989 (Biggins, Hanebury, et al. 1990)—it seemed logical to incorporate the release-cage idea into the experiment. Perhaps one technique would appear preferable, or the research would refine one of the methods or indicate benefits to blending both strategies. The 1988 U.S. Fish and Wildlife Service recovery plan called for precisely this type of comparative approach.

At a June 1990 meeting in Cheyenne, Wyoming, to discuss these ideas, Wyoming officials said comparisons were moot because all ferrets would be released without pre-release conditioning (B. Miller pers. obs.). During a break in the meeting, one official remarked to Miller, "I'm afraid the other idea [pre-release conditioning] will work better than ours [the Wyoming plan]. Then we'll be criticized for not using it." Issues of turf and control were clearly still a very important component of decision-making in the black-footed ferret program.

We performed those release experiments in fall 1990 (see Biggins, Hanebury, et al. 1991). One group of Siberian ferrets ($N = 14$) was raised in cages similar to the captive conditions of black-footed ferrets, with no previous experience of burrows or live prey, but was released onto the prairie dog colony at 4.5 months of age from elevated cages with supplemental feeding at the cage after liberation; these conditions resembled those in Wyoming's reintroduction plan.

The other group was raised in cages until the age of 3.5 months, then introduced into one of two 200-square-meter enclosed prairie dog arenas where they lived in prairie dog burrows and were exposed to live prey for one month. One prairie dog arena containing Siberian ferrets ($N = 10$) was free of predators, but Siberian ferrets in the other arena ($N = 15$) were harassed by a domestic dog several times a week to see if pre-release exposure to a potential predator would enhance survival (Figure 9.2). The dog, a Labrador retriever with a soft mouth, chased the animals and occasionally grabbed one but did no damage. Even so, the dog enjoyed the experiment far more than the Siberian ferrets did. Animals raised in both prairie dog arenas were released to the prairie dog colony at 4.5 months of age without the use of elevated cages. (Because we had a limited number of Siberian ferrets, we wanted to test techniques that were as distinct as possible.)

Because of experiments performed during their development, all the captive-raised Siberian ferrets had had extensive contact with humans and novel situations. Indeed, even the animals with pre-release conditioning spent developmentally sensitive periods in cages before entering the seminatural prairie dog colonies. These conditions may have affected juvenile development, but they could not be helped. There was much to learn and time was short (Figure 9.3).

A third group of five wild-caught Siberian ferrets was translocated from China. They too were neutered and released onto the same prairie dog colonies for purposes of comparing translocated wild-raised animals with reintroduced captive-raised animals. All the Siberian ferrets were monitored with radio-telemetry to collect information on movements and survivorship and to refine the telemetry system for the black-footed ferret releases.

Siberian ferrets with pre-release conditioning in the two prairie dog arenas exhibited movement and activity patterns similar to those of the wild translocated Siberian ferrets (Biggins, Hanebury, et al. 1991). The cage-raised Siberian ferrets without pre-release conditioning behaved differently than the wild-caught and arena-preconditioned groups. For example, most animals stayed on the prairie dog town, but those with pre-release conditioning moved more rapidly from burrow to burrow than did the cage-raised animals, which tended to loiter

Figure 9.2. A dog chasing a Siberian ferret in a 200-square-meter arena with prairie dog burrows fabricated by researchers. Photo by Courtney Conway.

on the surface (Biggins, Hanebury, et al. 1991). Moving quickly from the shelter of one prairie dog burrow to another should reduce susceptibility to surface predators. Also, the only Siberian ferrets that were verified as having killed prey in the wild had been through pre-release conditioning with prey (Biggins, Hanebury, et al. 1991). We regularly left food at burrow sites in an attempt to ease transition to the wild, but the overall value of this tactic is uncertain: the food attracted badgers, essentially substituting one risk for another.

Although there were significant differences among the four groups when we measured behaviors related to survival, there were no significant differences in survival rates. Longevity ranged from 0.2 to 21 days for cage-raised animals, from 0.4 to 33.3 days for both groups of preconditioned animals, and from 4.3 to 41.9 days for wild-caught animals (Biggins, Hanebury, et al. 1991). Given that a number of factors, including luck, affect life span after release, it is not surprising that the behavioral dissimilarities we found did not generate statistical differences in survival. Because of higher variability (statistically) when comparing survival rates, confirming significant differences probably requires a larger sample than we were able to monitor in the 1990 release.

Known causes of mortality in our experiments included coyotes (in 21 cases), badgers (8), owls (1), and starvation (3). Exposure to a live dog in one prairie dog arena increased the predator-avoidance response during captive experiments,

Figure 9.3. The release cage used for the reintroduction of black-footed ferrets into Shirley Basin, Wyoming. Photo by Rich Reading.

but did not translate into a postrelease survival advantage over the group raised in the predator-free prairie dog arena. Perhaps the antipredator response generated by exposure to the dog was not efficient enough to improve chances against a coyote (the ferret shock collar might have improved that response). It is possible that the hunting strategies of the dog did not sufficiently resemble those of coyotes. It is also possible that the enriched environment of the prairie dog arena, with or without predators, was the most important component of pre-release conditioning. Alternatively, we had the ability, through telemetry, to measure movement and activity behaviors in free-ranging animals, but predator avoidance behaviors could be measured only in captivity. Thus we can only speculate on the effects of pre-release predator experience on postrelease awareness. Larger sample sizes are necessary to statistically prove a survival difference.

Even though there were no statistically significant survival differences, our experiments revealed behavioral differences between cage-raised animals and those with pre-release conditioning. The behaviors of Siberian ferrets with only one month of pre-release experience in the prairie dog arenas more closely resembled the behaviors of wild-caught Siberian ferrets. The results of this research with Siberian ferrets were presented at the 1990 meeting of the Black-Footed Ferret Interstate Working Group. Tom Thorne, the Wyoming veterinarian, then announced that Wyoming would not recognize the pre-release conditioning research because the reintroduction method for black-footed ferrets had already been determined.

Reintroduction of Black-Footed Ferrets in 1991

The National Ecology Research Center and Larry Shanks of Region 6 continued to push for using two release methods in the 1991 black-footed ferret reintroduction. Shanks, head of enhancement for the U.S. Fish and Wildlife Service in Region 6, was a man with the courage of his convictions. They proposed providing half of the black-footed ferrets with pre-release experience in an enriched environment and releasing the other half via release cages with no pre-release experience. The proposal was favorably reviewed by outside specialists. The release was planned for fall, the normal time for family breakup among black-footed ferrets (although releasing pregnant females in the spring could also prove interesting in future attempts).

As a result of Shanks's persistence, Wyoming and Region 6 agreed that any black-footed ferrets above the 50 scheduled for the 1991 release and surplus to the captive-breeding program would go to a pre-release conditioning program at the Pueblo army base (L. Shanks, U.S. Fish and Wildlife Service memo, 20 May 1991). This seemed an acceptable compromise: if there were enough surplus ferrets, they could undergo limited pre-release experience in enclosed prairie dog colonies and be released in 1991. If there were only a few surplus ferrets, they could breed in the enclosed prairie dog colonies and their offspring could be released during a later reintroduction. But Wyoming controlled the captive population and allocated only 49 animals for the 1991 reintroduction.

The U.S. Fish and Wildlife Service recovery plan called for experimental and comparative releases during the early reintroductions. Despite the recovery plan, as well as the alternative recommendations and the reintroduction research, Wyoming raised all 49 animals in cages without pre-release experience and liberated them via on-site elevated release cages where they were supplementally fed. Thirty-seven black-footed ferrets were monitored by radiotelemetry during the period of release in September and October 1991, and there was additional monitoring by occasional spotlighting and snow-tracking (Biggins, Miller, and Hanebury 1992).

Twenty-seven of the 37 telemetered black-footed ferrets (73%) abandoned the release-cage area within 30 hours. About half of the 37 rapidly dispersed from the release area, moving 4.1–17.1 kilometers. Observation and scat analysis verified that some black-footed ferrets killed prairie dogs. Four ferrets survived the winter and two produced litters (*Drumming Post*, 1992). This was a major breakthrough. There was now proof that captive-born black-footed ferrets could reproduce in the wild (Figure 9.4). The remaining issues involved making the reintroduction process more efficient and preserving the prairie dog ecosystem.

Figure 9.4. A black-footed ferret above ground during daylight hours. Photo by Louise R. Forrest.

A poor release design prevented a scientific comparison of many variables that might have influenced survival. Even so, the significance of being from the same litter was apparent. The fate of a given animal was the same as that of its littermate in 77% of all possible comparisons, but nonsibling pairs shared the same fate only 51% of the time (Biggins, Miller, and Hanebury 1992). We could not find statistically significant correlations between survival and time of release, place of release, human disturbance, or weather.

Planning Releases after the 1991 Reintroduction

Following the 1991 reintroduction, Region 6 began looking for a way to reduce the conflict that was again afflicting the program. Larry Shanks's strong stands in favor of comparative reintroduction techniques and monitoring via radiotelemetry (in accordance with the 1988 recovery plan) had apparently angered Wyoming. In an effort to relieve tension, Region 6 decided that Larry Shanks would no longer work with ferrets in Wyoming. Instead of looking at the organizational weaknesses of the program, Region 6 was taking the easier route of blaming personalities. Shanks was assigned to work with other states on ferret issues and Steve Torbit, a former employee of Wyoming Game and Fish, would coordinate with Wyoming.

Larry Shanks continued to press for pre-release conditioning of a sample of black-footed ferrets. He hoped to use the empty warehouses in Pueblo, Colorado, during the Montana reintroduction scheduled for 1992. The captive black-footed ferret population was outproducing its space; there were excess females over three years of age—as of 1991, only captive females three years old or younger were officially counted in the SSP tally because they are the most fertile—and excess males of all ages (1991 Black-Footed Ferret Interstate Working Group meeting minutes). Additionally, one female had been rescued from starvation twice during the 1991 release, and was being held at the Pueblo army base. These excess ferrets seemed like a viable source to test enriched environments without using animals valuable to the captive population.

Wyoming declared, however, that the enriched environment (or "halfway house," as some have called it) would have to meet the disease-prevention criteria established at Sybille because such excess animals might have to be recalled into the captive population at a later date (F. Petera, Wyoming Game and Fish Department memo, 25 February 1992). Additionally, the genetics work was not complete, so the SSP did not know which ferrets were really surplus (F. Petera, Wyoming Game and Fish Department memo, 16 April 1992).

These stipulations may sound reasonable, but they embody several contradictions. During the 1987 breeding season, Wyoming had introduced every male black-footed ferret to a female Siberian ferret so the males could acquire breeding experience. At that time, there were only 18 black-footed ferrets (7 males), and each one was extremely valuable, but breeding experience was worth the risk of potentially contracting a disease from the Siberian ferrets that had just arrived from a Russian zoo. In 1992, however, when there were nearly 300 black-footed ferrets, probably representing quite a bit of genetic redundancy, the threat of disease was invoked as a roadblock to pre-release experience.

The second contradiction involved genetics. Region 6 had budgeted funds for genetic work in 1988, when there were several animals of disputed parentage. Yet, by 1992, Wyoming had still not taken the necessary blood samples (see Chapter 8). Wyoming also rejected a request for a male to breed the rescued black-footed ferret female at the Pueblo army base; artificial insemination would be acceptable, they said, if Region 6 agreed that resulting offspring would not be reintroduced anywhere (F. Petera, Wyoming Game and Fish memo, 16 April 1992). Because release to the wild was the reason to test pre-release conditioning, agreeing to that stipulation would have made no sense.

Finally, there was one more detour from testing pre-release conditioning. Montana was scheduled to reintroduce black-footed ferrets in 1992 and wanted to compare conditioned animals to cage-raised animals. Wyoming, however, through its governor, requested Montana to delay that state's 1992 black-footed ferret reintroduction until 1993 (F. Petera, Wyoming Game and Fish Department memo, 3 March 1992). Wyoming wanted to test the effects of telemetry on survival and claimed they needed 40 animals in each group (telemetered and non-telemetered) (F. Petera, Wyoming Game and Fish memo, 3 March 1992). That would require the entire stock of black-footed ferrets available for reintroduction. It was an election year, and black-footed ferrets were a political issue (because many ranchers dislike prairie dogs and endangered species), so the governor of Montana readily agreed (Reading 1993). The delay also gave Montana, in its governor's words, "time to make concrete strides toward control [poisoning] of prairie dogs to the 1988 levels as they have agreed to do." He added, "I am appreciative that we could have extra time granted by Wyoming's proposal to see results in this area" (S. Stephens, State of Montana memo, 5 March 1992).

Wyoming could have used a smaller number of animals by spreading its telemetry tests over two years, with equal samples represented in both years, but that option was rejected. Wyoming's request to study the effects of telemetry thus stopped reintroduction in another state, and diverted time and resources from finding the most efficient release techniques early.

Wyoming's telemetry study was based on the hypothesis that "Survival of ferrets released in best habitat, without telemetry and with good logistics for spotlight surveys is higher than survival in habitat that is possibly less than best, with telemetry, and possibly poorer conditions for spotlighting" (B. Oakleaf, unpublished document, Wyoming Game and Fish Department, 26 August 1992). This hypothesis is a lesson in confounding variables. For example, would any differences in survival be attributable to telemetry, to habitat quality, or to different shrub densities that made it easier for biologists to spotlight and count the ferrets at the location without telemetry? Indeed, the habitat quality where all radio-collared animals were released was 50% poorer than the habitat where all non-telemetered animals were released (according to a 1993 Wyoming Game and Fish Department unpublished report). The National Ecology Research Center suggested that samples of both groups be released in both locations, which is a sounder scientific design (D. Biggins pers. com.). But the Wyoming hypothesis stood, and it appeared to stack the deck against telemetry monitoring (telemetry monitoring was done by the National Ecology Research Center). In sum, a reintroduction in Montana was postponed, and the telemetry experiments in Wyoming produced no conclusive results.

Reintroduction of Black-Footed Ferrets, 1992–1994
Very little would have been learned about release techniques in 1992 had it not been for the doctoral research of Astrid Vargas, under the auspices of Stan Anderson in the University of Wyoming Cooperative Research Unit. Vargas was investigating the effects of different captive environments on black-footed ferrets. Although Wyoming had opposed sending black-footed ferrets to the pre-release

conditioning arenas in Colorado, they now said that the technique could be tested if it were done at the Wyoming research facility (F. Petera, Wyoming Game and Fish Department memo, 25 February 1992). Vargas incorporated the opportunity into her work, and she and Dean Biggins produced a scientific study plan that would test the enriched environment.

The 1992 reintroduction liberated 90 black-footed ferrets, 17 of which were raised in 35-square-meter outdoor arenas with access to prairie dog burrows and live prairie dogs. The other 73 were raised in the standard small cages. Of the 14 animals that survived the first month, 7 were from the pre-release-conditioned group of 17 and the other 7 were from the group of 73 raised in cages (Biggins, Godbey, and Vargas 1993; Vargas 1994). This represents a 39% rate of survival for pre-release-conditioned ferrets and a 10% rate for cage-raised ferrets, statistically a highly significant difference. The next summer four litters were sighted, but Wyoming did not trap and identify the adults that had survived the winter (1993 Black-Footed Ferret Interstate Working Group meeting minutes). We therefore do not know which group experienced long-term success.

The animals with pre-release conditioning also dispersed less frequently from the prairie dog colonies and generally made shorter movements (Biggins, Godbey, and Vargas 1993). This is particularly interesting because one would assume that ferrets raised in a large arena with access to prairie dogs would be in better physical condition than ferrets raised in small cages; they would thus have the capability to move farther (Biggins, Godbey, and Vargas 1993). Perhaps they did not do so because they were better adjusted to the environment they needed for survival (the prairie dog colony). Indeed, the Siberian ferret research also found that animals familiar with burrows used them more readily than animals raised in cages when both groups were introduced into an unfamiliar prairie dog arena (Miller, Biggins, et al. 1992). Staying on the prairie dog colony probably aids survival: dispersing black-footed ferrets are more subject to predation, often find themselves on poorer habitat, and spend more energy to get there.

Armed with these results, Region 6 argued for further pre-release conditioning and the National Ecology Research Center received 12 black-footed ferrets for the warehouses at the Pueblo Army base. The ferrets sent to Colorado were declared outside the control of the SSP, but they could be used to test the potential benefits of pre-release conditioning strategies during the Montana reintroduction.

Region 6 had scheduled a second attempt to reintroduce black-footed ferrets into Montana, this time in the fall of 1993. Meanwhile there were calls for Region 6 to assume authority of the soon-to-be-national recovery program. The "7-Point Plan" was a new Region 6 idea for changing the focus of the black-footed ferret project from Wyoming to a national scope (unpublished document, U.S. Fish and Wildlife Service, Region 6, undated). This plan called for the SSP to be jointly chaired by a representative of the zoo community and a Region 6 representative. Although there was little initial controversy over the 7-Point Plan, a February 1993 Wyoming memo asserted that Region 6 (which has oversight authority over the ferrets) and the American Association of Zoological Parks and Aquariums (the parent organization of the SSP) should worry about finding funding for black-footed ferret recovery instead of removing the Wyoming veterinarian from the SSP chair (A. Reese, Wyoming Game and Fish Department, 18 February 1993). In other words, the issue of control had risen again. Support for the 7-Point Plan quickly withered at the higher levels of Region 6, and Tom Thorne remains in the SSP chair. Region 6 still says that the 7-Point Plan is a high priority, but has not acted upon it as of October 1994.

Shortly after the episode of the 7-Point Plan, Region 6 relieved Larry Shanks of all black-footed ferret responsibilities. He had continued to push for testing pre-release conditioning and had recently worked to implement the 7-Point Plan. Even though he had coordinated ferret-related issues among all states except Wyoming, the issues he addressed still involved contact with Wyoming and conflict had persisted. Shanks's transfer occurred at the same time that Steve Torbit, who coordinated black-footed ferret work between Region 6 and Wyoming, left for other employment, creating a vacuum at the federal level just before the scheduled Montana reintroduction.

The Montana biologists had made it a primary goal to research the most efficient release technique leading to reintroductions across the entire former range of the ferret. They recognized that this path would pay higher dividends for national recovery, even if did not produce an immediate benefit to Montana. This unselfish and refreshing attitude was shared by officials of the Montana Department of Fish, Wildlife, and Parks, the Montana offices of the U.S. Fish and Wildlife Service, and the U.S. Bureau of Land Management. The black-footed ferret biologists at the National Ecology Research Center accordingly planned to move their field operations to Montana.

As the Montana reintroduction grew closer, however, friction began to develop between some Montana state employees and the federal government. As in Wyoming, different participants had different philosophies; because the program design was similar, similar conflict and control-oriented behavior surfaced in Montana. The black-footed ferret program had learned very little about organizational design from the Wyoming experience.

Then Montana was denied reintroduction for the second consecutive year. An early hint was a June memo from Region 6, stating that "The captive breeding program continues to produce ferrets ready for reintroduction. However, based on unconfirmed reports from Wyoming Game and Fish, production has not kept up with anticipated goals" (Issue Statement, Black-Footed Ferret Program, U.S.

Fish and Wildlife Service Region 6, 28 June 1993). It is disturbing when the federal agency that exercises oversight authority and pays for most of a program is limited to unconfirmed reports as a source of information.

Following an August 1993 meeting in Fort Collins, Colorado, between officials of Region 6 and Wyoming, it was announced that there would be no reintroduction in Montana because of low captive production. There were 127 surviving juvenile ferrets as of 2 August 1993, but only 69 could be allocated to reintroduction (Tom Thorne, Wyoming Game and Fish Department memo, 2 August 1993). In other words, there were only enough ferrets for Wyoming. We do not know why production dropped so drastically in 1993. Husbandry and inbreeding are both possible explanations (see Chapter 8). We hope that it was the former. If genetic chickens are coming home to roost, terrible consequences could ensue for the program.

In preparation for the 1993 Montana reintroduction, the National Ecology Research Center, the Charles M. Russell National Wildlife Refuge in Montana, the U.S. Bureau of Land Management, and the Montana Department of Fish, Wildlife, and Parks had already expended a significant amount of time and money. The expenditure of federal tax money is hard to estimate, but the National Ecology Research Center alone appears to have spent $70,000 for the monitoring and $230,000 for research into the best techniques for reintroduction (D. Biggins pers. com.). That research would be delayed at least another year. At least one of the federal entities learned about the cancellation via press releases several days after the actual decision.

Again there was only one reintroduction site. But this time Wyoming and Region 6 agreed that the federal biologists from the National Ecology Research Center, who had planned to monitor the reintroduction in Montana, would not transfer their efforts to the Wyoming release (even though the 1988 recovery plan stated the need to monitor early reintroduction attempts intensively). As a result, little new information was collected during the 1993 reintroduction. After the 1993 reintroduction, Wyoming estimated that 24 ferrets were alive in the wild: 4 from the 1993 release, 9 born in the wild in 1993, 2 from the 1992 release, and 9 that were not captured (1993 Black-Footed Ferret Interstate Working Group meeting minutes). Wyoming's November 1993 census was the last data collected until the summer of 1994.

In summer 1994, only five individuals were sighted from previous years' releases. Because no one trapped and identified them, it is not known whether they were reintroduced animals or members of the four wild litters born the previous year. No one carefully monitored the 1993 release, and no one could explain why the wild population had declined so drastically. After release of about 190 black-footed ferrets into Wyoming, only 5 remained in the wild and the program managers were only guessing at the reasons.

In 1994, black-footed ferrets were reintroduced into Wyoming, South Dakota, and Montana. Only time will tell if these new sites will be successful, and if the U.S. Fish and Wildlife Service will effectively coordinate a national program. Alvarez (1993), who worked on the Florida panther *(Felis concolor coryi)* program, remarked that, even though the U.S. Fish and Wildlife Service is the agency designated to take the lead in the recovery of endangered species, it is "a political weakling easily elbowed to the side." At least prior to 1994, it seemed that the black-footed ferret program had walked the same path.

SOME BIOLOGICAL RECOMMENDATIONS FOR REINTRODUCTION

Determine Reintroduction Criteria

Kleiman, Stanley Price, and Beck (1993) have proposed reintroduction criteria grouped into four basic categories. First they considered the condition of the species, posing questions such as: Is there a need to augment the wild population? Is there available stock that is surplus to the genetic and demographic needs of the captive population? And will reintroduction pose any threat to the existing wild population?

The second category addresses environmental conditions. For example, are the causes of decline still present? Is there sufficient protected habitat? And are populations below saturation in the habitat?

The third category involves biopolitical conditions. Will there be any negative impact on people near the reintroduction site? Is there community support? Are all relevant governmental and nongovernmental organizations involved, with a clearly defined structure for decision-making? And does the reintroduction comply with laws and regulations?

The fourth category pertains to biological resources. For example, does the program include research and development to devise tactics for reintroduction? Is there sufficient knowledge of biology to evaluate the success of the reintroduction? And are there sufficient resources to conduct reintroduction, monitor results, and perform a cost-benefit analysis of the techniques?

Here, drawing on Chapters 8 and 9, we will offer some recommendations for biological techniques in the reintroduction of black-footed ferrets (see also Miller, Biggins, et al. 1993). Later we will propose an organizational structure for endangered-species management (Chapter 14) and discuss how well the overall program has performed (Chapter 15). The biological recommendations below are therefore narrower than the measure of Kleiman, Stanley Price, and Beck (1993) or the gauge of program success discussed in Chapter 15.

Test the Effects of Different Captive Environments

Data indicated that pre-release conditioning in seminatural conditions provided benefits to captive-raised animals scheduled for release to the wild. By raising young ferrets in large enclosed prairie dog colonies, the captive environment may provide stimuli similar to those encountered by developing juveniles in nature. This approach seems safe when developmental processes are incompletely understood, and may provide a holistic pre-release preparation for captive-raised animals. It also provides a way to reduce human contact and habituation to people. This consideration may be particularly important for animals that are easy prey for humans, or for animals that could pose a threat to human safety.

Any captive program should analyze the effects of different captive environments on behavioral development. If data on behavioral development or behavioral traits critical to survival are unavailable from the field, they should be collected from a sample of wild-caught individuals as soon as the animals enter captivity. Comparison of trait expression among captive generations can provide valuable information about the long-term effects of captive environments on behavior. Data may also be gathered on the possibilities of restoring eroded behaviors, perhaps by testing a sample of reintroduced animals after a period of time in the wild.

In addition, the different captive-rearing methods should ultimately be compared via field releases. It is one thing to demonstrate significant differences during experiments in captivity, but another to demonstrate that those differences will translate into increased survival after release into the wild. Advantages demonstrated in captivity may not translate into survival differences because the behavior must interact with other behaviors for success in the wild (e.g., fishers that could kill but not hunt, or an animal that can hunt but cannot avoid predators while doing so).

Test More Than One Release Strategy

The black-footed ferret recovery plan (U.S. Fish and Wildlife Service 1988) suggested that the first three releases experimentally test variables that could affect success. The results of those early tests could then be incorporated into an operational technique for later large-scale releases. Comparing reasonable but widely divergent release strategies would assure that the fastest road to recovery would not be overlooked. The most promising strategy could be refined further with comparative tests. Furthermore, pursuing more than one technique when little information is available would increase the chances that at least one would be successful. Developing and testing the most efficient reintroduction technique early would ultimately save money, time, and animals and speed the process of recovery.

By contrast, lack of comparison can be very costly if the sole technique considered fails. The financial expense is obvious, but extra time in captivity can also increase behavioral and genetic erosion. In general, the faster a captive species can be returned to the wild, the easier reintroduction will be. Similarly, lack of comparison can lead to uniform adoption of a partially successful technique when there actually may be a more efficient and effective method. In the face of known (but modest) success, fear of failure may prevent some people from looking for a better technique. The program can still make progress toward recovery, but at a less efficient rate.

In these times of shrinking budgets and escalating conservation problems, efficiency must be a prime consideration. There may also be situations in which a given technique produces a slight benefit to individual animals, but the financial costs outweigh any advantages to the population. Comparing a given strategy one year to a different strategy the following year, without considering interyear variability, is an inferior scientific design.

Monitor Animals Effectively
Early reintroductions should be intensively monitored to determine causes of mortality, movements of released animals, and life-history attributes that could guide future releases. Accurate records should be kept on the fates of reintroduced animals and their offspring. Failing to collect adequate data makes it difficult, if not impossible, to evaluate the various procedures used and improve the efficiency of the program. Because reintroduced populations are destined to be small and vulnerable for a time, constant vigilance is necessary to prevent their extirpation.

Encourage and Stimulate Communication with Outside Expertise
Data should be made accessible in the peer-reviewed scientific literature. Accessibility of information generates the creative input necessary for solving the complex problems of reintroduction. We also recommend that all management plans, research protocols, and results be sent out for independent external review by qualified experts.

Evaluating the Methods
The primary goal of reintroduction is to establish a wild population, which may preclude the rigorous scientific schedules applied to laboratory animals. This does not mean, however, that the principles of science can be ignored when de-

signing captive programs or reintroduction techniques. A well-designed and well-monitored program increases efficiency and allows biologists to determine why a given process did or did not work. The latter is essential if techniques are to be improved (either increasing efficiency or "fixing" unanticipated problems), and if the program is to provide useful insights to other programs.

There are various measures for defining success of biological techniques for reintroduction, and the definition should be carefully chosen. Financial expense is a favorite of accountants, but it is much easier to count costs than benefits. A cheaper technique that establishes significantly fewer animals may not be thrifty over time. It is difficult to assess financial costs until survival rates are established.

Ultimately, the number of animals surviving to reproduce is the best comparative measure of techniques. But mortality is usually elevated in early reintroduction attempts, and survival comparisons are subject to high variability, making large sample sizes necessary. Postrelease evaluation of behavioral traits may therefore provide important information about release strategies that can be applied to increase survival in future attempts. Selection of behavioral attributes to be analyzed is primarily determined by two considerations: what attributes can be reliably recorded in free-ranging animals, and what traits seem most important to the animal's overall success (Biggins, Miller, and Hanebury 1992). We recommend using as many survivorship and behavioral indexes as possible. To evaluate the first black-footed ferret reintroduction, we analyzed causes of mortality, daily survival rate, fidelity to release site, litter effects, diet, and movements (Biggins, Miller, and Hanebury 1992).

Gaining knowledge for purposes of designing an optimum release technique may be the most important technical goal during initial releases. High mortality is not a failure unless biologists fail to learn enough to increase survival in future reintroductions. The comparative process associated with a rigorous and well-designed release offers the best opportunity to improve reintroduction and proceed rapidly toward recovery.

10

IDENTIFYING AND EVALUATING BLACK-FOOTED FERRET HABITAT

IDENTIFYING HABITAT FOR REINTRODUCTION

When it became clear in 1988 that the captive population would soon reach 200 breeding adults, previously established as the minimum necessary to begin reintroduction of surplus ferrets into their natural habitat (Wyoming Game and Fish Department 1987; U.S. Fish and Wildlife Service 1988), Region 6 formed the Black-Footed Ferret Interstate Working Group to coordinate states' efforts and help identify potential reintroduction sites. Ron Crete of Region 6 took on the herculean task of coaxing the various participating agencies to move in the same direction. The first reintroduction was slated to take place in Wyoming, a political decision that acknowledged the state as the original source of the captive ferrets. It was agreed that all other potential sites would be ranked by biological merit, using a comparative model devised by Biggins, Miller, et al. (1993).

Reintroduction requires finding and protecting healthy habitats, which for many endangered species is not an easy task. We are currently witnessing a worldwide decline of biotic diversity unmatched since the Cretaceous period, and the rate of biological depreciation is accelerating (Myers 1979; Wilson 1988). Destruction of habitat is one of the major reasons for this loss, and reintroduction attempts must carefully assess the remaining fragments of habitat. Biological evaluation should consider the animal's requirements, the presence and density of predators and competitors, the presence or absence of threatening diseases, spatial characteristics, and management considerations, among other assorted variables. Habitat evaluation must be standardized, and potential sites should be quantitatively assessed and compared before reintroduction is attempted.

Not surprisingly, Griffith et al. (1989) found that the success of reintroduction

137

and translocation increases with increasing habitat quality. In some projects, reintroduction has been a component of a broader program to restore habitat (Holloway and Junigus 1973; J. L. Anderson 1986; Kleiman 1989; Stanley Price 1989; David 1990). Interestingly Griffith and his colleagues found that such programs were no more successful than those that did not improve habitat. It is possible, of course, that in the latter programs the habitat was already of sufficient quality, and enhancement was not necessary.

The decisiveness of several general habitat features is obvious. Is the original cause of the species' decline still present? If so, reintroduction or translocation may be a waste of time and money. Some variables (such as food, water, refugia, nesting or denning sites, and presence of endemic diseases) may be relatively easy to assess. Others, such as the degree of conflict with potential predators, are more difficult to analyze but very important. If natural predators are present at high densities, or if exotic predators are present, short-term predator-control programs may be warranted until the reintroduced animals adjust to their new environment (Kleiman 1989). Studies of captive-raised Siberian ferrets released to the wild indicated that survival was greater when predator numbers were lower (Biggins, Hanebury, et al. 1991). Such habitat variables as ecosystem resilience and stability are less intuitively important, but worthy of attention in systems characterized by frequent natural disturbances such as fires, volcanoes, and droughts (Kleiman 1989; Stanley Price 1989). The impact of reintroduction on other rare, sensitive, or endangered species must also be examined when assessing and comparing sites.

It is important to reintroduce animals into their former range. Griffith et al. (1989) found that translocations to the center of a species' former range were more likely to be successful than those occurring on the edge of or outside the former range. But the species' former range is not always suitable, especially when it is plagued by the presence of exotics (Witteman et al. 1990; J. W. Wiley et al. 1992).

ANALYZING THE MONTANA REINTRODUCTION SITE

Preliminary Evaluation of the Site

Site selection for the 1991 reintroduction was predicated on returning ferrets to their original location near Meeteetse, Wyoming. But plague, which had been active since 1984, continued to undermine the potential of the area to support ferrets. By 1989 the site had an estimated capacity of only 14 ferret families, and by summer 1990 this number had declined to fewer than 6 families. In September 1990, therefore, Wyoming substituted the backup site in Shirley Basin, which had the potential to support an estimated 142 ferret families (56 Fed. Reg. 41473–41490, 1991), as the location for the first reintroduction. The prairie dog colonies at Shirley Basin had been mapped and analyzed by the University of Wyoming Cooperative Research Unit for a potential ferret reintroduction (C. Conway 1989), and searches for other populations of ferrets had been performed sporadically in the area for nearly 10 years.

The black-tailed prairie dog complex in north-central Montana was another of the earliest sites identified and developed for reintroduction. A *prairie dog complex* is defined as a group of distinct prairie dog colonies, none more than 7 kilometers from its nearest neighbor (Biggins, Miller, et al. 1993). Seven kilometers—the longest move made in a single night by a black-footed ferret at Meeteetse—represents a wild-born ferret's ability to move between patches of habitat. Beginning in 1988, biological studies gathered data on the prairie dog ecosystem, searched for ferrets, censused potential predators, and monitored diseases in the area (Reading, Grensten, et al. 1989; Reading 1991, 1993).

Prairie Dog Colony Dynamics and Species Associations

Both the dynamics of black-tailed prairie dog colonies and the vertebrate species associated with them had been monitored and analyzed on the Montana reintroduction site between 1981 and 1988, but after the site was selected for potential ferret release the research and monitoring became more intensive. The prairie dog colonies were mapped using aerial photographs and 7.5-minute topographic maps, and colony area was determined from these maps with an electronic planimeter. This information made it possible to calculate annual expansion (or contraction) rates of prairie dog colonies. We also calculated burrow density and compiled lists of vertebrate species associated with prairie dogs. In 1988 there were some 170 prairie dog colonies, totaling 19,223 hectares, in the complex (58 Fed. Reg. 19221–19231, 1993).

Average size of the black-tailed prairie dog colonies in the reintroduction area increased between 1981 and 1988, but the rate of expansion decreased (Reading, Grensten, et al. 1989; Reading 1993). This reinforced the findings of Knowles (1982) and Garret, Franklin, and Hoogland (1982) that prairie dog populations exhibit logistic growth. Initial rates of increase were rapid, but eventually increased competition, reduced resources, less favorable habitat at the colony's edge, and physical barriers (such as steep slopes and dense vegetation) slowed growth.

The Montana prairie dog complex was compared to others across North America as a reintroduction site for black-footed ferrets. The 170 colonies averaged 103.8 ($\pm$ SE of 3.3) burrows per hectare, but density was not significantly related to colony size (Reading 1993). Because density of burrows per se is not a reliable indicator of prairie dog population size (Menkens, Miller, and Anderson 1988), density of *active* burrows (Biggins, Miller, et al. 1993) was used to estimate the potential for 561 ferret families on the Montana prairie dog complex in 1988 (58 Fed. Reg. 19221–19231, 1993). Over 14,000 hours of surveys failed to produce evidence of a single living black-footed ferret (Reading 1991).

We compiled a list of 171 vertebrate species sighted on black-tailed prairie dog colonies, and found that larger colonies contained more species of birds (Reading 1993). Because prairie dog colonies resemble islands, the application of island biogeography theory has important implications for the preservation of species. The theory posits that patches of habitat maintain larger numbers of species when their area is larger and when sources of immigration (other islands) are closer (MacArthur and Wilson 1967). In other words, complexes of prairie dog colonies that are relatively large and linked like stepping-stones for dispersing prairie dogs and associated species can support more species than small distantly spaced colonies.

Other variables of the prairie dog complex were analyzed using a Geographic Information System (GIS), a computerized mapping system that represents a powerful tool for habitat analysis and management. The variables we examined included vegetation, soils, slope, aspect, land ownership, patch size, patch shape, and intercolony distance; actual colonies were compared with randomly distributed control areas.

Prairie dog colonies at the Montana reintroduction site are more prevalent on slopes of less than 4% and on elloam soil associations, suggesting that prairie dogs actively select these conditions (Reading 1993). On relatively level areas, it is easier to detect predators. Elloam soils, consisting of well-drained sandy loam to silty clay, provide the necessary depth and structural support for burrow systems and are unlikely to flood. Land ownership of prairie dog colonies is predominantly federal, which is unsurprising given the antagonistic attitudes of private ranchers toward prairie dogs. Such information can be used to develop a cartographic model of preferred habitat, which may facilitate prairie dog management, identification of potential habitat, and assessment of areas of possible expansion.

Predator and Disease Monitoring

Predator studies were undertaken in Montana to identify potential sources of predation, the primary source of known mortality in the 1991 and 1992 Wyoming black-footed ferret reintroductions. Between 1989 and 1991 predators were assessed by means of roadside raptor counts to identify diurnal avian predators (see Craighead and Craighead 1956) and scent-station surveys to identify mammalian predators (see Conner et al. 1983). Spotlight searching along transect routes also produced an index of predator densities. In general, predator densities were lower on the Montana reintroduction site than in other parts of the ferret range (Reading 1993). A relatively low density of coyotes at the Montana site may be partially explained by the intensity of coyote-control programs in the area.

Plague and canine distemper are of supreme concern to biologists. Plague devastates the prairie dog prey base, and distemper attacks ferrets directly and fatally (E. S. Williams et al. 1988). The most effective methods of detecting both diseases are analyzing carnivore blood serum taken from coyotes and examining whole carcasses (Barnes 1993). Carnivore blood serum (derived from a 5- to 15-milliliter blood sample from the animal) can detect titers to both plague and distemper, but because many coyotes survive canine distemper a few animals should be sacrificed to examine for brain lesions. These lesions can indicate past infections of distemper even if blood titers show no immediate threat. Fresh feces, collected from the trap site or rectum of the coyote (by workers using latex gloves), can provide additional data on distemper (E. S. Williams 1990). Plague may be detected by collecting fleas from prairie dog burrows, but attempts to do so were not very successful in Montana (Knowles 1993). Montana has therefore tracked plague throughout the prairie dog complex by sampling coyotes. Successfully collecting flea samples would also identify the local flea species, which might provide important information about the movement and ecology of plague through the prairie dog complex.

Although canids, mustelids, and procyonids (raccoons) can all carry canine distemper, coyotes are probably the most important reservoir of the virus for black-footed ferrets (E. S. Williams 1990). Ten coyote carcasses from a given population should be sufficient to reveal presence of canine distemper about 97% of the time, and seropositivity can be detected from 20 blood samples about 95% of the time (E. S. Williams 1990). It is more difficult to predict the number of blood samples needed for plague detection; if plague is present at low densities, it may take as many as 250 (E. S. Williams 1990).

Wyoming has done a thorough job of disease survey at the Shirley Basin reintroduction site, with testing carried out at the Wyoming state veterinary laboratory in Laramie. In January 1983, 85 coyote carcasses were shipped from the Montana reintroduction site to the Wyoming laboratory for evaluation. Forty-six of those carcasses tested positive for plague antibodies (*Phillips County News* [Montana], 17 February 1993).

This was bad news. The Montana reintroduction site had experienced a 52% reduction in prairie dog hectares between 1988 and 1992. In other words, the site's potential had decreased from an estimated 561 ferret families to about 290 ferret families. Although most of this drop was due to plague, there was also evidence of illegal prairie dog poisoning (Reading 1993).

Because black-tailed prairie dog populations often decline by 95–98% in the presence of plague (Barnes 1993; Culley 1993; J. P. Fitzgerald 1993), the Centers for Disease Control recommended application of the pesticide permethrin to counter the spread of the disease (Barnes 1993). Plague is passed through a flea vector, and the pesticide works against the fleas. Evidence from black-tailed prairie dog colonies on the Rocky Mountain Arsenal in Colorado suggested that permethrin slows the spread of plague. During summer 1993, field workers applied the chemical to several colonies at the Montana reintroduction site. That effort significantly reduced the number of fleas (Knowles 1993), and dusted colonies showed no further declines by late 1993. Permethrin was not used by Wyoming at either Meeteetse or Shirley Basin, and plague was documented at both places. The prairie dogs near Meeteetse crashed, whereas those in Shirley Basin have remained stable.

In summary, for any release site investigators should evaluate ecological features, quantify habitat, census potential predators and competitors, analyze disease potential, map land-ownership patterns, and search for wild populations of the reintroduced species. Thorough knowledge of all these phenomena makes management of the species, and the natural system on which it depends, considerably easier. But finding a site suitable for reintroduction, though difficult, is only the first step. The second step is protecting the area from further degradation.

TAKING INTO ACCOUNT THE SIZE AND SHAPE OF PROTECTED AREAS

As we have seen, prairie dog colonies resemble islands. Although the prairie between colonies may not present a formidable barrier to dispersal for some vertebrates associated with prairie dogs, it may for others. If there are many habitat patches in proximity to each other, it is easier for immigrants to repopulate vacated patches.

Several discrete release sites could constitute metapopulations (separate subpopulations), with artificial migration or colonization forming a single large population (Gilpin 1991; Hanski 1991). Gilpin found the effective population size of metapopulations to be at least 10 times smaller than the number of individuals in the actual population (a typical N_e:N ratio is 1:3—see Chapter 8). To improve the ratio, Gilpin suggested maximizing persistence times of local populations, increasing the number of populations in existence, and augmenting gene flow between sites.

Although debate about metapopulation principles persists, most people agree that, for any given individual patch, larger is better (MacArthur and Wilson 1967;

Diamond 1975; Gilpin and Diamond 1980; Hanski 1991). More specifically, the biology, genetic history, and ecology of the animal often suggest an appropriate reserve design. For example, there is little disagreement over the metapopulation approach for black-footed ferrets, whose susceptibility to canine distemper calls for natural barriers against transmission of the disease between distinct prairie dog complexes. Species with low genetic diversity may benefit from population subdivision if patches provide different selective pressures (Gilpin 1987). Factors such as high rates of predation along habitat edges may also influence shape requirements.

Buffer zones and corridors may benefit black-footed ferrets. Large colonies connected by corridors mean that ferrets spend less time traveling through the no-man's-land of burrowless prairie when moving among the colonies of a complex (although this benefit must be balanced against disease risk, even within a complex). Buffers necessarily imply some level of protection for the prairie dogs near a protected area. Even if the prairie dog densities in the buffer zone are not equal to those of the core refugia, they can still provide restless young ferrets with peripheral areas in which to operate, heightening their probability of persistence until a better territory opens up.

It is generally accepted that a protected area should provide for interactions of ecosystems across a landscape. Buffer zones can assure that corridors wide enough to encourage the movement of species link habitats. The use of buffer zones and corridors can help conserve the biotic integrity of a region—that is, the presence of the species native to an area, as opposed to generalists that invade fragmented habitats (Ratcliffe 1986). When generalists invade, the total species count may actually increase while the number of native species declines; thus simple species richness does not measure the quality of an area (Sampson and Knopf 1982; Van Horne 1983). The maintenance of native species usually requires large areas of relatively undisturbed original vegetation, whereas many generalists seem to survive almost anywhere (Kitchener et al. 1980; Humphreys and Kitchener 1982; Noss 1983).

But there is more to habitat protection than theories of metapopulations, island biogeography, and landscape ecology. When conservationists are faced with the prospect of trying to save what little habitat remains from overexploitation, debates about size and shape are moot; you have to take what you can get. In most cases, protecting habitat has remained a contentious and politically charged issue. As a result, only 16% of listed endangered species have critical habitat designated under the Endangered Species Act (U.S. General Accounting Office 1992). The black-footed ferret, for example, has an extremely simple and well-understood dependence on prairie dogs. Yet the federal government has not designated critical habitat for ferrets, and prairie dog poisoning programs continue to receive federal financial support. In the next section, we will examine how Mexico is handling prairie dog management.

PROTECTING A PRAIRIE DOG COMPLEX IN CHIHUAHUA, MEXICO

Potential Value to Conservation

The Centro de Ecología of the Universidad Nacional Autónoma de México is initiating a high-plains protected area in northern Chihuahua, Mexico, about 70 kilometers south of the New Mexico bootheel. The project holds tremendous promise for protecting the largest remaining black-tailed prairie dog complex in North America and for reintroducing the black-footed ferret.

The Chihuahuan Desert, which sprawls across the Mexico–U.S. border extending from New Mexico and Trans-Pecos Texas south to San Luis Potosi, is critical to the maintenance of regional and hemispheric biodiversity. The area is evolutionarily unique, biotically diverse, sensitive, threatened, and one of the least-studied parts of North America (Wauer and Riskind 1977; Tanner 1985). As evidence of Chihuahua's remoteness, the endemic Bolson tortoise *(Gopherus flavomarginatus),* North America's largest land tortoise, was discovered there only 30 years ago (Morafka and McCoy 1988), and a small herd of wild bison *(Bison bison)* still roams the area.

Grasslands in and around the proposed protected area support the largest black-tailed prairie dog complex in North America, some 55,000 hectares containing as many as 1.6 million prairie dogs (Ceballos et al. 1993). One single colony of the complex measures 34,000 hectares, and approximately 60% of the land area in the complex is covered by prairie dog colonies (typically, only about 20% of the area in a complex is covered by prairie dogs).

The Chihuahuan prairie dog complex houses the full diversity of life supported by the keystone species. A keystone species is an organism that is essential to the structure and process of a community or ecosystem—in other words, a species that in some way supports other forms of life. Ecologically, the prairie dog ecosystem is an oasis of species diversity on the arid plains. In the United States, due to poisoning programs, several species dependent on the prairie dog ecosystem are either listed or proposed for listing under the Endangered Species Act, including ferruginous hawks, mountain plovers *(Charadrius montanus),* swift foxes *(Vulpes velox),* and black-footed ferrets. Burrowing owls *(Athene cunnicularia)* have also declined and are designated as species of concern in several states. Ferruginous hawks, burrowing owls, mountain plovers, and kit foxes (considered a subspecies of *V. velox* by Hall 1981) are all found on the prairie dog colonies of the Chihuahuan prairie dog complex.

The protection of Chihuahuan habitats is important to large and small mammals, to the biological diversity of the prairie dog ecosystem, to herpetological fauna, to insects, and to resident and migratory birds. Indeed, Raitt and Pimm (1977) emphasized that the northern Chihuahuan grasslands are the principal winter habitats for many North American grassland birds. As a group, endemic populations of grassland birds have declined more rapidly, more consistently, and over a wider geographic area in the last 25 years than any other group of birds (Knopf 1993). For example, three western grassland birds, the lark bunting *(Calamospiza melanocorys),* the mountain plover, and the Cassin's sparrow *(Aimophila cassinii)* have declined more than 60% since 1968 (Knopf 1993).

Approximately 500 plant species with economically valuable genetic resources also exist along the Mexico–U.S. border, and 60–75 of those plants are threatened by inappropriate land uses (Nabhan 1990). Nabhan suggests that protected areas would enhance the economic potential of these resources. He specifically mentions the Chihuahuan Desert's unique richness and encourages management practices that would enhance long-term persistence.

Threats to Biodiversity in Chihuahua

The recent population shift toward the Mexico–U.S. border has imposed sudden and heavy demands on surrounding ecosystems. Migrants from other parts of Mexico, who come to speculate on a border economy, do not understand or appreciate the arid environment (Ezcurra and Halffter 1990). Economic and technological development following this population increase has not integrated ecological considerations. Proximity to an international border, with striking income differences on the two sides, aggravates the problem. The resulting environmental degradation has depleted biodiversity and economically valuable natural resources. Desertification in Mexico is rapidly becoming a reality, with erosion and greater pressure on semiarid areas (Sonnenfeld 1992). The unique prairie and montane habitats of northern Chihuahua are declining, and biodiversity in Mexico and the United States is at risk (Dittmer 1951; J. Brown 1971; Wauer and Riskind 1977; Ezcurra and Halffter 1990). The protected area thus offers a tremendous opportunity for international action toward conservation, and the black-footed ferret represents an excellent bridge to that cooperation. The species, the supporting ecosystem, and hemispheric biodiversity would all benefit.

Potential for Black-Footed Ferret Reintroduction

Application of the model developed by Biggins, Miller, et al. (1993) indicated that the Chihuahua prairie dog complex could accommodate 1,280 adult female black-footed ferrets with families (Ceballos et al. 1993). With the inclusion of adult males and offspring, the total summer black-footed ferret population could exceed 6,000 individuals, by far the largest existing or proposed reintroduction site. Although there is yet no evidence about the history of plague, large numbers of prairie dogs have been present on this complex for at least 100 years without major population crashes. Because of its enormous size and density, the Chihuahua prairie dog complex represents the best opportunity for the long-term recovery of the black-footed ferret, and of many other species that depend on prairie dogs. As an appealing symbol of the declining prairie grasslands, the black-footed ferret will give as good as it gets by focusing international attention on the protected area.

The reintroduction could also provide employment opportunities for the local population around the proposed protected area, stimulate further research on managing complex biological interactions, enhance career development of conservation biologists in Mexico, and augment environmental education. The cooperative bonds forged by this venture could benefit the conservation of many other sensitive species presently managed in both Mexico and the United States and enhance conservation strategies that span the international political border.

The reintroduction in Mexico also presents opportunities to address many of the obstacles to recovery that have been discussed at recent Black-Footed Ferret Interstate Working Group meetings. For example, Region 6 funding to help states manage endangered species (called Section 6 funding) was recently reduced from $1 million to $442,000 (1992 Black-Footed Ferret Interstate Working Group meeting minutes).

As a result of the cuts, several Region 6 representatives to the 1992 Interstate Working Group meeting recommended that the ferret program pursue partnerships with private entities and creative funding to replace the shrinking Section 6 funds. They predicted very little Section 6 money for reintroduction after 1994 (1992 Black-Footed Ferret Interstate Working Group meeting minutes). The cuts occurred when the program was expanding to develop more reintroduction sites than the single one in Wyoming.

The site in Mexico offers an opportunity to utilize sources of international money unavailable for recovery efforts in the United States. For example, both the U.S. Agency for International Development and the Mexican government have made generous contributions to this project. The benefits of these contributions would extend north of the Mexico–U.S. border as well, in that the development of a viable wild population in northern Mexico could reduce the expenses of captive-breeding centers in the United States and Canada. With the potential production of ferret offspring in Mexico, the translocation of wild-caught juveniles from Chihuahua to other sites across the former range would be less expensive, and would probably enjoy a higher success rate, than use of captive-born stock. If successfully repopulated with ferrets, the reintroduction site in northern

Mexico could eliminate total dependence on captive breeding, and could serve as a wild ferret farm to supply other United States and Canadian reintroduction sites. Because there are no recognized subspecies of black-footed ferrets (E. Anderson et al. 1986), it is unlikely that problems would arise from moving animals across their former range. The climate in Chihuahua is typical of high-plains grasslands, with snow from December to February. Temperatures vary from −10° to +45°C. Plains vegetation in Chihuahua consists of short grasses (grama grasses, *Bouteloua* spp.; muhley grasses, *Muhlenbergia* spp.; three awns, *Aristida* spp.) and prostrate herbs, similar to that of the high-plains grasslands that extend north into Canada (Warnock 1977).

The lack of subspecies makes biological sense. The black-footed ferret hunts the same prey across its range, and prairie dog burrows offer a relatively constant environment regardless of the surface temperature (F. R. Henderson et al. 1974). The evolutionary forces that selectively shaped morphology, genetics, and behavior were therefore uniform across the animal's entire range.

The U.S. Fish and Wildlife Service (1988) recovery plan specified that 10 or more self-sustaining black-footed ferret populations are necessary for downlisting (reclassification to a less threatened status in accordance with the Endangered Species Act). In 1994 black-footed ferrets were reintroduced in Wyoming, Montana, and South Dakota. The cutback in Section 6 funding may hinder the development of new sites if the potential financial burden combines with opposition from the local agricultural community to delay or eliminate reintroductions.

The Chihuahua site could come close to producing a viable population of black-footed ferrets all by itself. It could therefore be critical to the long-term recovery requirements of the animal. The 1990 Interstate Working Group meeting recognized the importance of complex size to survival potential, and passed a resolution that all reintroduction sites should be ranked in terms of their biological potential to the ferret. Many reintroduction sites are vulnerable to poisoning or severe fluctuations in the prairie dog population. In 1992 potential reintroduction areas in Wyoming and Colorado suffered prairie dog population crashes (1992 Black-Footed Ferret Interstate Working Group meeting minutes). In 1990 a similar prairie dog crash had occurred on the proposed Utah reintroduction site (1990 Black-Footed Ferret Interstate Working Group meeting minutes). Prairie dog populations on the Montana reintroduction site have declined by 50% or more since 1988. South Dakota poisoned 185,600 hectares of black-tailed prairie dogs between 1980 and 1984 (Hanson 1988) and another 90,000 hectares in 1986 and 1987 (Tschetter 1988). The Bureau of Indian Affairs proposed poisoning on approximately 24,000 hectares of black-tailed prairie dogs on two South Dakota reservations, and several Montana reservations want to poison their prairie dogs (1992 Black-Footed Ferret Interstate Working Group meeting minutes).

The consistently high numbers of prairie dogs in northern Chihuahua for the last 100 years, the comparative rarity of poisoning in Mexico, and the proposed protected area offer some insurance against population crashes and threats of poisoning that occur in other parts of the historical range. Indeed, the local government in Chihuahua recently chose the plan for a protected area over a proposal to poison the prairie dogs. This attitude is not apparent at any other existing or potential reintroduction site.

At present, the published range of the black-footed ferret extends into the Chihuahuan Desert of southern New Mexico but not into Mexico (Hall 1981). The nearest modern museum specimen was located 70 kilometers north of the border. Nevertheless, black-footed ferrets were probably coterminous with prairie dogs. The U.S. Fish and Wildlife Service (1988) recovery plan and agreements with Wyoming, Montana, and South Dakota all characterize black-footed ferrets as probably endemic to northern Mexico (1993 U.S. Fish and Wildlife Service draft rules for South Dakota and Montana; also, 56 Fed. Reg. 41473–41490, 1991).

Fossil ferret specimens from the northern (A. H. Harris 1977) and southern (Messing 1986) portions of the Chihuahuan Desert were both found with prairie dog remains. The lack of modern museum records south of the border is probably due to lack of investigation. According to S. Anderson (1972), the first scientific collections in the state of Chihuahua occurred in 1907, when 190 specimens were analyzed; very few specimens were collected from 1911 to 1930 because of the Mexican Revolution. Only about 6,300 museum specimens had been collected from all parts of the state of Chihuahua (one-twelfth of the entire area of Mexico) as of 1970, about 4,800 of them obtained between 1930 and 1970 (S. Anderson 1972). By 1930, northern Mexico had already suffered some of the effects of fragmentation and islandlike extinction patterns (Dittmer 1951; J. Brown 1971). It is unsurprising that scanty investigations over an area this large failed to produce a modern specimen of a nocturnal, semifossorial species as secretive as a ferret.

Findley and Caire (1977) argued that describing the fauna of a region solely by referring to recorded specimens can be inaccurate; the completeness of the published record can be dictated by chance and by the relative vigor of search efforts. They proposed an alternative way to define the fauna of a region by investigating the assemblage of mammalian species co-occurring over a geographic area with the same overriding biological factors as the region in question. By statistically analyzing quadrants, they presented evidence in support of the technique. Coincidentally, their statistical sample included the Chihuahuan grassland of northern Mexico, and the mammals of the sampled areas coincided with similarly adapted fauna of the Great Plains in Kansas (Findley and Caire 1977). By applying this technique, one can conclude that black-footed ferrets probably lived with black-tailed prairie dogs on the grasslands south of the Mexico–U.S. border, just as they did throughout the rest of the Great Plains.

The Mexico reintroduction site was first proposed to the Interstate Working Group in 1989 by Gerardo Ceballos of the Centro de Ecología, Universidad Nacional Autónoma de México. Since then searches for ferrets have continued, and several graduate students are now working full-time in the region. It was proposed as a black-footed ferret site again at the 1992 and 1993 Interstate Working Group meetings, but as of mid-1994 there had been no decision about including the Chihuahua prairie dog complex in the ranking process for future black-footed ferret reintroductions. If Region 6 decides to rank the Chihuahua prairie dog complex with the other potential locations, the area will be prepared along the lines described earlier in this chapter.

11

CONSERVING THE
PRAIRIE DOG ECOSYSTEM

Man is always marveling at what he has blown apart, never at what the
universe has put together, and this is his limitation. He is at heart a fragmenting
creature.

Loren Eiseley

FRAGMENTATION OF THE PRAIRIE DOG ECOSYSTEM

The prairie dog ecosystem provides biological niches to dozens of vertebrate
species that rely on prairie dog activity, at least in part, for survival (Reading
1993). Ecologically, this ecosystem is an oasis of species diversity on the arid
grasslands. It sustains higher numbers of small mammals and arthropods, nearly
six times the number of terrestrial predators, higher numbers of avian predators,
and greater avian species diversity and density than does the surrounding prairie
(Hansen and Gold 1977; Clark, Campbell, et al. 1982; O'Meilia et al. 1982; Agnew et al. 1986; Kreuger 1986). The presence of prairie dogs favors plant diversity and promotes growth of perennial grasses and forbs grazed by livestock and
large native ungulates (hoofed animals) (Bonham and Lerwick 1976). Before the
onset of poisoning campaigns, prairie dogs extended across the Great Plains and
created an ideal habitat for hundreds of millions of bison, elk *(Cervus elaphus),*
and pronghorn antelope *(Antilocapra americana),* as well as prairie birds such as
mountain plovers and burrowing owls. Their burrows provided refugia for myr-
iad small mammals, reptiles, and amphibians, and their biomass supplied the nu-
tritional needs of innumerable carnivores and raptors. In sum, prairie dogs are
ecosystem regulators that enrich primary productivity, species densities, species

150

diversity, soil structure, and soil chemistry by their burrowing and grazing activities (Detling and Whicker 1988; Sieg 1988; Reading, Grensten, et al. 1989).

Several of the other species that rely on prairie dogs may soon join the black-footed ferret on the federal endangered-species list. The black-footed ferret is charismatic enough to serve as a flagship species, whose protection could enhance the other components of the prairie dog ecosystem by educating people about the folly of destroying the prairie. However, the black-footed ferret recovery program has not yet adequately addressed attitudes toward prairie dog eradication.

As we saw in Chapter 2, the program to exterminate prairie dogs began because ranchers wanted potential competitors with livestock eliminated. Livestock eat grass, and prairie dogs eat grass. So prairie dogs must go. The historical rationale was that simple. Since the turn of the century, prairie dog ranges have been reduced from a historical level of 40 million hectares, by conservative estimate, to about 600,000 hectares by 1960 (Marsh 1984). These figures represent at least a 98% decline in the original geographic distribution of the five species of prairie dogs (other estimates of historical prairie dog distribution go up to 100 million hectares). The few remaining prairie dog colonies are both fragmented and isolated, and thus more susceptible to extirpation by a number of factors, most prominently sylvatic plague.

A decline of this magnitude would be sufficient to qualify most species for some level of protected status, but the prairie dog suffers from a century of misinformation and bad publicity. Prairie dogs, particularly the black-tailed species, are maligned by strong western agricultural interests, and protection by the U.S. Fish and Wildlife Service would be a politically controversial act. Indeed, prairie dog colonies are not even listed as critical habitat for the endangered black-footed ferret.

Some proponents of the status quo argue that the prairie dog population is not seriously threatened because prairie dogs can still be found across their historical ranges. But to conclude that prairie dog populations are safe because remnant colonies are still scattered throughout a geographical region between Canada and Mexico masks the severity of habitat fragmentation. Fragmentation threatens species that depend on a particular habitat in three ways: demographic units are eliminated or reduced in size, and the remaining small isolated colonies are more susceptible to extinction by means of disease, genetic problems, demographic events, or natural catastrophes; sources of immigration are destroyed; and habitat alteration between colonies precludes recolonization and genetic exchange (Wilcox and Murphy 1985). As a result, the risk of extinction from habitat disruption may rise disproportionately to the extent of habitat reduction (Wilcox and Murphy 1985; Wilcove et al. 1986). In some cases, reductions in the numbers of one species can cause a wave of secondary extinctions that affects species diversity (Wilcox and Murphy 1985; Wilcove et al. 1986). This is undoubtedly true of the prairie dog.

Although prairie dogs may meet the biological criteria for legal protection under the Endangered Species Act, political antipathy runs deep. Several state governments have legally declared the prairie dog a pest and mandated its extermination on private, state, and even federal lands. The South Dakota Department of Agriculture even went so far as to "order and require" the U.S. Bureau of Reclamation to eradicate 24 hectares of prairie dogs deemed "a menace to neighboring lands" (South Dakota Department of Agriculture memo, 12 December 1992). In Montana, similarly, state regulations require that lessees of state lands poison the prairie dogs on those lands or risk losing their leases (Reading 1993).

"Pest status" has legitimately been granted to introduced exotics, but the prairie dog is an endemic species of the Great Plains. In fact, prairie dogs were a critical element in developing and maintaining the integrity of the short-grass and midgrass prairies. To label such an important keystone species a pest is unsound conservation policy with a high price tag in lost biodiversity.

PRAIRIE DOGS AND LIVESTOCK:
FINANCIAL ASPECTS OF POISONING

Prairie dog control policies remain largely unaffected by the results of scientific studies. Policy is usually strongly influenced by past policies, internal resources, and preferences of key decision makers. Thus it is not surprising that ecological findings have not brought about change in prairie dog poisoning programs. Even the theory of incompatibility between livestock and prairie dogs has not been supported by rigorously collected data.

Some livestock studies have reported no significant difference in market weight between steers that coexist with prairie dogs and those that do not (Hansen and Gold 1977; O'Meilia et al. 1982). Because grass is shorter on prairie dog towns, range managers in earlier eras concluded that there was less food for cattle. But in reality both the nutrient content and the digestibility of forage are enhanced when prairie dogs are present. Thus the reduction in standing crop is apparently compensated for by increased quality, digestibility, and productivity of grasses and forbs (O'Meilia et al. 1982; Coppock et al. 1983; Krueger 1986).

In fact, domestic cattle and bison prefer to graze on prairie dog towns because the grass is more succulent (Coppock et al. 1983; Wydeven and Dahlgren 1985; Krueger 1986; Detling and Whicker 1988). Uresk (1987) reported that early successional range conditions were best for cattle management, and that prairie dogs promoted such a situation. Indeed, later successional stages were not found on prairie dog colonies. In light of these studies, and the fact that 300 prairie dogs eat only about as much as 1 cow-calf unit (Uresk and Paulson 1989), poisoning campaigns do not seem to be worth the financial expenditure.

In fact, a cost-benefit analysis revealed that poisoning programs operate at a net financial loss (Collins et al. 1984). The poison simply costs more than any grazing benefits to cattle after prairie dogs are poisoned. Because the federal government subsidizes the costs, there is little incentive for ranchers to worry about cost-effective actions. In one area of southeastern Colorado, the poisoning costs would have exceeded the market value of the land.

The economic analysis of Collins et al. was conservative and did not consider the long-term costs of a degraded ecosystem, costs that are later transferred to society as a whole. For example, the eradication of prairie dogs may have eliminated a natural control of mesquite in the Southwest (J. A. Miller 1991). Prairie dogs eat mesquite seeds and contribute significantly to seedling mortality by stripping bark. Coincidental with recent prairie dog decline, mesquite has proliferated and now interferes with the livestock industry, preempting grass for livestock and making roundups difficult (J. A. Miller 1991). Additionally, 32% of the winter diet of prairie dogs is prickly pear cactus *(Opuntia polycantha),* a plant that cattle do not eat and that proliferates when livestock overgraze an area (Summers and Linder 1978). Furthermore, the Collins et al. (1984) economic analysis did not consider the intangible value of biological diversity as a public benefit or recognize depletion of biotic resources as a loss of potential or actual wealth (McNeely 1988).

Federally owned land is also poisoned, though by definition it is protected in the interests of the entire nation, because a handful of grazing lessees influence management policy. For example, permittees on South Dakota's Buffalo Gap National Grassland, managed by the U.S. Forest Service, make up only 2% of the state's livestock industry (Sharps 1988) yet influence poisoning policy. And less than 5% of the beef weight produced in the United States is on public land in the West (Ferguson and Ferguson 1983; U.S. General Accounting Office 1988a). Many ranchers perceive financial losses when they share rangeland with prairie dogs, and this deep-seated view is not easily countered with facts.

As a result, local livestock interests continue to pressure agencies to poison these federally owned lands. There is a total of 357,059 hectares on Buffalo Gap National Grassland in South Dakota and Nebraska, and it is prime prairie dog habitat. As recently as 1980, 17,520 hectares of prairie dogs had persisted through earlier poisoning campaigns. In 1988, the U.S. Forest Service proposed restricting prairie dogs to only 1,248 hectares; alternative proposals ranged up to 3,520 hectares (unpublished U.S. Forest Service biological assessment, 17 August 1988). Similar examples of prairie dog poisoning occur on other national grasslands, on public lands managed by the U.S. Bureau of Land Management, and even in a few national parks.

The sway of local agricultural interests is well illustrated by a memo from the state government of South Dakota about black-footed ferret reintroduction, which would require a certain population of prairie dogs:

You are hereby advised that the Governor is totally opposed to the reintroduction of black-footed ferrets into South Dakota. Direct your staff to cease their work on evaluating black-footed ferret recovery potential and its effect in South Dakota. The reintroduction of black-footed ferrets meets with adamant opposition from the agricultural community and has no economic benefit to the state. (State of South Dakota, 8 November 1988)

The historical composition of prairie communities has all but disappeared because of this intolerance. Poisoning afflicts the wildlife community both by eliminating a critical link in the food chain and by inadvertently poisoning nontarget species. Specialized predators are the most vulnerable, and the black-footed ferret was a major casualty of the campaign against prairie dogs.

THE RESULT: AN ENDANGERED SPECIES

Black-footed ferrets evolved to utilize prairie dog colonies with extraordinary economy, but the cost of this specialization is vulnerability to habitat disruption. Eradication of habitat via prairie dog poisoning campaigns (a deterministic event) eliminated some black-footed ferret populations entirely and reduced overall numbers; the remaining habitat was fragmented. Thus black-footed ferrets lived in small isolated populations, which have a higher probability of extinction caused by diseases, disaster, demographic variance, and genetic problems (stochastic events): the smaller the population, the higher the probability of collapse. Black-footed ferrets at Meeteetse each used about 50 hectares of white-tailed prairie dogs (Forrest, Clark, et al. 1985a). Under those circumstances, a 1,000-hectare prairie dog colony could hold several thousand prairie dogs, but would only support about 20 ferrets. Thus it is easy to see how the forces of small-population biology can eliminate a ferret population even though the prairie dog colony survives.

When a given black-footed ferret population winked out, fragmented habitat made recolonization difficult, a difficulty compounded with each lost colony. These losses in turn reduced gene flow and genetic diversity via genetic drift. The small litter size of black-footed ferrets, particularly when compared to the conspecific Siberian ferret, may be a result of inbreeding in isolated populations (an ecological explanation was also discussed in Chapter 6). In short, the black-footed ferret followed a general pattern of extinction set off by a deterministic event (poisoning) and knocked out by stochastic events.

The black-footed ferret recovery plan requires protection of at least 75,000–100,000 hectares of prairie dog complexes strategically placed within the former range to minimize vulnerability to catastrophe (U.S. Fish and Wildlife Service 1988). Because ferrets can be compatible with livestock grazing, that amount of land—a mere 0.1% of the total western rangeland—can easily be sheltered from poisoning without financial loss to ranchers (Turnell 1985; U.S. Fish and Wildlife Service 1988). Indeed, 0.1% is very modest considering that prairie dogs historically covered about 20% of the natural short-grass and midgrass prairies (Summers and Linder 1978). But poisoning policy has developed a great deal of momentum, and the philosophy has been ingrained by a century of misinformation. Livestock producers cling to traditional beliefs, and agency decision makers remain unconvinced by ecological evidence—or unwilling to face the wrath of the agricultural community. Significant policy changes are therefore unlikely to occur without greater receptivity to scientific information on the part of decision makers and a change in the attitude of the ranching community. As long as the federal government continues to subsidize poisoning, there is little incentive for either change to occur.

AN INTEGRATED SOLUTION

Legal Intervention via the Endangered Species Act

Protecting individual species has been an important step in slowing the decline of many species toward extinction (Bean 1992). During the early years of environmental action, a number of species were already in desperate straits, and action was necessary to prevent further loss. However, conservation is much more complex than biologically analyzing the status of each species separately and then applying legal protection to those that have reached a state of crisis. Acting only when crisis is full-blown narrows opportunities for success, increases financial costs, and escalates conflict between conservation and local interests (Wemmer and Derrickson 1987). Handling species individually is also slow and laborious. In the United States about 650 species are listed as threatened and endangered, and another 600 candidate species await possible inclusion (U.S. General Accounting Office 1992). Yet the U.S. Fish and Wildlife Service has added an average of only 44 species a year to the endangered-species list, so it could take years to address these candidates (U.S. General Accounting Office 1992).[1] Between

3,000 and 5,000 other species in the United States may be threatened with extinction, based on available data, but are not yet included as candidates (U.S. General Accounting Office 1992). In the 1980s, 34 species went extinct while awaiting federal listing (Cohn 1993). Only 16 species placed on the endangered-species list have been officially removed (delisted): 4 because the original data were in error, 5 that recovered, and 7 that went extinct (U.S. General Accounting Office 1992).

As a result of such statistics, legal experts and biologists have begun advocating a shift of focus from managing individual species toward managing entire ecosystems (E. M. Smith 1984; J. M. Scott, Csuti, et al. 1987; Rohlf 1991). Ecosystem management would address plants and animals in groups, and could potentially speed the process of protection considerably. But agreement is lacking about what ecosystem management entails. The concept is widely cited as a panacea, and the U.S. Department of Interior has invoked a need to manage systems instead of species. But what is to be managed, how, and by whom are seldom defined. The concept is therefore palatable to all political persuasions. It can be cited to generate research support for conservation biologists, but also to gut the protection provided by the Endangered Species Act before an alternative exists to replace it. And there is another reason to move carefully toward ecosystem management: given our poor record with single species, why should we assume that working at a more complex level will be easier or more successful?

But the prairie dog, as a keystone species, provides an excellent opportunity to forge a gradual transition from traditional single-species management to management of a system. It is preferable, of course, to manage species proactively, before legal intervention is necessary, but prairie dogs have already declined too severely to avoid some kind of legal recognition, particularly with poisoning programs still active. The Endangered Species Act can play an enormous role in the preservation of biodiversity by offering protection to a keystone species and therefore to all species dependent on it (Rohlf 1991).

Protecting a threatened keystone species would have fiscal and educational benefits as well. Protection of keystone species gives managers an avenue to educate the public about the value of ecosystem conservation and the links between animals and their habitat. The transition from species to system would be straightforward because the keystone species helps maintain the system. Fiscally, the federal government would be spared the burden of maintaining an expensive support system for other species that would become imperiled as the keystone species continued to decline. No matter how polemical the situation, protecting a keystone species is far more cost-effective than trying to protect each individual species dependent upon it. This is particularly true for the prairie dog. Each year, the federal government and several state governments subsidize both prairie dog poisoning and preservation of species that depend on the prairie dog. In 1991 the federal government spent more than $1.5 million on recovery of the black-footed ferret (U.S. Fish and Wildlife Service 1992); the same year, it probably spent several million dollars poisoning prairie dogs. As a direct result of poisoning expenditures, ferret-recovery expenses will continue to rise and more species will need to be placed on the federal dole. By the time this book reaches print, for example, it is likely that the mountain plover—a bird that selectively nests on prairie dog colonies throughout much of its range—will have been added to the threatened- or endangered-species list.

In 1994 Region 6 rejected an internal proposal to list the black-tailed prairie dog as a candidate species. Candidate status would have focused attention and money on the problem, and because of the prairie dog's reproductive potential, it could have reversed the downward trend without the restrictions of full endangered status. Assigning candidate status to the prairie dog would have been an excellent step toward the systems management that the Department of Interior says it favors. It appears, however, that Region 6 has chosen instead to list individual species that depend on prairie dogs and not to list the root cause of lost diversity.

Habitat Protection and Conservation Issues

Conservation of most species depends on more than legal protection. Many species are protected by law, but enforcement in the field can be difficult, and legal maneuvers can both circumvent the intentions of endangered-species legislation and create unproductive conflict.

Initiating sustainably usable protected areas on the grasslands of Canada, the United States, and Mexico (see Chapter 10) would allow for integration of conservation and economic potential, and a system of incentives or rebates could assure ecologically sound use. Federally owned lands in the United States offer excellent opportunities to use this strategy, although in many cases federal lessees wield tremendous power over government agencies and use the lands at a level above their ecologically sound carrying capacity.

Overgrazing—forage consumption that exceeds the regenerative capacity of natural vegetation—is a serious and continuing threat to the health of many federal lands (Vale 1975; U.S. General Accounting Office 1988a). According to F. R. Henderson (1980), "Over-abundance of prairie dogs, in many cases, is a sign of poor range management. We perpetuate poor rangeland management by advocating killing prairie dogs only." Total production is higher on pastures supporting only prairie dogs (and even on those supporting both prairie dogs and cattle) than on pastures supporting only cattle; thus cattle reduce total production more than prairie dogs do (Uresk and Bjugstad 1983). Furthermore, the presence of prairie dogs may just amplify problems caused by excessive livestock densities; poisoning prairie dogs when livestock are the major offenders will only increase the economic and ecological burden on the land. Yet grazing-reform proposals are routinely defeated by powerful western Congressmen representing the livestock industry (or timber and mining). This is despite the fact that the West is heterogenous and there are many other groups with a direct stake in the wise stewardship of federal lands.

Local socioeconomic issues and conservation of natural resources cannot be separated. Large corporations may have the capacity to exploit an area for a quick profit and then move to another region after its resource wealth has been drained. The average working family, however, is considerably more limited in its options. When the trees have all been cut, the ground is barren, or the environment is otherwise degraded, the local human population eventually suffers. Local residents are left with fewer economic opportunities and the environmental costs that exploiters have left behind. A watershed fouled by deforestation, food productivity lost because of eroded soil fertility, desertification, pollution, and decline of clean water supplies are examples of economic costs to society directly related to a degraded environment (Lovejoy 1986). In short, areas that fail to maintain environmental quality are also least successful at providing a decent standard of living (Mishra et al. 1987; Durning 1989; Homer-Dixon et al. 1993).

The majority of the human population depends on basic resources for immediate survival, and if those resources are not managed well, people's fundamental needs cannot be met (Frazier 1990). Environmental protection does not necessarily mean conflict, and human land uses can be part of ecosystem management if development uses the potential as it exists rather than imposing exotic agricultural uses (Cloudsley-Thompson 1988). With an integrated plan, the economic needs of the local population and preservation of biodiversity can be balanced.

Western (1989) asserts that wildlife has a better chance of survival when linked with humanity than when isolated from it, and various biomes of our planet provide value to both humans and wildlife. For example, La Tigre National Park in the cloud forest of Honduras produces high-quality water throughout the year, accounting for 40% of the water supply in the capital city of Tegucigalpa (McNeely 1988). McNeely's *Economics and Biological Diversity* (1988) presents a compelling argument that the fundamental constraint on conservation is the ability to exploit short-term profits without paying the full social and economic costs. These costs are usually undervalued or ignored in the present, then transferred to society as a whole when payment comes due. Accurate assessment of future costs, combined with present-day economic incentives to use resources wisely, is necessary to change attitudes and move from overexploitation to sustainable use.

We offer a philosophical caveat about the term *sustainable development*. Like *ecosystem management,* this term is frequently undefined, and as a result is used by many people in many different ways (often in self-interest). Genuine sustainable development is not a mechanism to further concentrate or maintain wealth and power in the hands of a few. Poverty and environmental problems feed on each other in a vortex of despair, and overconsumption in one region combined with poverty in another will prevent us from living within the carrying capacity of the planet. The ramifications of unequal distribution of wealth, exploding birth rates, and limited resources could be catastrophic, and they should not be glossed over by a buzzword.

In conclusion, because people are part of the ecosystem, separating ecological concerns from socioeconomic ones simply does not work very well. Many people depend heavily on local natural resources for sustenance, and setting aside a large chunk of land for the exclusive use of vacationers (or scientific researchers) can create bitter feelings. In many cases, positive economic incentives can balance the slate.

An Economic Incentive to Conserve Prairie Dogs

Establishing protected areas, reserves, and conservation areas will do a great deal to benefit the prairie dog ecosystem. But constraints on the size of protected areas, combined with habitat fragmentation, will limit the safety net for large or specialized species. The federal government needs to find a way to restore biological integrity on private lands as well, without adversely affecting the dominant consumptive uses of the range.

The Endangered Species Act addresses the need for incentives:

Encouraging the states and other interested parties, through Federal financial assistance and a system of incentives, to develop and maintain conservation programs which meet national and international standards is a key to meeting the Nation's international commitments and to better safeguarding, for the benefit of all citizens, the Nation's heritage in fish, wildlife, and plants. (Endangered Species Act, Section 2[a][5])

Instead of spending money to poison prairie dogs, the federal government could offer financial compensation to ranchers whose land-management practices are compatible with the prairie dog ecosystem (Miller, Wemmer, et al. 1990). Tax breaks, product-marketing help, and free publicity might also be appropriate incentives for ranchers who manage their lands both for livestock and for black-footed ferrets and prairie dogs (e.g., "This beef produced on a privately owned and managed black-footed ferret reserve"). Because attitudes are entrenched in the western agricultural community on the issue of prairie dog management, it may take such positive incentives for any public-education program to work. In

Montana, Reading (1993) showed that increased knowledge alone did not change negative perceptions of black-footed ferrets and prairie dogs (see Chapter 12). Similar results were obtained from other wildlife studies (Arthur et al. 1977; Kellert 1990).

Because of these entrenched attitudes, it will not be possible for education programs to address misconceptions about the prairie dog ecosystem while federal and state agencies continue to subsidize prairie dog poisoning. Words may say one thing, but actions quickly override them. To continue the poisoning subsidy will reinforce misconceptions and undermine all other efforts to conserve biological diversity on the western grasslands.

A positive incentive can be accomplished by reallocating money and personnel now used for prairie dog poisoning to monitoring activities for prairie dog conservation (establishing the policy of paying the incentive, allocating the money, etc.). Because such an incentive is outside the traditional prairie dog management paradigm, it would require a comprehensive education program (see Dietz and Nagagata 1986) and an economic model demonstrating the financial feasibility of environmentally sound livestock practices. For long-term effectiveness, this plan would probably require legislative action as well.

Public land should simply not be poisoned. The environmental and fiscal costs of prairie dog poisoning are too great, and the percentage of U.S. beef weight produced on western public land is too small. On leased public land, ranchers are charged a federal grazing fee based on the amount of forage they use. Forage is measured in *animal unit months* (AUMs), and one AUM sustains a cow-calf unit, a horse, or five sheep for one month (U.S. General Accounting Office 1988a). Lessees using public land could receive compensation for the policy change in the form of grazing-fee credits (free AUMs). There is also a move afoot to increase grazing fees on public lands. But simply raising grazing fees without addressing the factors that are degrading the prairie benefits no one. A portion of that increase could be rebated to ranchers who graze their cattle on land that includes prairie dogs.

Conservation incentives, whether on private or public land, will work only when stocking rates are within the carrying capacity of the land. A balance between grazing impact and forage capacity is an elusive but essential goal, and even today livestock overgrazing persists on public lands (Vale 1975; U.S. General Accounting Office 1988a). Carrying capacity depends on the quality of forage as well as its quantity, so livestock numbers are related to that tradeoff. In proper balance, cattle and prairie dogs can coexist (Krueger 1988).

One part of a Region 6 strategy to make ferret reintroduction more palatable to ranchers is "prairie dog block clearance," whereby ferret reintroduction sites are not poisoned but poisoning is made easier elsewhere (U.S. Fish and Wildlife Service 1990). Region 6 is considering changing the term "block clearance" to the more innocuous "ferret-free areas." Whatever the strategy is called, it still means poisoning, and it has five serious problems. First, block clearance does not address antiquated but prevailing misconceptions about the prairie dog ecosystem. By sanctioning the use of poison, Region 6 is reinforcing the view that prairie dogs have little value in the prairie ecosystem.

Second, even if block clearance is only part of an overall Region 6 strategy, it will probably remain the central tool simply because poisoning is familiar. It always seems easier to walk a known path, but the urgency of the prairie dog situation indicates that we should be examining other ideas. We cannot find adequate solutions by confining our thought within the paradigm that caused the problem.

Third, block clearance potentially rewards regions that have pursued vigilant poisoning campaigns. If formerly excellent prairie dog habitat was poisoned, leaving just a few small colonies, that area could be a candidate for block clearance to obliterate the remaining fragments of the prairie dog community.

Fourth, poisoning is not cost-effective. The federal budget is already overburdened and growing, and scientific evidence does not support the idea that prairie dogs are range pests.

Fifth, block clearance is a political maneuver subject to the pressures of local political whims. To quote Lynn Greenwalt (1988), former director of the U.S. Fish and Wildlife Service:

In spite of its strength, the [Endangered Species] Act is vulnerable; its armor is not seamless. The Act is vulnerable to political intervention and to decisions based on political expediency rather than what is best for the species. It is not easy to resist the pressure to make special arrangements which provide for the advance of projects or programs or political proposals.

An example is a memo from the South Dakota Department of Agriculture (R. Scheide, 17 December 1992) about the risk of poisoning an area inhabited by ferrets in the course of block clearance:

In reference to your letter, I must reiterate that it is our position that surveys are not required for use of zinc phosphide as the label states "Do not apply in areas known to be inhabited by black-footed ferrets." There are presently no such areas in South Dakota. If you have any questions, please contact me.

Simple as that—no muss, no fuss.

During negotiations with local ranchers about prairie dog block clearance, there will be heavy pressure from livestock interests to limit colony size at the black-footed ferret reintroduction site. It is easy to envision a scenario in which well-intentioned biologists must settle for less than they believe adequate because of such political pressure. Ferguson and Ferguson (1983), Montgomery (1990), and Boyle (1993) have discussed the unfortunate fate of several federal biologists who raised environmental concerns in the face of exploitative forces.

During negotiations about prairie dogs and ferrets, one of the first questions posed is always "What is the minimum necessary?" If a minimum area or population size is offered, it tends to become the absolute best that can then be achieved. Minimum population sizes are purely speculative even with the best of intentions, and their management would be unlikely to provide for long-term stability in the carrying capacity of the environment. The resulting minimum area would be eligible for black-footed ferret reintroduction, but it would probably be a small population vulnerable to random events and lacking opportunity to expand. In this situation, maintenance of a wild population would require intensive management. R. B. Harris et al. (1989) have estimated that population sizes below 120 will periodically go extinct within 100 years (the smaller the population, the more likely it will be lost). Thus the ferret colony would probably require periodic restocking from captive or other wild populations. Some ferrets would be out of captivity, but the federal government would be bankrolling a long-term and expensive project. And, while the federal government continues to pay for prairie dog poisoning, the U.S. Fish and Wildlife Service will eventually need to add other species to the list of endangered and threatened organisms.

Black-footed ferret recovery must be based on conservation of the ecosystem on which it depends. The black-footed ferret has the charisma necessary to be a flagship species, shedding light on the decline of the prairie dog ecosystem. But if we fail to recognize the endangered black-footed ferret as a symptom of an imperiled ecosystem, the drain on species diversity and the federal budget will only increase. Continuing to destroy the prairie dog ecosystem, and the diversity that it supports, while reintroducing black-footed ferrets into a few isolated sites is nothing more than an expensive and cosmetic attempt to cover our inability to preserve prairie biodiversity. Yet this is what is happening. The integrated management program that we have discussed in this chapter is an alternative to the conflicting directives of poisoning policy and endangered-species management (Miller, Wemmer, et al. 1990; Miller, Ceballos, and Reading 1994). An ecologically and fiscally sensible program that educates the public, restores the integrity of the western grasslands, and rewards environmentally sensitive members of the livestock industry would be far more responsible than continued mass poisoning.

12

PUBLIC ATTITUDES ABOUT BLACK-FOOTED FERRETS AND PRAIRIE DOGS

They're not concerned about the small picture; they're concerned with the overall picture.

Wyoming Farm Bureau executive, denouncing conservationists' efforts on behalf of grizzly bears, September 1993

On a sunny day in north-central Montana, a muddy and well-used pickup truck tops a small butte. The two biologists inside scan the expanse of short-grass prairie, which extends to the horizon. Almost without noticing what they are doing, they abruptly stop talking and switch off the truck's radio. Something is amiss. Although prairie dog mounds dot the landscape, the only visible animals are a few sheep, the only sound an occasional bleat muffled by a stiff, dry wind.

Domestic oats growing from the mouths of the burrows betray the reason for the prairie's emptiness. The prairie dog colony was poisoned, thoroughly and illegally. Not a single prairie dog remains alive. The colony is on public land administered by the U.S. Bureau of Land Management, and it is part of a large complex slated for a future black-footed ferret reintroduction. But many ranchers do not like prairie dogs, and they do not like black-footed ferrets because they believe the Endangered Species Act gives animals and plants priority over people.

Favorable public attitudes are obviously crucial to successful conservation efforts. By assessing public views and knowledge of wildlife, conservationists can design effective education programs and public-relations campaigns. But it is not just the attitudes of the general public that matter; so do the attitudes of recovery-program participants. Because the decisions and actions of key players are influ-

163

enced by different goals, philosophies, and constituencies, it pays to understand their perceptions as well.

Public attitudes toward wildlife are influenced by a number of factors, including knowledge of the species, the physical characteristics of the animal, human–animal relationships, and the species' economic or cultural value. When reintroducing an endangered species, we can add attitudes toward the Endangered Species Act to the list.

Some disastrous consequences have resulted from failure to investigate public beliefs and attitudes before reintroduction of a wildlife species. Developing local support was the most commonly stressed nonbiological factor influencing success (program analysis in Reading 1993). Yet few programs evaluate existing attitudes before launching their public-relations efforts. Notable exceptions—and splendid examples of solid education programs—are the golden lion tamarin project in Brazil and parrot conservation programs in the eastern Caribbean (Dietz and Nagagata 1986; Butler 1992). Knowledge and attitude surveys preceding education and public-relations efforts equipped these programs to design different support-building strategies for different sectors of the local populace.

Obviously, the more antagonistic the general public is to a species, the greater the challenge to that species' recovery program, especially if opposition is concentrated in powerful interest groups. Charismatic vertebrates, species with economic value, and those with cultural significance are less problematic. Using an appealing species as an umbrella can often protect other organisms that use the same habitat, and can provide a vehicle for broader conservation-education programs. The black-footed ferret has such potential for the prairie dog ecosystem.

AN ATTITUDE STUDY IN MONTANA

Black-footed ferret reintroduction faces several significant public-relations challenges. Because the ferret is an obligate dependent of the prairie dog, recovery programs must address values and attitudes associated with that species. An attitude study in Montana focused on ranchers within the proposed reintroduction site who are heavily dependent on public lands for grazing (Reading 1993; Reading and Kellert 1993). The survey also sampled the knowledge, attitudes, and opinions of ranchers statewide, other residents of Phillips County (the site of the reintroduction), residents of Billings (the largest city in Montana), and members of conservation organizations in Montana. Information was obtained from informal meetings and interviews, public comments provided to the agencies, and a mail survey. It was then developed into attitude scales showing differences among the various groups.

As expected, the study found local residents, especially ranchers, to be antagonistic toward prairie dogs, black-footed ferrets, and the proposed reintroduction of ferrets into Phillips County. Most of the negative attitudes associated with the reintroduction were rooted in the ferret's association with prairie dogs and the ferret's status as an endangered species, which ranchers perceive as a hindrance to ranching operations on both public and private rangeland. Local ranchers, consistently the most hostile group, also received the highest scores in categories indicating a preference for dominating nature. They scored lowest in categories indicating sympathy or affection for prairie dogs and ferrets, and showed little concern for the ecological value of those species. By contrast, groups either less directly affected or strongly interested in conservation (Billings residents and members of wildlife or conservation organizations) were the most supportive and sympathetic. The greatest challenge clearly lies in gaining the support, or at least the grudging consent, of the local populace.

Moralistic, altruistic, and utilitarian values of black-footed ferrets were generally more important to ranchers and the local public than were scientific, ecological, and recreational values (Reading 1993). Thus effective public-relations programs should focus on the former set of values. Emphasizing the potential of black-footed ferrets to attract recreationists would probably be unsuccessful at increasing support for reintroduction, given the low recreational value most ranchers place on ferrets. Indeed, such appeals failed to garner support in the past.

Despite recent research indicating that competition between prairie dogs and livestock for forage is exaggerated and poisoning programs are not cost effective (see Chapter 11), negative attitudes toward prairie dogs persist, as quotes from surveyed ranchers attest: "I don't believe the results of those studies [prairie dog–cattle experiments]. Sure, my cows prefer to graze on prairie dog towns, but they have to leave them to fill up." Another rancher asserted, "I don't care what those studies say. It's just different here." Similarly, a Wyoming rancher once told us that six prairie dogs eat as much as one cow. However, most nonranchers surveyed (and even some individual ranchers) want to preserve at least some prairie dog colonies on public lands. This finding suggests that the majority of Montanans place at least some value on prairie dogs (Reading 1993).

Ranchers, especially those living near the reintroduction site, also feared that ferret reintroduction would hamper ranching and farming operations, result in a loss of control over grazing lands, and affect their traditional western rural lifestyles. To a lesser extent, the same was true of other Phillips County residents. Similar fears have been generated by other threatened and endangered species (notably wolves and bears), and especially by plans for habitat protection.

These fears are not unfounded. Western livestock producers have traditionally used public lands as they saw fit, at minimal cost, but recent years have seen a gradual shift in philosophy. Pressure is growing to manage public lands in the interests of the entire nation, and to take a hard look at federal subsidies for grazing, logging, and mining. Ranchers are thus fighting to maintain their traditional access to public lands. Recent initiatives include the Sagebrush Rebellion, an antifederal movement in which state or county interests tried to snatch federal land, and various court cases speared by a Wyoming lawyer to define ranching and logging on public land as a "culture and custom" that have precedence over federal powers. Both strategies have failed in court but have polarized attitudes. Reintroduction of an endangered species clearly represents an additional threat to traditional rancher power, and fear of change is not an uncommon phenomenon.

Studies of rural residents dependent on natural-resource extraction have revealed similar attitudes (Boggess 1982; Bath 1989; Kellert 1990). People employed in such industries are typically very hostile to government control and inclined toward dominating and exploiting wildlife. They are also often directly affected by wildlife-conservation initiatives, especially endangered-species restoration programs. So it is not surprising that resource-dependent groups are antagonistic toward endangered-species programs. Addressing this opposition is one of the greatest challenges facing the field of conservation biology.

The Montana attitude study found only a few significant differences among demographic or participatory groups for Billings and Phillips County residents (Reading 1993). People who were younger, more educated, female, and not employed in agriculture or natural-resources extraction were more supportive of prairie dogs, ferrets and the proposed black-footed ferret reintroduction. Hunters were significantly more antagonistic toward the proposed reintroduction than were nonhunters, but they also valued ferrets more than did nonhunters for altruistic and utilitarian reasons. Perhaps the apparent discrepancy arose from hunters' fears of hunting restrictions after reintroduction. The study suggested that hunters respect the natural world, and that if their concerns over hunting restrictions were adequately addressed, they might become important supporters of ferret reintroduction and prairie dog conservation. Kellert (1990) found hunters supportive of wolf restoration in Michigan, and recommended eliciting their support to counter antagonism in the agricultural community.

Past studies have found demographic and socioeconomic variables such as age, income, and level of education to be the important indicators of values and attitudes (Kellert 1979; Kellert and Berry 1987). In the Montana study, these variables were far less important than membership in one of the primary sample groups (rural-urban residency, livestock dependence, and membership in wildlife or conservation organizations), which correlated with antagonism or support (Reading 1993).

Knowledge of prairie dogs and black-footed ferrets varied significantly among the primary sample groups in the Montana study. Local ranchers and members of conservation organizations both scored high on knowledge, yet their attitudes were consistently at opposite ends of the scale. In other studies, Minnesota and Michigan farmers demonstrated more knowledge of wolves than did the general public or members of wildlife organizations (Kellert 1990), and in Wyoming ranchers and the general public scored equally on knowledge about wolves, but members of conservation organizations scored highest (Bath 1989). These results highlight the difference between knowledge and attitudes, a difference with significant implications for education and public-relations programs. Simply providing facts and information will not necessarily result in a more supportive public, because knowledge is only one of several factors influencing attitudes (Rokeach 1972; P. J. Brown and Manfredo 1987). Although public-relations and education programs have successfully generated support for some reintroduction programs, they have rarely been successful at changing attitudes and values, especially those that are strongly held (Chaiken and Stangor 1987). The data on attitudes toward prairie dogs suggest that personal experiences, and resulting perceptions, are the most important contributing factor to attitudes (Cutlip and Center 1964; Tessler and Shaffer 1990). Nevertheless, public education programs are critically important. Even if knowledge does not change entrenched negative attitudes, it can make people who were previously uninformed or neutral more sympathetic. For example, the general population in the Billings area had more sympathy for reintroduction after they had more knowledge of ferrets (Reading 1993).

The results of the Montana study suggest that newspapers, books and articles, and to a lesser extent television, may provide the best venues for an education and public-relations program. In addition, certain agencies, such as the U.S. Bureau of Land Management, may be effective locally. A large percentage of the proposed black-footed ferret reintroduction site in Montana lies on the Bureau's lands, and the agency regularly contacts landowners about the reintroduction effort. These overtures probably account for the high proportion of Phillips County residents, especially local ranchers, who identify the Bureau of Land Management as a source of information about prairie dogs and black-footed ferrets. They probably also account for local ranchers' high scores on knowledge about black-footed ferrets.

IMPLICATIONS AND RECOMMENDATIONS
OF THE MONTANA STUDY

The findings of the Montana attitudinal study suggest that the ferret recovery program must adequately address the antagonism of ranchers and local residents while simultaneously developing support among uninformed or undecided individuals and maintaining the support of conservationists and residents of Billings.

There are three basic approaches to accomplishing these goals: pressure, purchase, and persuasion (Cutlip and Center 1964). Ideally, all three methods should
be employed in a coordinated, carefully planned public-relations program.

Power and authority (in the form of law enforcement, control over use of resources, and penalties) can be used to apply pressure. The prohibitive aspects of
the Endangered Species Act represent a potentially powerful use of authority, but
they should be very carefully employed. Since carrots generally work better than
sticks, programs should consider offering financial benefits or other incentives.
An example is the suggested conversion of federal dollars allocated for prairie
dog poisoning to a financial incentive for ranchers who manage for prairie dogs
and livestock (see Chapter 11 and Miller, Wemmer, et al. 1990). Direct purchase
of land is also an option for protection. Finally, education and public-relations
programs should persuade people to support species reintroduction, or at least
not to actively oppose it. Receptivity can be enhanced if these efforts are made by
someone familiar and trusted, such as another rancher. Perhaps the most effective
long-term method of inducing broad changes in values and attitudes is to focus on
the social institutions that shape and reinforce values.

Persuasion was the only educational technique employed in the Montana program, and the involvement of trained public-relations professionals was minimal. Instead, this task fell largely to wildlife professionals. While working on a
management plan for black-footed ferret reintroduction, managers from the key
agencies took into account the concerns of local ranchers but largely ignored
other important constituent groups. This tactic appears to have been largely unsuccessful in garnering local support and may have alienated some urban and
conservationist supporters.

Generating support for a controversial wildlife program is a complicated un-
dertaking. Wildlife professionals should strive to incorporate educational and
public-relations goals into their work, but the onus of responsibility should not
fall on people untrained in public relations and already burdened by complex biological and technical tasks. Instead, an education and public-relations program
should be developed by the appropriate branches of key agencies or conservation
organizations, or preferably both, in collaboration with social scientists and professionals trained in education and public relations.

There is compelling evidence that the public is strongly supportive of efforts to
conserve wildlife but poorly informed about wildlife and conservation issues
(Kellert 1976). Too often, education programs fail to inform citizens about the real
issues, skirting sticky matters entirely and instead offering chatty self-promoting
newsletters that highlight the achievements of the organization or reinforce the
dominant philosophy (Alvarez 1993).

In contrast, one proposal states that wildlife and environmental professionals should provide the fundamentals of environmental and wildlife conservation to the general public, thus giving citizens the tools to pressure agencies toward better decisions regarding conservation (Duda 1987, as cited in Alvarez 1993). While some with power may be nervous over this prospect, an informed public can reduce the number of decisions based on politics instead of biology, and conservation can only benefit from such a change.

13

LEGAL DIMENSIONS OF BLACK-FOOTED FERRET RECOVERY

At least 26 federal laws currently provide protection to animal and plant populations in the United States. Two of the most influential examples are the Endangered Species Act of 1973 (ESA)[1] and the National Forest Management Act of 1976 (NFMA).[2] Both of these statutes mandate protection of biological diversity[3] through protection of certain key species and their habitats. The coverage provided by these two Acts, however, is hardly adequate to protect biodiversity in general. The ESA provides protection only for individual species of animals or plants listed as endangered or threatened, and the NFMA covers only lands under U.S. Forest Service jurisdiction, a fraction of the nation's land surface. Furthermore, the two Acts typify the weaknesses of any legislation, in that their intent is often undermined by conflicting regulatory interpretations and poor agency implementation.

This chapter discusses how knowledge of the legal landscape assists recovery of species like the black-footed ferret. The first section reviews the four major pieces of federal environmental legislation that define the legal context for efforts to protect biological diversity. The remainder of the chapter examines strategies to improve implementation of existing and proposed legal protection of biodiversity.

UNDERSTANDING THE STATUTORY FRAMEWORK

The Endangered Species Act

When Congress enacted the ESA, it expressed "concern over the . . . loss of *any* endangered species" (emphasis in original).[4] But not just any endangered spe-

170

cies qualifies for protection under the ESA. A species must first be listed pursuant to procedures mandated by the Act. Two agencies, the National Marine Fisheries Service (within the Department of Commerce) and the U.S. Fish and Wildlife Service (within the Department of Interior) are responsible for listing and for managing these listed species.

The listing process begins when a petition is submitted to the appropriate secretary.[5] In the case of marine fishes, whales, seals, and sea turtles at sea, it is the Secretary of Commerce; in all other cases, and when sea turtles are on land, it is the Secretary of the Interior.[6] Following review, the species can be listed as endangered or threatened, placed in Category 1 (taxa for which sufficient information exists to warrant listing but which are precluded from listing due to backlogs in the process) or Category 2 (species for which listing is probably appropriate but about which insufficient information is available), or dismissed.[7]

If a species is listed as endangered or threatened, it receives the full protection of the ESA. The substantive differences between the two classifications (which are based on degree of threat) differ only slightly, in that certain absolute prohibitions against "taking" threatened species may be modified by the Secretary. Most other requirements of the ESA apply equally to endangered and threatened species. Category 1 species receive limited protection[8]; under Section 7 of the ESA, the appropriate secretary must act only to "prevent a significant risk to the well-being of any such species."[9] Category 2 species are often suspended in a limbo of scientific uncertainty, receiving virtually no protection.

The listing process presents a formidable barrier for many species in need of the Act's protection. At least 34 species have gone extinct while awaiting a decision (Cohn 1993). While Congress recognized the importance of plants and invertebrates, directing the agencies to consider taxonomic uniqueness, and not charisma, as the primary basis for requiring protection (Rohlf 1988), only a small portion of the total agency budget goes to listing of these life forms. State fish and wildlife agencies frequently oppose petitions to list,[10] and the U.S. Fish and Wildlife Service often chooses not to list even when their own scientists support listing, as was the case with the northern spotted owl.[11]

Responsibility for implementation of recovery efforts dovetails with the assignment of agency jurisdiction under Section 7 of the ESA. Section 7 requires that federal agencies consult with the U.S. Fish and Wildlife Service (or the National Marine Fisheries Service) to ensure that "any action funded, authorized, or carried out by such agency . . . is not likely to jeopardize the continued existence of any endangered species or threatened species or result in the destruction or adverse modification of habitat of such species which is determined . . . to be critical."[12] In most cases, Section 7 imposes only procedural constraints on federal agency action; that is, it requires an interplay between the agency and the Fish and Wildlife Service, which occasionally results in modification of agency proposals for action. However, Section 7 also imposes substantive obligations on agencies. Among these are obligations to conserve endangered species through protection of habitat.[13] At least one commentator has observed that this obligation probably extends to the implementation of recovery plans, particularly when the agency has already taken steps to conserve a species pursuant to a recovery plan (Rohlf 1988). While this requirement makes recovery plans that are highly specific more enforceable, it also means that the design of such plans becomes more contentious and difficult (Houck 1993). Recovery plans are thus increasingly the target of litigation and controversy.

The U.S. Fish and Wildlife Service is also under increasing pressure, from within and outside the agency, to remove restrictions imposed by listed species and the ESA by delisting or modifying species' legal status. While Section 4 requires the same rigor of analysis to delist species as it does to list them,[14] the Service has settled on occasion for "recovery" objectives that have been openly questioned by scientists as inadequate for long-term maintenance of a listed species or population, reflecting instead what many view as politically attainable recovery. Despite these attempts, only 16 species had been delisted by 1992, and half of those had gone extinct (U.S. General Accounting Office 1992).

A strategy the Service has employed more frequently is the use of Section 10(j) "experimental/nonessential" designations for recovery of listed species. The secretary may designate a population of a species as "experimental," thus "downlisting" it from endangered to threatened status, if the population is established "outside the current range."[15] Because species are typically endangered precisely because their ranges have been reduced through habitat destruction, nearly all reintroductions and translocations will necessarily occur outside the species' current range. Potentially all species recovery is thus affected by this provision.

Section 10(j), which was added to the ESA in 1982, came into being through the efforts of several conservation groups to provide an exemption to the Act's strict taking provisions in order to promote recovery efforts for the red and gray wolf. Both wolves have been eliminated from much of their former range through a long history of predator control. Section 10(j) was designed to permit local rules to be tailor-made to fit local demands for control of wolves to protect livestock, including killing or manipulating introduced wolf populations.[16] While Section 10(j) may have provided wolf-recovery advocates the carrot needed to gain the acceptance of farmers and ranchers in the wolf-recovery areas, its use in recovery programs for other species—black-footed ferrets in particular—has had bizarre consequences. For example, when the Meeteetse population was brought into captivity, all of the captive animals and their progeny were fully protected as "endangered," a status all captive populations still maintain. In 1991 Wyoming and the U.S. Fish and Wildlife Service promulgated rules designating any populations returned to the Meeteetse area as "experimental/ nonessential."[17] The result is a transformation of the species' status from full protection by the ESA in the wild to less protection by the expedient of declaring them "extinct" and then returning them to the area from which they came.

The problems caused by this sleight of hand are compounded by the Service's insistence that all experimental populations be designated as "nonessential."[18] *Essential* populations are those "whose loss would be likely to appreciably reduce the likelihood of the survival of the species *in the wild*" (emphasis added).[19] A species designated "nonessential" that lives outside a national park or national wildlife refuge is treated as a "species proposed for listing"[20] or a Category 1 species. In other words, it enjoys no Section 7 protection, which means that federal agencies are under no obligation to conserve these populations.[21] In the case of the black-footed ferret, the Service has justified a nonessential designation because the ferret genome is protected in captivity. But protection of the species in captivity is not the intent of the ESA, which clearly envisions species recovery in the wild through its many references to ecosystems, critical habitat, and habitat acquisition.

All ferret reintroductions to date have relied on "nonessential" designations, even though the best recovery sites were presumably those selected for the first releases. Logically, one or more of these sites must be "essential" to recovery of ferrets in the wild, because there are no other wild populations of the species. There seems little question that the ferret is one of the "special cases" envisioned by Congress in which "experimental" populations are necessarily "essential" as well.[22] Region 6 has attempted to finesse this apparent contradiction by arguing that, for black-footed ferrets, "the captive population will be the primary species population,"[23] but this statement is troubling in that it implies the Service believes it can meet its obligation to conserve species by housing them in zoos or herbaria. This assertion opens a wide front along which those burdened by the restrictions imposed by the ESA could successfully argue that removal of species from the wild is one solution to land-use conflicts. Section 10(j) may be a slippery slope leading to serious weakening of the ESA's protection.

If one means of protecting species is to protect the species' habitat, then, conversely, "protecting the habitat of a species may conserve an ecosystem or community."[24] The ESA accomplishes this end through Section 4, which requires that the Secretary of the Interior or Commerce "shall, concurrently with making a determination of whether to list . . . designate any habitat of such species which is then considered to be critical habitat" to the "maximum extent prudent and determinable" based on the best biological information available.[25] However, economic and other impacts can be taken into account in the designation of habitat, and any area may be excluded, unless extinction will result without a designation.[26] In general, the secretary has broad discretion to balance the imminence of extinction against economic concerns, and critical-habitat designation has often been delayed or ignored (Rohlf 1988). When no critical habitat is designated, the protection afforded species on federal lands is limited to whether an agency action jeopardizes the existence of the species, which means federal agencies' actions that fall short of severe impact yet affect habitat are largely shielded from judicial review (Houck 1993). No critical habitat has been designated for the black-footed ferret.

Section 9 of the ESA offers another route to protection of habitat by interpreting the Act's prohibitions on "taking"[27]—a legal term for harm to an animal—to include significant habitat modification. The ESA regulations define "harm" as "an act which may include significant habitat modification or degradation where it actually kills or injures wildlife by significantly impairing essential behavioral patterns, including breeding, feeding or sheltering."[28] The courts have supported this broad definition of harm through habitat modification in numerous cases, finding harm from fragmentation of habitat that impaired essential behavioral patterns correlated with a decline in numbers, even though no actual deaths could be proven *(Sierra Club v. Lyng)*,[29] and where the state has permitted activities that modify critical nesting and feeding areas *(Palila v. Hawaii Department of Land and Natural Resources)*.[30] More recently, the Supreme Court, in its landmark decision in *Babbitt v. Sweet Home Chapter of Communities for a Greater Oregon*,[31] upheld the definition of harm in the regulation, but noted that questions of proximity and degree—will the farmer who tills the field be liable for the silt that enters the stream that poisons the fish?—will necessarily be difficult ones in individual cases.

In passing the ESA, Congress observed that "it is in the best interests of mankind to minimize the losses of genetic variations" existing in the natural world.[32] The ESA attempts to capture existing natural genetic diversity by protecting the species that express this diversity. While crude, protection on a species-by-species basis has proven effective in preserving a measure of existing biological diversity, particularly where species protection is strongly linked to protection of the ecosystems on which they depend. Yet over one-third of the nearly 650 species listed under the Act do not have completed recovery plans (Houck 1993); few of the completed plans address the need for population sizes sufficient to arrest genetic loss (Culbert and Blair 1989), and many, like that of the black-footed ferret, provide no protection for critical habitat. The ESA requires more—that the federal government take affirmative steps to recover species to the point where ESA protection is no longer necessary.[33] Like many other species, the black-footed ferret requires no less.[34]

The National Forest Management Act

The National Forest Management Act of 1976 (NFMA) requires the Secretary of Agriculture to promulgate such regulations as "specifying guidelines for land management plans developed to . . . provide for diversity of plant and animal communities based on the suitability and capability of the specific land area . . . within multiple use objectives of [the] land management plan . . . [and] to preserve the diversity of tree species similar to that existing in the region."[35] National grasslands, where most ferret habitat is located, are part of the National Forest System and subject to all rules and regulations of that system.[36] Grazing lands are to be managed "in accordance with direction established in forest plans."[37]

The NFMA mandate to create forest plans that specify how to protect species diversity is one of the most perplexing provisions of the NFMA (Wilkinson and Anderson 1985). The requirement resulted from concern that some eastern hardwood forests were being converted to monoculture pine plantations, and that the Forest Service had ignored nonconsumptive resources like wildlife (Wilkinson and Anderson 1985). The NFMA regulations require management and planning to preserve diversity on national forests "at least as great as that which would be expected in a natural forest."[38] However, site-specific management plans that reduce diversity can be allowed "where needed to meet overall multiple-use objectives."[39] Thus all that is necessary to evade diversity protection is the existence of a conflicting multiple-use objective. This loophole raises the question of whether the NFMA has any functional diversity mandate at all.

Yet the NFMA may not be entirely without protective standards. Diversity is addressed at several points in the NFMA regulations, some of which are relevant to the National Grasslands. First, planners must "provide for the diversity of plant and animal communities . . . consistent with the overall multiple-use objectives of the planning area."[40] The same provision appears to impose a procedural requirement that "such diversity shall be considered throughout the process," and places no limits on the amount of diversity to be conserved. It does require the plan to address diversity issues with quantitative data.

In addition, Section 219.19 of the NFMA requires that "habitat shall be managed to maintain *viable populations* of existing native and desired non-native vertebrate species in the planning area" (emphasis added) and "that habitat must be well distributed so that those individuals can interact with others in the planning area."[41] (Wilkinson and Anderson [1985] have suggested that this section requires the Forest Service "to treat the wildlife resource as a controlling, co-equal factor in forest management.") A viable population is defined as "one that has the estimated numbers and distribution of reproductive individuals to insure its continued existence."[42] This definition appears to encompass all factors affecting viability, such as genetic considerations and population demographics (Wilkinson and Anderson 1985). If an existing population is not viable, it presumably is not being properly maintained and its numbers should be increased.

The viability regulations have been the source of some controversy. The "viability" concept has undergone an enormous transformation since the rule was promulgated in 1982 (see, e.g., Soulé1989). It is now the subject of an extensive literature laden with quantitative analysis not envisioned at the time the rule was promulgated. The complexity and shifting definition of what constitutes viability has led the Forest Service to agonize over how to implement the regulation.[43]

For each planning unit, furthermore, selected species must be monitored to determine whether management is preserving ecosystem processes and diversity. These "management indicator species" are selected from the following list:

[(1)] endangered and threatened plant and animal species . . . [(2)] species with special habitat needs that may be influenced significantly by planned management programs . . . [(3)] species commonly hunted, fished, or trapped, [(4)] non-game species of special interest, [and (5)] additional plant or animal species selected because their population changes . . . indicate the effects of management activities on other species of selected major biological communities.[44]

Because it is not feasible to account for all or even most of the species within a planning unit, the idea is to select representatives of a suite of species. These representatives presumably "indicate" that the manager's activities are consistent with preserving ecosystem processes and diversity.

In *Seattle Audubon Society v. Evans,* plaintiffs challenged the Forest Service's management guidelines for the northern spotted owl *(Strix occidentalis),* an indicator species in the national forests of Oregon and Washington.[45] Plaintiffs were able to show that the plan adopted by the Forest Service had a low probability of maintaining a viable population of owls. As a result, the court halted further timber harvest in the owl's habitat until the Forest Service came up with a plan to maintain species viability.

The NFMA also specifies that "habitat determined to be critical for threatened and endangered species shall be identified, and measures shall be prescribed to prevent the destruction or adverse modification of such habitat."[46] It is not clear whether "critical habitat" means habitat officially designated by the U.S. Fish and Wildlife Service or habitat that is viewed by scientists and managers as critical to survival of a species. Regardless, planners are required, where possible, to "include special areas [within the National Forest lands] to meet the protection and management needs of such species."[47]

In 1995, responding to the success of suits like that over the spotted owl and to an agency emphasis on "ecosystem management," the Forest Service proposed changes to the NFMA regulations.[48] The changes essentially abandon the concept of species "viability," replacing it with a directive that forest plans be written to prevent the listing of any species under the ESA. This goal is to be accomplished under the proposed rule by providing adequate "habitat capability" for "sensitive" species; habitat capability includes the "quantity, quality, and distributions of habitats needed by a species."[49] Critics have pointed out that this directive applies to far fewer species and is considerably less concerned with distributions of species throughout the forest than the existing rule. Furthermore, while the viability requirement posed a "formidable challenge,"[50] it provided a point of departure for measuring agency compliance with the NFMA. The revisions also include explicit recognition of the ESA's requirement for conservation of species listed under the ESA, calling for strict compliance. Whether or not the proposed rule is adopted in its current form, it is clear that Forest Service management is moving away from data-intensive population analysis toward habitat analysis. How the agency will measure its success and compliance with the NFMA remains to be seen.

The National Environmental Policy Act

The National Environmental Policy Act (NEPA), passed in 1969, sets out a broad policy of restoring and maintaining environmental quality for future generations "without degradation."[51] While NEPA does not require actual protection of the environment, it has essentially opened the planning process for managing federal lands to public participation and judicial review (Grumbine 1992). NEPA requires all federal agencies to prepare an environmental-impact statement for any "major federal actions significantly affecting the quality of the human environment."[52] The NEPA's requirements are essentially procedural; so long as an agency's decision is fully informed and well considered, it is entitled to deference.[53] But if new information becomes available after completion of the environmental-impact statement, or if the agency has not fully revealed some important aspect of the environmental impact, the agency must prepare a supplemental environmental-impact statement and take a hard look at the alternatives in light of the new information. While the effect of NEPA is to delay actions that could adversely impact biodiversity, often delay is sufficient to discourage poorly thought-out proposals from going forward or to provide a window of opportunity for other alternatives to appear.

The Federal Lands Policy Management Act

The Federal Lands Policy Management Act of 1976 (FLPMA) gives the U.S. Bureau of Land Management authority to manage lands under its jurisdiction in a manner that will "protect the quality of scientific, scenic, historical, ecological, environmental . . . values."[54] The FLPMA also requires the Bureau of Land Management to develop "regulations and plans for the protection of public land areas of critical environmental concern."[55] Unfortunately, there are no clear FLPMA guidelines governing the relative weight of ecological concerns in relation to other mandates such as oil and gas development or grazing. Thus the degree of protection for environmental values that this Act provides is untested.

MOVING TOWARD LEGAL PROTECTION OF BIODIVERSITY

Diversity is not easily defined. As Sagoff (1980) has observed, "it seems plain that we would prefer to preserve a variety of very different species, rather than to preserve every species in a narrow class." But this approach is defensible only if there is no utility associated with a species. The best example of the costs of this attitude is the oft-cited case of a variety of wild corn found in Mexico that holds out the promise of disease resistance in domesticated corn.[56] In other words, even varieties of species may have unique economic as well as genetic value. The common law action of waste, which protects the reasonable expectations of succeeding estates in land, also lends support for preserving species with high utility for future generations (Rogers 1983). The shortcoming of utility as a standard is, of course, that we cannot predict the future uses of species or ecosystems.

Existing legislation imposes several nonutilitarian standards—including aesthetic, ecological, educational, historical, recreational, and scientific value—for diversity preservation.[57] It is questionable, however, whether a statute like the Endangered Species Act recognizes an existence right for certain classes of organisms and ecosystems or simply views genetic variation as another potential resource.[58] The latter interpretation would explain congressional reluctance to expand ESA coverage or to extend protection to the ecosystems housing these resources.

Foreshadowing the debate that could ensue from attempts to define biodiversity legislatively, the 1988 Congress considered amending the National Environmental Policy Act to address biodiversity concerns. The U.S. Forest Service expressed concern that defining biodiversity broadly "would subject the NEPA process to . . . litigation based on the almost unlimited interpretations and meanings of biological diversity" (Carlson 1988). The Wilderness Society suggested more concrete criteria: a federal action would not be considered adverse unless it created losses of regionally rare, native animal or plant species or scarce natural floral or faunal communities, or losses of fish, wildlife, or plant species or natural wildland communities that had already shown significant declines over a sizable portion of their historic ranges.[59]

The Wilderness Society proposal essentially called for legal recognition of "pre-endangered" species. Such a continuum approach to legal protection of species based on their scarcity has intuitive appeal, in the sense that what is rare may also be more valuable. However, it assumes that the data or tools exist to measure the abundance and distribution of natural communities. Worse, we are probably not equipped to assess intelligently the amount of community diversity that ought to be conserved. Ensuring maintenance of a baseline population would be an acceptable starting point, but of course we have little empirical data about the size of natural communities in earlier eras.

A triage approach to biological conservation has also been proposed. Society would direct its conservation efforts toward the species and communities most likely to benefit, as opposed to those that may or may not survive despite our endeavors (see D. O. Linder 1988). This approach would require a formal assessment of the risks associated with forsaking some elements of diversity, but no such assessment mechanism currently exists. Furthermore, no one can seriously doubt that charismatic species would receive more funding regardless of their ranking.

If statutes such as the Endangered Species Act and the National Forest Management Act provide the authority on which to base more extreme protection measures, how can diversity be more effectively conserved? First, it has been argued that the National Environmental Policy Act process is the best place to begin (Carlson 1988) because NEPA implicitly requires that "cumulative action, which when viewed with other proposed actions [has] cumulatively significant impacts," should be considered in environmental-impact statements.[60] Such cumulative-impacts analysis, if coupled with an inventory of the existing species and community types in a region, would provide insight into the relative health of the species or communities in question. Moreover, because it is likely that only one or two impacts will be at issue in any given region (e.g., loss of wetlands, loss of grizzly bear habitat, loss of swan breeding grounds), the data will be focused. The resulting databases, which are feasible to construct given computer-driven information systems, can be refined over time as new information becomes available.

It is not clear why the NEPA's cumulative-effects requirements have not been appropriated in the service of the biological-diversity cause. In *Natural Resource Defense Council, Inc. v. Hodel,* the court practically outlined the sort of modeling exercise required to comply with the NEPA in its discussion of the impacts of offshore oil leasing on marine mammals.[61] The court suggested that the Secretary of the Interior look at the effects of simultaneous interregional development, including identification of various species, distribution of the species, extent of activities, and the "synergistic effect of those activities on the . . . species," and that the secretary then "examine alternatives to simultaneous development (e.g., staggered development) that would mitigate any synergistic impacts."[62] In essence, this is a blueprint for explicitly raising diversity concerns within the NEPA process.

The environmental-impact statement should probably also address the full range of activities with potential impact on a particular ecosystem, community, or species. Others have proposed that a revision of the Council on Environmental Quality regulations would address diversity issues more effectively than the NEPA (Carlson 1988). The letter is probably a more efficient means to prompt agency compliance, since the NEPA has already been interpreted to accommodate biodiversity considerations.

In addition, federal legislation is needed to inventory and evaluate the nation's biodiversity. The only way to assess accurately whether cumulative effects will significantly influence biodiversity is to know more precisely what resources are present.

Finally, it is necessary to establish conservation objectives for biodiversity. This may be accomplished by formally addressing the potential risks that current scientific knowledge enables us to identify. The objectives receiving the most attention will doubtless be determined by our perceptions of what is likely to be most valuable in the future, from economic, psychological, aesthetic, and biological standpoints. We can start by adopting a national policy of no net loss from our larger ecosystems—not only wetlands, but prairies and forests as well—until we gain further insights into the processes necessary to sustain long-term biodiversity.

The prairie dog provides an excellent opportunity to forge a transition from traditional single-species management to management of a system. Prairie dogs live in discrete communities that are (in the absence of disease) fairly stable over time. Therefore, like wetlands, the boundaries of these ecosystems can be given a legal or jurisdictional definition.

CONSERVING PRAIRIE DOGS

As we have seen, the U.S. government continues to fund programs that destroy the habitat of the black-footed ferret while billing the taxpayer for the costs of a ferret recovery program (see Chapter 11). Though there has been little concerted opposition to poisoning programs, they are clearly amenable to legal and political challenge.

For example, state laws designating prairie dogs as pests could be challenged based on federal preemption. The supremacy clause in Article VI of the U.S. Constitution allows state statutes and authority that conflict with federal law to be overridden. The U.S. Supreme Court is particularly skeptical of state laws deemed "hostile to federal interests," striking down, for example, state statutes passed to thwart the acquisition of easements under the Migratory Bird Treaty Act.[63] It has been observed that "the Supremacy Clause creates an implied right of action for injunctive relief against state officers who are threatening to violate the federal Constitution or laws."[64] It is clear that state laws requiring mandatory poisoning of prairie dogs, such as in South Dakota (see Chapter 11), are in conflict with the purposes of the Endangered Species Act, the National Forest Management Act, and the Federal Lands Policy Management Act where prairie dogs are needed to provide habitat for species like the black-footed ferret.

There are reasons, however, why suits have not been filed to strike down state statutes requiring prairie dog poisoning. State officials, despite their rhetoric, are aware of the limitations imposed by federalism. Western states in particular are dependent on enormous federal subsidies that supply funds for everything from payments in lieu of taxes to food stamps. It is unlikely that state officials would force compliance with a state law to poison prairie dogs if they thought doing so could lead to an explicit ruling that the law was invalid, or would complicate their participation in federal benefit programs. If a state attempted to enforce state laws requiring prairie dog poisoning on unwilling federal managers, there is little question that the state would be amenable to suit in federal court. However, it is unlikely that states would press the issue for reasons of comity.

A more intriguing question is whether the state can force its poisoning regulations on private landowners who have an interest in protecting prairie dogs. This could be a critical issue should private conservation trusts become involved in restoration of black-footed ferrets. Clearly, there are good arguments that the state cannot enforce its law if the habitat is part of a recovery scheme to protect a listed species.

Another area that remains untested is whether the National Environmental Policy Act (explicitly) and several other statutes (implicitly) could be used to require analysis of the cumulative effects of all federal programs on the total prairie dog resource for recovery of ferrets and other listed species dependent on prairie dogs. Indeed, accurate estimates of the total numbers of prairie dogs or of the area occupied by prairie dogs nationally are lacking. If such an inventory existed, federal actions such as "animal damage control" poisoning programs, land management plans, and cooperative agreements with states that impact prairie dogs could be cumulatively analyzed to assess effects on prairie dogs and other species protected by the ESA that are dependent on prairie dogs. None of the poisoning programs on federal lands has analyzed cumulative effects on the prairie dog ecosystem.

Without an inventory, the U.S. Fish and Wildlife Service has no scientifically supportable means to assess cumulative effects, which exposes the agency to political pressure. In 1991, for example, Congressman Hank Brown of Colorado moved Region 6, on behalf of northeast Colorado landowners, to approve prairie dog poisoning. Region 6 had no basis for claiming that the taking of habitat would jeopardize black-footed ferrets, even though one of the complexes was biologically qualified as a ferret reintroduction site. If the Service had effectively used existing environmental laws to gather the scientific information necessary to assess the impact of this program on the overall ferret recovery effort, it could very well have supported a position resulting in less or modified poisoning.

ADDRESSING INEFFICIENCIES ARISING FROM STATE AND FEDERAL CONFLICT

Conflicting Roles in Implementation of the Endangered Species Act

The Endangered Species Act stands for a national commitment to species conservation; it also represents the pinnacle of federal intervention into the arena of wildlife management and preservation, an arena once occupied exclusively by state governments (Rohlf 1988). Although state wildlife agencies share the ESA's laudable goals, the creation of a federal role in state wildlife-management decisions necessarily throws together state and federal actors who may, for various reasons, hold incompatible views on how the ESA should be implemented. Turf battles, conflicting definitions of federalism, and organizational dynamics are among the spheres in which this conflict plays out.

There is little question that the federal government has a significant role to play in wildlife management. Beginning with the Migratory Bird Treaty Act of 1918,[65] Congress and the courts have affirmed that managing wildlife resources is a transboundary problem often best addressed at the federal level. Furthermore, federal trusteeship of wildlife resources is often necessary because the costs of missed short-term economic opportunities at the state level are seldom offset by the benefits of species protection; the benefits, like increased tourism or regional quality of life, often become apparent only at the regional level or over time.

Issues of federalism and agency jurisdiction were never far from the minds of the legislators who drafted the ESA. As Senator Tunney noted after vigorous debate in 1973 about the state role in endangered-species management, "Some argue that the States should have their chance. I argue that the States have had their chance."[66] The federal government was assigned the role of fundamental authority under the ESA, but the final compromise over the federalism question resulted in a different alliance. The House assigned the fundamental responsibility for endangered-species programs to the federal government, while the Senate amended the legislation to shift basic responsibility to the states. The conference committee retained language giving the states an opportunity to participate in the protection of endangered and threatened species in cooperation with the federal government.[67]

The mechanism for cooperation is Section 6 of the ESA, described thus in 1977 amendments to the ESA:

Section 6 places the fundamental responsibility for establishing and overseeing an endangered species program in the Federal Government. However, Section 6 mandates that the appropriate Secretary, depending upon the species involved, cooperate with the States in carrying out the endangered species program. The cooperation envisioned by Section 6 includes consultation with the States concerned before acquiring any land or water under the Act, and the development of cooperative management agreements with States that establish an adequate and active program for the conservation of endangered and threatened species. Section 6 resulted from the realization that the successful development of an endangered species program depended upon a good working arrangement between the Federal and States [*sic*] agencies. Although the Federal agencies have the broad policy perspective and authority to carry out the Act, the State agencies have the physical facilities and the personnel to see that State and Federal endangered species policies are properly executed.[68]

Section 6's grant-in-aid provisions represent a formidable carrot to assure state participation in ESA programs. Eligible states qualify for two-to-one matching grants and exercise greater control over listed species within their boundaries, a tremendous incentive for states to participate. Millions of dollars have been appropriated for Section 6 programs since 1977, but there is no evidence that Section 6 has promoted true cooperation between state wildlife agencies and the federal government. In the case of ferrets, in fact, it appears to be a point of contention, judging by the following excerpt from a state-agency memo:

We would like to use two specific examples . . . of how the partnership role for the states is eroding. . . . Subsequent conflicts arose [with respect to the proposed black-footed ferret reintroduction]. . . . The [U.S. Fish and Wildlife] Service resolved the dispute by asserting that this decision and all future ones were solely theirs to make. This came despite the protocol document's assurance to local landowners that they would be working with the state. (Montana Department of Fish, Wildlife, and Parks, Endangered Species Act reauthorization materials, n.d. [1993])

And from the federal response:

Extensive efforts were made to maintain cooperative functions for BFF [black-footed ferret] reintroduction, recognizing each agency's capacities and legal responsibilities. [Montana Department of Fish, Wildlife, and Parks] created much of the strife with lack of team playing, un-reviewed news releases, changing already agreed upon decisions, and inopportune communication of internal agency affairs with landowners. (U.S. Fish and Wildlife Service response to Montana's reauthorization materials, 22 September 1993)

Not only is cooperation lacking, but Montana (and other states) appear to be unimpressed by the Section 6 incentives in light of the workload associated with the ESA:

Our chief concern with funding is that Sec. 6 allocations to the states are inadequate and inconsistent. . . . The state of Montana was faced with the dilemma of either picking up the slack or abandoning our commitment to the endangered species. We filled the needs, but are unable to continue to do so particularly because of the increased number of listed species. (Montana Department of Fish, Wildlife, and Parks memo, 1993)

Implicit too is the age-old issue of who gets to run the show:

State commitments made to preserve . . . species are being undercut by federal management. Our inability to conduct some activities . . . because of a lack of a permit, has resulted in extreme negative public reaction . . . to the Department. Many of the [Western] Governors' concerns were addressed in the language of those [reauthorization] bills . . . their chief concern—state authority. (Montana Department of Fish, Wildlife, and Parks memo, n.d. [1993])

Game Theory: Models of State and Federal Roles

Regardless of who is "right" in such conflicts, the species of concern do not benefit from the unproductive conflict introduced into programs by interagency friction. Models of cooperation and conflict, often referred to collectively as game theory, help explain why such situations arise. One of the simplest models is known as "the prisoner's dilemma."

The prisoner's dilemma typically involves two participants—envisioned as prisoners—each of whom has two choices: to keep mum about their joint crime or to defect (squeal) on the other prisoner and thus go free. Because defection always yields a higher payoff than does cooperation, there is always the temptation to defect. The dilemma is that if both prisoners defect, they will be worse off than if they had cooperated with each other by staying silent about the crime, in which case the police would have been less likely to obtain a conviction. The prisoner's dilemma is often used to explain "commons" (shared resource) problems: if all nations were to cut back on whaling, for instance, there would be a collective benefit (more whales) to be shared. Yet it pays an individual country to engage in whaling to the detriment of the resource (Hirshleifer 1982). While this model oversimplifies complex interactions, it nonetheless captures the essence of many two-party interactions, such as those between state and federal wildlife managers. Where the noncooperator strategy prevails, cooperation "failures" may result in payoffs sufficient to move the program forward, but inefficiently, because one participant's gain is offset by the other's loss. On average, this state of affairs reduces the overall reward to both, who are trapped in a stable equilibrium of tolerating and anticipating defection.

Hirshleifer (1982) has modeled ways to escape (mathematically) from the traps created by symmetrical relations dominated by noncooperation. Participants could adopt a strategy of retaliation (reacting favorably to cooperation while punishing defection with counter-defection), but this strategy is not viable if there are benefits to be gained by defecting on the very last interaction. In such cases there is no incentive to cooperate on the next-to-last interaction, and so forth, until the game unravels. A more efficient strategy is to create an asymmetry in the power relations between the participants—assigning a superordinate ("Big Daddy") role to one participant. Big Daddy can then effectively force cooperation by sanctioning noncooperation or rewarding cooperation.

In a multiparty prisoner's dilemma, a third viable strategy is "moralistic aggression" on the part of "uninvolved" third-party enforcers on the side of the victim of uncooperative behavior. For instance, the provisions of Section 11 of the ESA for lawsuits by citizens can be used by an informed public to ensure cooperation between the states and the federal government, or among federal agencies.

Game theory captures some of the fundamental problems stemming from state-federal conflict in the ferret program. The program continues to move forward, but inefficiently, because interactions between the participants are dominated by the noncooperator strategy. Early in the program Region 6 could have assumed the role of Big Daddy, but instead chose to place itself in a symmetric power-sharing role with Wyoming and the other states. The lack of incentives to cooperate has led the states to look first to their own interests, often to the detriment of ferrets. For example, Wyoming maintained throughout that it would stock its own reintroduction sites first, regardless of opportunities to establish ferrets elsewhere. Hundreds of ferrets and many years later, Wyoming has only a handful of ferrets in the wild and no active release program. Meanwhile, other sites where ferrets might have fared better are still waiting their turn. Had the U.S. Fish and Wildlife Service taken a more active and dominant role in determining where ferrets were going, the pace and direction of recovery might have taken a different turn, with a more efficient outcome.

Granting increased authority at the federal level is at odds with the prevailing conventional wisdom. Perhaps inefficiency is part of the legacy of our federal system, an artifact of democracy to be factored into the work of government. However, endangered-species programs will not move forward at a pace necessary to accomplish the tasks of recovery in the current environment of state self-interest. The resulting tension will not be alleviated by giving more authority to the states, but by exercising more rational authority at the federal level while taking state concerns into account. Conservation groups, too, have been noticeably unassertive about forcing cooperation between state and federal agencies to accomplish recovery tasks. Multiparty recovery efforts may be a sounder basis for policy-making, resulting in more efficient solutions at a lower cost; such efforts may promote greater cooperation between the key participants in the ferret program as well. The U.S. Fish and Wildlife Service is the natural entity to facilitate broad-based participation in the program, and its role as final authority under the ESA should be maintained in future revisions of the Act.

14

ORGANIZING A RECOVERY EFFORT

SAPISMO AND ENDANGERED SPECIES

In an article on human nature and science, Mares (1991) notes that science is a human endeavor and is thus replete with ambition, arrogance, insecurity, egomania, paranoia, and jealousy. Describing mammalogy research in Latin America, where there are few mammalogists, Mares observes that each area of study tends to be dominated by a single researcher. He invokes the analogy of a big toad in a small pond and calls the resulting phenomenon *sapismo* (*sapo* means "toad" in Spanish, and *sapismo* is toadlike behavior). The term describes many endangered-species programs perfectly. We embellish his analogy with our observations of black-footed ferret research and recovery efforts.

When there are very few toads in a pond, Mares explains, one will soon dominate and then use its power and influence to reduce the field even further, often extending its authority into areas where its experience is limited at best; this can be particularly easy to accomplish if the *sapo grande* (big toad) is in a position to grant money or permission to others. The sapo grande may invoke nationalism (or state pride) to prevent the entry of other participants. The sapo grande is easily threatened, particularly when operating outside its area of expertise.

When threatened or countered, sapos grandes often react by belittling the source rather than addressing the issues at hand. On the ferret project, people with alternative ideas were often labeled "negative to the program" because a sapo grande failed to differentiate between his or her own interests and the interests of the species.

Sapismo often restricts a project to a "limited learning syndrome," for several

187

reasons. Generally speaking, sapos grandes only support cooperative research when it benefits them or is controlled by them. In order to maintain control, the sapo grande may continually erect barriers to each new idea originating outside its sphere of influence. When presented with an idea that threatens the prevailing philosophy, a sapo grande may try to prevent the concept from being tested. If the idea can only be delayed and turns out to be good, the sapo grande will often adopt it but rewrite history to claim credit for the idea. Press releases and documents that create and reinforce legitimacy are important weapons in battles for control. By forcing people out of the program, either by withholding permits for study or by generally making life miserable enough to burn out other biologists, the sapo grande can maintain enough continuity to promote the "official version" of the story. The number of good ideas arising from a given source may not influence the sapo grande's decision-making as much as the perceived threat to its power and authority. In fact, a source that produces a number of good ideas may be perceived as particularly threatening. Finally, the sapo grande may be intelligent but typically is not humble, and unless intelligence is tempered by humility it is usually not used effectively.

According to Mares, participants' salaries or permission to work often depend on the sapo grande, a situation that leads to the sapo grande being surrounded by sycophants. The combination of having its ego fed by these people, being isolated from intellectual competition, and gaining power over other specialists leads the sapo grande to develop a greatly overblown self-image.

In endangered-species and conservation programs, well-intentioned people sometimes contribute to sapismo. Agencies and nongovernmental organizations often choose to "throw money at a problem" rather than enlisting competent, dedicated people to do careful planning (Frazier 1993). Money and resources are desperately needed, but when they are freely dispensed with little oversight or accountability, the potential arises for empire-building. Monetary contributions promote an image of commitment, but the true measure of dedication is investing time and attention as well (Frazier 1993).

Similarly, people with the power to change the situation often unwittingly contribute to sapismo by choosing not to rock the boat. Many bureaucrats fear that overt discord will generate bad publicity, to the detriment of fund-raising opportunities (and career advancement). To enhance the program's image and obtain more financial support, bureaucrats often nominate an undeserving sapo grande for awards, honors, or other positions of power. The sapo grande in turn uses public recognition to establish credibility and further entrench power.

As time passes, some sapos grandes make enough enemies to cause their own fall from authority. Unfortunately, others accumulate enough power to rule indefinitely. Regardless, endangered-species conservation efforts are far too complex to be limited to a single person or philosophy. Mares (1991) posits that the antidote to sapismo is people; large ponds make it more difficult for a sapo grande to emerge. Our aim is not merely for an antidote but for preventive medicine. In *The Book of Laughter and Forgetting,* Milan Kundera stated, "The struggle of man against power is the struggle of memory against forgetting" (1981:3). It is in this light that we have written the recent history of black-footed ferret conservation and offer some general policy suggestions.

The U.S. Endangered Species Act is one of the most far-reaching conservation documents ever produced by any nation (Rohlf 1991; Bean 1992), yet its effectiveness could be vastly improved (Yaffee 1982; U.S. General Accounting Office 1988b; Kohm 1991). Although some endangered-species programs have been successful, very few have been efficient. The problem resides less in the Act itself than in its administration and implementation (O'Connell 1992). This is not surprising, in that endangered-species management usually occurs in an environment of uncertainty, complexity, conflicting jurisdictions, and public scrutiny. Programs conducted in such an atmosphere are typically vulnerable to a host of administrative challenges.

Common problems include slow decision-making, decision-making without the benefit of outside expertise, decision-making that consolidates control at the expense of scientific and management priorities, rewarding of organizational loyalty while penalizing creativity and initiative, faulty information flow or deliberate communication blockage, failure to develop concrete objectives that can be used to evaluate progress, deviation from established plans during implementation (for political reasons), and an overly rigid or conservative organizational hierarchy that impedes effective action. Yet, of all the factors influencing efficient and successful species recovery, organizational issues are perhaps the most poorly understood by the participants.

The Importance of Program Effectiveness and Efficiency

There are six main reasons to improve the efficiency and effectiveness of endangered-species recovery programs (see Miller, Reading, et al. 1994). First, programs that experience even moderate success are imitated by other programs. It should be noted, however, that the biology of some species may partially mask programmatic shortcomings. An inefficient organizational model may demonstrate progress toward recovery for one species but provide poorer results if applied to a species that has a smaller margin of error (e.g., slower reproductive rate, smaller effective population size, fragmented habitat, a local human population that is more antagonistic toward the species, etc.).

Second, programs with organizational problems use more resources (time, money, personnel, animals, etc.) than necessary, resources that could be applied to other equally pressing conservation problems. Many programs are already hindered by insufficient funding, making efficiency a necessity.

Third, if the species inhabits the jurisdictions of two or more agencies, the lack of a comprehensive plan hinders interagency cooperation. For example, the first joint meeting of the U.S. and Canadian whooping crane *(Grus americana)* recovery teams was held in 1991 (1992 *Endangered Species Technical Bulletin* XVIII:3). Prior to that time, the two nations had separate recovery plans, even though the whooping crane is a high-profile endangered bird that migrates between the two countries. Obviously, lack of interagency cooperation can give rise to duplication of effort or ignoring of important tasks. Poorly defined programs (or stacked recovery teams) also create friction between agencies. The resulting antipathy may create distrust and unnecessary delays, which can contaminate future joint efforts on behalf of other threatened species.

Fourth, recovery programs that span agency jurisdictions or geographic boundaries need statistically comparable information. Many recovery programs that reintroduce or translocate species over a broad geographic or jurisdictional range have been burdened by noncomparable, or inadequate, scientific designs. Because such data fail to meet qualifications for publication, peer review of the program is inhibited.

Fifth, small populations are very vulnerable to collapse because of chance genetic, demographic, or environmental events. Delays and diversions in policy setting or implementation only make recovery more difficult.

Sixth, when an agency restricts creative input and limits itself to self-orchestrated positive reinforcement (e.g., stacked recovery teams and limited critical review), the repercussions can be grave. Internal self-deception can lead an organization to harden its position, polarize the political situation, and jeopardize the recovery of a species.

We argue that the efficiency and effectiveness of recovery programs must be improved. Many countries offer legal protection for endangered species but do not specify procedures for developing and implementing recovery plans. For example, in the United States, the Endangered Species Act does not specify how the secretary of the interior will ensure that protective actions are actually accomplished. This ambiguity contributes to multiple problems.

THE NATURE OF THE PROBLEM

Organizational Issues

Most people assume that conservation decisions are based on science, but a number of nonscientific factors affect their outcome. Science may claim to be the pure pursuit of knowledge, but any practical application of that knowledge involves personalities, attitudes, economics, administrative procedures, politics, and so on. Discretionary judgments are influenced by past policies, the preferences of decision makers, economic consequences, legal constraints, individual goals, and fear of taking risks. Decision makers' receptivity to information is often a function of the source and context of the information, and changes of direction during implementation result from ambiguous plans, conflicting goals within and among the involved agencies, limited resources, and variability in the competence of the participants (Warwick 1975; Yaffee 1982).

All the groups that shape and enact endangered-species recovery programs, including federal agencies and nongovernmental organizations, are afflicted by these problems. Wildlife biologists often mistakenly believe that the problems of their particular species-recovery effort are unique, but in reality the structure of the managing organization accounts for 50–75% of the way that individuals behave in any group (Galbraith 1977). In other words, similar patterns of behavior will appear in programs with similar organizational designs regardless of the species in question, geographic area, and even the agencies or personnel involved. We can thus learn valuable lessons by examining other endangered-species programs with similar mandates and constraints, and by applying some of the principles of organizational theory (Loucks 1992).

Most people who work directly with endangered species, however highly trained in the biological sciences, have had little exposure to organizational theory. They are therefore rarely able to diagnose or solve organizational problems (Clark and Kellert 1988; Clark, Schuyler, et al. 1992; Reading 1993). Biologists also prefer to plunge into the biological and technical work for which they are trained, particularly when much needs to be accomplished in the field and laboratory (Phenicie and Lyons 1973). In such circumstances, organizational problems are often conveniently blamed on biopolitics or on personalities (Schon 1983; Jackson 1986; Clark and Cragun 1991). However accurate these assessments, they do not define the problem suitably to permit the development of an effective solution (Schon 1983). No one denies that politics, personalities, and personal motivations influence programs, but appropriate policies and organizational arrangements can help prevent or ameliorate such problems. Unless biologists explicitly recognize and address organizational and policy issues, even obviously rational solutions to important conservation problems may be undermined, distorted, or misapplied.

In addition to the scientific skills necessary to collect and evaluate biological information, conservation biologists need enough political savvy to function effectively in the policy-setting and implementation processes (Clark, Schuyler, et al. 1992). Developing these skills may require extensive consultation with a social scientist, comparable to consulting a statistician about experimental design.

Organizational Culture

All organizations have their own distinctive cultures, which mold how their members view and respond to the situations they face. An organization's culture can influence how its members perceive goals, and even the goals they pursue for the organization and themselves (Warwick 1975; Clark 1986; Reading, Clark, and Kellert 1991). Consciously or unconsciously, furthermore, they tend to select people with similar perspectives (Janis 1972). A homogeneous workforce in turn makes internal functions efficient by minimizing conflict, but it also stifles creativity. Organizational cultures can be perpetuated indefinitely by built-in strategies of hiring and promotion (e.g., the good-old-boy system) and by the proclivity of many bureaucrats to focus mainly on pleasing their bosses. Eventually, internal rules and regulations, standard operating procedures, rewards, and sanctions act to institutionalize an organization's culture, making it more rigid and difficult to change.

In his study of organizational behavior, Harrison (1972) found three typical cultures: task-oriented cultures, which reward achievement of goals; power-oriented cultures, which strive to consolidate control of programs, power, and money; and role-oriented cultures, which emphasize legitimacy, hierarchy, and status. The latter two types tend to become rigid bureaucracies whose primary goal is procedural correctness rather than performance (Clark, Crete, and Cada 1989). Rigid bureaucracies in turn allow their individual members to hide from accountability behind the shield of the organization.

Organizational Structure

Formal organizational structure, or hierarchy, is perhaps the most obvious feature of any organization. Less obvious but equally important are its informal organizational structures, which often represent the real chain of command and the way things are actually accomplished.

Many of the federal and state agencies charged with endangered-species management long ago developed rigid hierarchical structures (long, narrow chains of command) because they began as regulatory bodies. State game and fish agencies, for example, originated to regulate hunting and fishing. Although most states have recently instituted nongame programs, the primary focus of these agencies is still enforcing game laws and establishing harvest limits.

When routine and familiar tasks are the main function of an agency, rigid structures can be productive and efficient (Clark 1986). Regulation, for example, involves fairly routine comparisons of conduct against a defined standard. But endangered-species programs must react quickly in an uncertain and complex environment subject to factors outside of the agency's control—conditions that require rapid assimilation of new information and implementation of creative, cost-effective solutions. Inefficiency and ineffectiveness often result when agencies organize endangered-species programs using rigid templates derived from their historical regulatory tasks. If the lead organization is also strongly oriented toward a power or role culture, its policies are likely to have objectives incongruent with recovery goals for the species.

Policy-Setting Issues

Brewer and deLeon (1983) have outlined six broad stages through which any policy passes: (1) *initiation,* when the problem is first identified; (2) *estimation,* when the problem is analyzed and defined; (3) *selection,* when a specific policy is formed and adopted; (4) *implementation,* when the policy is executed; (5) *evaluation,* when the policy's effectiveness is analyzed and recommendations are made for improvement, and (6) *termination,* when the overall effort is revised or ended. An understanding of these six phases can greatly enhance efficiency and effectiveness by enabling participants in recovery programs to manage the process rather than becoming preoccupied with individual personalities.

The policy-setting process encompasses the first three parts of Brewer and deLeon's (1983) model: identification of the problem, expert analysis of the problem, and formulation of a plan of action. The policy-setting process can be weakened by failure to use scientific information effectively, inaccurate or partial problem recognition, and stacking advisory groups (Miller, Reading, et al. 1994). Let us explore each of these pitfalls in more detail.

Ineffective Use of Information   The early stages of endangered-species recovery programs are often characterized by insufficient knowledge to develop a confident course of action. Particularly when biological data are scarce, matters of personality, program control, power distribution, organizational hierarchy, and administrative philosophy can dominate policy setting, often to the detriment of the program. This is how unsubstantiated ideas became established as policy for recovery programs aimed at the California condor (Snyder and Snyder 1989) and the black-footed ferret (Chapters 7–9). In both programs, issues of program control and administrative philosophy carried more weight than did scientifically collected data. Montgomery (1990), D. P. Hamilton (1992), Marshall (1992), and Boyle (1993) describe other cases in which scientific information was not used effectively in planning.

A sapo grande can counter scientific data simply by exercising its power to say no when confronted with a novel idea. A slightly more cunning sapo grande can request a huge amount of paperwork, memo transactions, documentation, and the like to drain the time and energy of its opponents before debunking the idea. A critical outside review by independent scientific specialists during policy formation can prevent the endorsement of plans that misuse or ignore scientific data. An outside review may also assure that information necessary for future decisions is collected scientifically.

Reluctance to Recognize Problems   The policy-setting process is also hindered by simple avoidance of problems and controversies, such as Wyoming's denial of the population declines at Meeteetse (see Chapter 7). The development of a plan can also be delayed if agency personnel are reluctant to admit that problems require analysis by outside experts. They may fear dilution of their power and control, or harm to their public image if explicit recognition of the problem is misconstrued as a sign of weakness and an invitation to public criticism. Some program participants seem to believe that a proactive approach invites criticism for taking action at a time when nothing needed to be done. These attitudes tend to delay action until it is absolutely clear that an emergency exists. This approach to endangered-species conservation must be changed. Crisis management is more expensive and has a lower probability of success than proactive strategies that could prevent future catastrophes, and it also deflects funds from such efforts (Wemmer and Derrickson 1987).

Stacked Recovery Teams   The third serious hindrance to the policy-setting process is "stacking" recovery teams. Stacked (biased) advisory teams are typically appointed by a control-oriented organization, or sapo grande, to recommend politically motivated policies, thus lending them a veneer of credibility and legitimacy. Stacked groups may be predominantly composed of employees of the dominant agency, or others whose first priority is maintaining smooth relations with the agency. Stacked groups often make recommendations in areas in which they have little expertise.

An examination of 32 recovery teams found that 76% of their members represented federal or state agencies, 11% were from nongovernmental conservation groups (private organizations), and only 8% from universities (Table 14.1). Needless to say, agency personnel have no monopoly on pertinent biological and social-science knowledge. As Clark and Harvey (1988) have noted, the black-footed ferret advisory team was composed almost exclusively of agency personnel who had no prior experience with ferrets or with managing small critically endangered populations, and W. B. King et al. (1977) and McFarlane (1992) make similar observations about the red-cockaded woodpecker recovery team.

When the decisions of stacked advisory groups are influenced by top-level agency personnel unfamiliar with the species, those decisions typically reflect the agency's political goals as well as recovery goals (Clark and Harvey 1988). When both types of goals are present, the political motives generally go unacknowledged. In some cases political goals may actually subvert the recovery goals (see Snyder and Snyder 1989 on the California condor program). This phenomenon, known as "goal displacement" (see Chapter 7), is the logical extension of battles for program control. Recovery programs can become powerful tools for legitimizing and enhancing organizational and individual power domains (Warwick 1975; Clark and Harvey 1988).

When the species' biological-recovery needs conflict with the dominant agency's political goals or philosophy, the agency may redefine the species' needs in terms of its own goals or objectives. In the black-footed ferret project, this phenomenon delayed captive breeding, impeded the collection of information important to recovery (genetic studies and reintroduction techniques), and postponed reintroduction outside Wyoming (see Chapters 7–9). In the recovery effort for red-cockaded woodpeckers, redefining the problem allowed for clear-cutting instead of uneven-aged timber management in the species' foraging areas, a practice that fragments habitat surrounding traditional colony sites (Jackson 1986; McFarlane 1992). Changes in problem definition also impeded important research on the California condor (Snyder and Snyder 1989).

The reports of stacked advisory groups typically consist of highlights from meetings instead of complete transactions (Loucks 1992). Such reports can misrepresent study results or meeting conclusions and further undermine the ability of outside experts to evaluate the program accurately.

An extreme case of team-stacking occurred in the red-cockaded woodpecker program, when a recovery team representing multiple organizations was disbanded and replaced by a single individual hired to formulate policy. In 1982 the red-cockaded woodpecker recovery team was disbanded and an employee of the U.S. Forest Service was given a contract to revise the recovery plan. A committee of biological specialists appointed by the American Ornithologists' Union was critical of the resulting recovery plan and of the mechanism by which it was developed (Ligon et al. 1986).

Stacking or eliminating recovery teams is a means to restrict the role of others and consolidate power. Reducing the influence of outside specialists assures control of information flow, which is the most powerful tool for legitimizing a particular doctrine. Indeed, the dominant agency or individual may feel threatened by people with alternative viewpoints and thus may eject them from the recovery program. When self-legitimization is an overriding goal, there are rarely methods of constructively resolving conflicting opinions. One of the most famous examples is the Craigheads' grizzly bear research in Yellowstone National

Species program	Number of recovery-team members representing:						Affiliation of team leader[b]
	Federal agency	State agency	University	Private organization	Industry	Self[a]	
American crocodile	3	2	0	1	0	0	State
Atlantic Coast piping plover	2	0	0	0	0	0	USFWS
Attwater's prairie chicken	1	1	1	1	0	0	University
Black-capped vireo	0	0	0	1	0	0	University
Black-footed ferret	1	0	0	0	0	1	?
California condor	4	2	0	4	0	0	USFWS
Dusky seaside sparrow	1	1	1	0	0	0	USFWS
Eastern brown pelican	3	3	1	0	0	0	State
Eastern cougar	1	0	0	0	0	0	USFWS
Eastern peregrine falcon	1	0	0	0	0	0	USFWS
Eastern timber wolf	5	3	0	0	0	0	State
Florida manatee	4	6	0	3	3	0	?
Florda panther (or puma)	5	4	0	0	0	0	USFWS
Florida snail kite	2	1	0	1	0	0	State
Grizzly bear	2	1	0	0	0	0	State
Hualapai Mexican vole	3	1	0	0	0	0	?
Kirtland's warbler	3	2	0	3	0	0	Private

Species							Affiliation
Least tern	1	0	0	0	0	0	USFWS
Light-footed clapper rail	3	3	2	1	1	1	USFWS
Mississippi sandhill crane	1	0	0	0	0	0	USFWS
Northern rocky mountain wolf	6	2	1	1	1	0	USFWS
Red-cockaded woodpecker	2	0	0	1	0	0	USFS
Red wolf	2	2	0	0	0	0	USFWS
Roseate tern	2	2	0	1	0	0	?
Salt marsh harvest and California clapper rail	3	1	0	0	0	0	?
Snail darter	1	2	0	0	0	0	State
Southern bald eagle	3	2	2	2	0	0	State
Southern sea otter	1	0	0	0	0	0	USFWS
Utah prairie dog	10	6	4	0	0	0	State
Whooping crane	2	2	1	1	0	0	USFWS
Wood stork	1	0	0	0	0	0	USFWS
Yuma clapper rail	3	2	0	0	0	0	State
All 32 programs (overall)	82 (47%)	50 (29%)	14 (8%)	20 (12%)	6 (3%)	2 (1%)	

Notes: These 32 recovery plans represent a sample of the vertebrate endangered-species programs that were in effect as of 1993 in the United States. Data were compiled by Courtney Conway.

a "Self" = Individual contractor.

b USFWS = U.S. Fish and Wildlife Service. A question mark indicates that the affiliation was not determined (in most cases because no team member was identified as leader).

Park. In that case, valuable long-term studies by independent researchers were eliminated, and the scientists who conducted them were replaced with agency personnel (Hornocker 1982). Another more recent example involved the work of Joel Berger and Carol Cunningham with rhinos in Namibia. Their investigations suggested that dehorning rhinos might not be the best conservation strategy, a finding that conflicted with existing government policy (Berger 1994; Brussard 1994). Even though they had kept the Namibian government informed through reports and drafts of manuscripts, after publication of their findings in *Science* (see Berger and Cunningham 1994) their research permits were not renewed.

Implementation Issues

Implementation, evaluation, and revision are the final three phases of the Brewer and deLeon (1983) policy model. Even when the first three phases produce an excellent plan, results ultimately depend on the plan's execution. Often the people who formulate plans lack crucial knowledge of important biological, technical, and social-science issues, and leave implementation plans vague. It is therefore important that policy be defined as clearly as possible at the outset. Otherwise, implementation can alter established policy, often consolidating substantial power in the hands of the implementing organizations and personnel (Yaffee 1982; Clark, Amato, et al. 1991). Those who implement policy can undermine an established plan in a variety of ways, including deliberate delaying tactics, yielding to parochial political pressures, and preventing an unbiased review of performance (Miller, Reading, et al. 1994).

Deliberate Delay   If the implementing agency opposes the policy it is charged with executing, policy execution can be deliberately delayed by failing to allocate sufficient funding, allocating funding to tangential work instead of the central project, raising last-minute obstacles that could have been easily resolved if revealed earlier (often called sandbag management), or intentionally failing to collect necessary data despite earlier agreement to do so. An example of the latter is Wyoming's failure to collect blood samples for genetic studies, despite recommendations by the Captive Breeding Specialist Group of the IUCN, agreement to do so, and funding for the work from Region 6.

Yielding to Local Political Pressures   Implementation can also be affected by local political and economic forces that oppose the recovery program for short-term economic reasons (Greenwalt 1988; Rohlf 1991). The Endangered Species Act bars consideration of economic and political factors during the process of identifying species in danger of extinction, but it fails to preclude these inhibitive factors from affecting the planning and implementation of recovery efforts. For example, land that hosted the last known red-cockaded woodpecker colony in Holly Springs National Forest was traded to a developer (Jackson et al. 1977). Similarly, property values combined with legal threats negatively influenced the implementation of a habitat-conservation plan for the Coachella Valley fringe-toed lizard *(Uma inornata)* (O'Connell 1992). In a third instance, political pressure from the shrimp-fishing industry prevented the National Marine Fisheries Service from enforcing or even clearly recommending the use of turtle excluder devices despite a decade of research demonstrating the benefits to endangered sea turtles and their minimal impact on shrimp catches (Allen 1990).

In reality, the ESA has not always succeeded in excluding economic and political factors from the initial listing process. Because of pressure from the U.S. Department of Interior and the timber industry, for instance, the U.S. Fish and Wildlife Service delayed listing the northern spotted owl as threatened (U.S. General Accounting Office 1989). The United States has succeeded in passing strong legislation to protect biodiversity but has not changed the basic political and economic incentives that militate for unsustainable overexploitation. As a result, vested economic interests can successfully use power plays and legal maneuvers to maintain access to land and resources at the expense of biodiversity (Salwasser 1990).

Dodging Critical Review   When self-legitimization is a high priority, organizations or sapos grandes may be reluctant to critically review their own performance (Yaffee 1982). They may close communication channels that would allow for outside critiques, or impede such critiques by coupling huge quantities of paperwork with a very brief time frame for evaluation and comment. Another strategy is to intentionally select a biased evaluating team, whose purpose is to endorse the program and discredit its critics. When honest and impartial evaluation of performance is not permitted, neither individuals nor organizations can be held accountable for their actions. As a result, recovery-plan implementation may be inefficient or actually misdirected.

FORMULATING A PLAN OF ACTION

The plan of action we propose employs a recovery team that integrates the best expertise, whether governmental or independent, into the planning process. It also introduces accountability into all phases of planning and implementation (Miller, Reading, et al. 1994). Such a cooperative panel of specialists would bring credibility and respect to the program and overcome a number of the previously identified pitfalls. Establishing a team of decision makers is also the first step in countering sapismo.

A sound recovery plan is crucial, but it cannot take the place of a team. Recovery plans spell out general goals, which is an important function, but they are difficult to keep timely because of rapidly evolving knowledge and events, combined with a slow approval process. Endangered-species management requires extreme flexibility, capacity to respond to changing circumstances (and mistakes), and an ability to take advantage of new opportunities and technologies quickly. These capabilities are best embodied by a team of specialists. The team should meet at least annually, and more frequently when necessary, to formulate recommendations for specific and pressing issues. And, of course, the problem should be accurately defined before strategies are developed. This point may sound basic, but too many programs seem to skip over problem definition, which can lead to an errant strategy.

The team should always include biologists who have substantial hands-on experience with the species. Representatives of the full range of biological perspectives can contribute skills and knowledge in such areas as genetics, habitat restoration, disease, and necessary biological techniques. It is equally important to include social scientists who can assess attitudes, economists who can predict economic benefits and costs, education and public-relations experts who can present the program to the public and raise necessary funds, organizational specialists who can help design effective organizational arrangements, attorneys who can address regulatory issues, and so on. These nonbiological experts can address specific problems in their respective fields that can be critical to a successful recovery program (and "in their fields" should be emphasized for all participants—an effective team has no room for a sapo grande). The composition of the team should also be fluid enough for advice to be obtained from any needed discipline.

The recovery team should not include—and in particular should not be chaired by—individuals whose primary function is to represent an agency. Interagency working groups are necessary to coordinate the tasks and responsibilities of implementation, but that is a very different duty from planning recovery. Membership on the recovery team should represent the best scientific and technical skill available, not the best skill available within the dominant agency. Political appointees pushing personal or agency agendas divert attention from recovery. It is important, however, for all team members to be aware of the political constraints within which agencies operate.

Scientific and conservation organizations could create a database of specialists qualified to serve on recovery teams. The agency mandated to direct recovery of endangered and threatened species could then cooperate with these organizations to form teams. The shared responsibility would make for teams composed of the best available expertise.

Team members should be shielded as much as possible from outside interference. Free flow of ideas and information is essential so that, during debate, criticism can be raised in a neutral context and evaluated in a rational way. The team should operate on a consensus basis, and the recommendations should be biologically and politically viable. Janis (1972) and Clark (n.d.) offer a number of excellent suggestions for avoiding "groupthink" and stimulating democratic discussion during meetings. It can be difficult to unify diverse perspectives, goals, and values, but an effective coordinator can enhance the exchange of information and ideas and keep participants on an equal footing. Clark, Crete, and Cada (1989) suggested that recovery teams function as free-standing entities parallel to the managing agency or agencies, as has been done in private businesses. We believe this is an excellent idea.

Recovery programs would also gain credibility if team decisions were published in a journal or the Federal Register. If some members disagree with a given decision, they should be allowed to write an accompanying dissenting opinion. The planning process should also be subject to periodic critical review by outside specialists in order to ensure a continuous focus on biologically sound efforts (Goldstein 1992; Marshall 1992). As a precedent, the National Science Foundation, the National Institutes of Health, and the U.S. Environmental Protection Agency have all established protocols for objective scientific and programmatic review.

Some of the above-mentioned recommendations have been implemented in decision-making on endangered species in Canada, where nongovernmental organizations contribute a great deal of scientific expertise (Prescott and Hutchins 1991). In the United States, the recovery team for pacific salmon species consisted of a group of specialists, not representatives of dominant agencies; they designed recovery efforts as a series of testable hypotheses and quickly modified management strategies as necessary (Volkman 1992). Similarly, in the black-footed ferret recovery program, an ad hoc team staffed by members of the Captive Breeding Specialist Group and the American Association of Zoological Parks and Aquariums provided expert advice to Wyoming and Region 6 that was critical in the inception and early success of the captive-breeding efforts.

Once the recovery team has outlined the program's priorities, it should send those recommendations to the national agency mandated to direct recovery of threatened and endangered species. It is crucial that national policy be determined at the national level. Local goals invariably differ from national recovery goals, and it would be far too chaotic for each region to develop its own program as part of a national effort. The establishment of national policies does not signify exclusion of local concerns, but their integration in a larger, consistent whole. The same principle applies to international cooperative efforts.

EXECUTING THE PLAN

When assigning implementation tasks, the federal agency mandated to direct recovery may wish to delegate some or all of its responsibilities to other organizations. For example, responsibility for captive breeding may be given to professionally managed zoological parks, field research may be allocated to independent researchers, or a population may be managed by a local wildlife agency. Formulation and execution of the plan need not be in the hands of a traditional federal or state agency. Other organizations—for example, Wildlife Conservation International, Jersey Preservation Trust, and the National Zoological Park—have historically brought high standards to recovery and reintroduction programs for endangered species.

If responsibilities are delegated, the arrangement should be contractual (Miller, Reading, et al. 1994). A contract reduces the probability of policy change during implementation and helps assure that all parties clearly understand their obligations and commitments. A contractual delineation of responsibilities could also reduce destructive conflict and power struggles. In the United States, such a contractual arrangement could be pursued, for example, through the permitting process of the U.S. Fish and Wildlife Service and Section 6 funding allocated to state agencies involved in endangered-species recovery efforts.

When programs involve more than one state, implementation must be a coordinated national effort. To promote this process, the permitting procedure could be shifted to the national level, and organizations wishing to participate in execution of the plan could submit proposals to the Federal Register for outside comment. Alternatively, proposals submitted to the U.S. Fish and Wildlife Service could be reviewed by the recovery team.

The contractual arrangement would also include a periodic (at least annual) review by the recovery team of progress to date, both to evaluate the contractor's performance and to revise policy recommendations. If the contractor fails to meet the contractual arrangement, the relationship could be terminated, and funding and permits extended to another contractor. In the black-footed ferret program, Region 6 had oversight authority that it did not always exercise. In politically delicate situations, a recommendation from the recovery team to extend or terminate a relationship with an implementing organization might relieve some of the pressure on the responsible agency. It may be impossible to prevent all deviations by implementing organizations, but the review process would allow such a situation to be rectified quickly.

In conclusion, the changes we have recommended would link power with responsibility, which would heighten overall performance in any recovery effort. A situation in which there is no expert team, no review, and no accountability can become tyrannical, producing problems like those recounted in this book. The fact that similar problems recur even though the cast of characters changes reinforces this analysis. Significant improvements can be made in the efficiency and effectiveness of endangered-species programs by addressing the organizational structure defining the base of operation. Our recommendations will harness the expertise of agencies and nongovernmental organizations efficiently to address conservation dilemmas. The resulting cooperation would promote sound policy goals and better use of information. Accountability during the policy-setting and implementation processes would make deviations from the plan more difficult. The synergistic effect of shared resources, both financial and human, would also disperse political pressure among several agencies, reducing the pressure on any single agency and producing better results in the process. That would be particularly advantageous in these difficult economic times, when cooperation and shared human and financial resources are rapidly becoming essential to a successful outcome.

15
DEFINING SUCCESS AND OTHER DILEMMAS

DEFINING SUCCESS FOR THE FERRET RECOVERY PROGRAM

Has the black-footed ferret recovery program been a success? The question is difficult to answer. Success means many things to many people; it can be measured using different time scales, and different criteria can produce different answers. Sometimes one method of evaluation masks deficiencies that another method reveals. For example, counting only the number of ferrets in captivity and reintroduced has created an impression of success, at least over the short term. These numbers are certainly a source of pride to recovery-program participants, and they represent a tremendous effort on behalf of the species. But they say nothing about efficient use of effort and resources, amount of genetic diversity conserved, unpursued opportunities, public support for the program, public attitudes about habitat destruction, broader issues of biodiversity, or what has been learned about black-footed ferret conservation and reintroduction.

Continuing to rely on narrow definitions of success hampers program evaluation (see Reading and Miller 1994). For instance, a recovery program can satisfy an overly narrow criterion even with inadequate and ineffective organizational arrangements. Organizational parameters should be used to evaluate how efficiently the whole process worked, not simply whether some limited objectives were achieved. In some cases, an animal's biology can mask organizational shortcomings (e.g., black rhinos and black-footed ferrets have vastly different reproductive potentials that would affect their apparent success in recovery programs). And increased human effort can partially overcome program inefficiencies, but usually by incurring greater costs and higher rates of burned-out biologists. Species with fewer biological advantages or less funding may go extinct if their recovery programs employ a poor organizational model. Because of organizational weaknesses, the black-footed ferret program has been saddled with poor information flow, delays that nearly caused the extinction of the wild population in 1985 and 1986, restricted use of outside expertise to produce proactive plans, high financial costs, and high levels of conflict that sapped the time and energy of participants.

Recovery programs may also progress without a rigorous use of science, experimental design, or adequate documentation. Numbers of animals may increase even when managers have little or no understanding of the mechanisms involved, so there may be no scientific basis to make adjustments when problems arise. In addition, without a solid base of knowledge to build on, there are fewer opportunities to improve efforts or to apply techniques to the reintroduction of other species. The first three black-footed ferret reintroductions (1991–93) lacked experimental design and were laden with confounding variables, making it difficult to determine whether the program was using the most efficient and cost-effective reintroduction technique. Such inability to evaluate the program slows the learning process. Identifying the optimum technique early means that the species will spend less time in captivity, minimizing the erosion of survival behaviors necessary for life in the wild. Determining appropriate techniques early on can also avoid saddling the program with a less-than-optimal method of operation.

Because conservation dollars and managerial time are both limited, efficiency is important both to the program at hand and to other programs that must compete for similar time and funding. Reintroduction programs are usually expensive, so their organizers should strive to limit the resources their programs consume by increasing efficiency and thus the likelihood that the species can be reestablished rapidly. This approach was not employed when Wyoming insisted that a new captive-breeding facility be constructed in their state although existing zoos could have been utilized, when research and management proposals were not sent out for peer review, or when research results were not applied in a timely fashion.

Recovery programs often make progress only at a cost to relationships between organizations. If the organizational design is poor, conflict between participants could poison future decisions involving the same agencies or other species in the same jurisdiction. For example, discussion of black-footed ferrets was delayed because of friction over grizzly bear management between Montana wildlife officials and Region 6. The black-footed ferret program may be one of the most strife-ridden in the United States, yet there has been no serious attempt at conflict resolution. Conflicts between agencies or with the public could prompt state agencies, ranchers, or resource extractors to lobby for weakening the Endangered Species Act.

Some recovery programs are handicapped by poor public relations. Species can be successfully established at a reintroduction site, but because the attitudes of the local public have been poorly assessed or addressed, other problems may arise in the same or different regions. For example, Montana residents feared changes in the black-footed ferret reintroduction plan because alterations had occurred in an earlier elk translocation there.

Finally, reintroduction programs may successfully establish a population but fail to educate the public or confront the broader issue of conserving biodiversity. The black-footed ferret can be a flagship species for conservation efforts, but the recovery program has not adequately addressed the prairie dog poisoning that is reducing biodiversity across the western Great Plains (see Chapter 11). In the future, the program's success may be defined by a few isolated and heavily managed black-footed ferret populations, while the actual species diversity of the prairie dog ecosystem continues to decline. Reintroduction could thus be labeled a success (at least from the perspective of agency self-aggrandizement), but in reality amount only to a cosmetic effort rather than true conservation.

In summary, captive breeding has produced an ample supply of black-footed ferrets, and three reintroductions have spawned several litters in the wild. So, using a short-term biological standard, the black-footed ferret program is cited as a model to be emulated. Yet, measured by the broader criteria we have discussed, the program is still far from "almost the conservation success of the century" as the director of the Wyoming Game and Fish Department termed it (*Casper Star-Tribune,* 22 October 1993). Broad criteria are essential to gauge the achievements of a reintroduction program and the ability of that program to serve as a model.

LEARNING FROM THE BLACK-FOOTED FERRET PROGRAM

Discussing the lessons learned from the black-footed ferret program is almost as complicated as defining success. Those involved in the recovery effort have all learned a great deal about the biology of the black-footed ferret and other issues pertinent to conservation, and the responsible agencies have adjusted their strategies after technical errors were detected. Yet we are still trying to recover individual species without adequately confronting the problems of the ecosystem on which they depend. Prairie dogs are still being poisoned, and more species dependent on them are being proposed for listing under the Endangered Species

Act. Though agencies continue to search for answers, they restrict their solutions within the paradigm that caused the original problem. Strategies such as block clearance (Chapter 11) are predicated on prairie dog poisoning and thus reinforce attitudes that promote destruction of the prairie and the species it shelters. Indeed, as long as the government sponsors poisoning campaigns, it will be very difficult to change attitudes about the role of prairie dogs on western grasslands. Federal endorsement of poisoning only encourages the negative perceptions that have persisted throughout the century.

A species cannot be separated from the habitat on which it depends; we have proposed a multifaceted solution to this issue in Chapter 11. The symptoms of conservation problems may be biological, but the root causes are social and political. Any cure limited to biology without addressing the other facets will fail. As we mentioned previously, animals' behaviors do not exist in isolation. The performance of a single behavioral trait depends on a host of external circumstances, or on other behaviors that must be simultaneously executed (for instance, predator-avoidance behaviors affect hunting strategies). Similarly, human "conservation behaviors" are intertwined. It is in this light that we have discussed legal aspects, habitat protection, attitudes and education, economic incentives to manage for diversity on the prairie dog ecosystem, organization structures for efficient planning, accountability for entities that make and implement policy, and biological techniques.

In terms of policy, the behavior of Wyoming and Region 6 has changed little throughout the life of the program. Early unresolved conflict produced a struggle for power, and Wyoming consolidated control at nearly every stage. Region 6, which has oversight authority, generally chose to avoid conflict and to appease Wyoming. Those appeasements only solidified Wyoming's grasp on the program.

The black-footed ferret recovery program is still centralized around Wyoming despite the need for an international scope. As Tim Clark (n.d.) points out, centralization is acceptable if the central point is the source of all information and ideas, but it rarely is. When an organization is oriented toward control, proposals from the periphery are seen as a threat to dominion, making the center more and more resistant to opinions originating outside its sphere of influence. In the black-footed ferret program, reaction to recommendations from the periphery was typically rapid and negative. That many of these recommendations were eventually adopted did not make for a more open response to the next proposal. Indeed, the next suggestion met the same type of roadblock. In other words, the black-footed ferret program learned how to adjust tactics, but it never learned how to improve the process of learning. The recovery effort resisted organizational learning because controlling participation was more important (Clark n.d.).

As an example, Clark and Harvey (1988) advocated the creation of task forces and project teams, and the inclusion of outside specialists in decision-making processes to make the recovery program more flexible and responsive. Wyoming responded in a memo, "How can horizontally coordinated task forces and project teams be controlled and directed to assure recovery of a species efficiently and economically?" (Tom Thorne, Wyoming Game and Fish Department, 10 January 1989). The point is not to control and direct but to democratically integrate different skills and viewpoints to generate solutions for complex problems. The dilemma with black-footed ferret recovery was not that groups with different ideas were involved (as Wyoming has maintained), but that the inflexible organizational structure could not extract benefits from those varied opinions.

The memo also stated that Clark and Harvey's recommendation promoted a negative image of Wyoming, which would hurt recovery by influencing states cooperating with Wyoming. This response blurs the interests of the species with the interests of Wyoming. Although criticism may affect the views of cooperators, silence may mean a continuation of program closure.

Collapsing the program around Wyoming has not only undermined the efficiency of recovery but may also have hurt the long-term funding prospects for ferrets. As a result, fewer and fewer people in the scientific and conservation communities had opportunities to participate. The loss of constituencies has translated into less advocacy at the national level, both within and outside the agencies. Charismatic as it is, the black-footed ferret competes in a stringent fiscal environment with many other deserving species. It is noteworthy that the lack of advocacy at the national level has coincided with declining budgets for the black-footed ferret. The only antidote to this declining interest is to open up the program to national participation. Doing so will bring expertise to bear on the difficult problems of recovery and will also increase public support and funding through both private organizations and the government.

It is our contention that Region 6 failed to make ferret recovery a national program. It may have been easiest for Region 6 to acquiesce to Wyoming's agenda in the short term, but that strategy has probably impaired recovery over the long run. People, or agencies, in a position to improve conservation should not simply throw money at a problem but invest time and attention as well (Frazier 1993). Without funding, conservation efforts will fail, but financial investment without commitment creates the foundation for empire-building.

We reiterate that local views must be recognized, but not at the expense of a broader perspective. The U.S. Fish and Wildlife Service can accomplish that broader outlook by establishing interdisciplinary teams of specialists to produce strategies by consensus and by linking federal funding to a contract specifying adherence to the plan. A well-organized planning process and clearly defined roles during implementation would do a great deal to discourage destructive conflict. Recovery programs do not necessarily have to be headed by government agencies. The U.S. Fish and Wildlife Service has contractually delegated responsibilities to private groups, a model that should perhaps be investigated further. It is noteworthy, however, that the same organization or agency can appear as the hero in one case and the villain in another. Organizations are not innately good or bad, and their performance often depends on how power and resources are dispersed and whose interests are at stake. This is another reason that interdisciplinary teams are important.

Regardless of who formulates and enacts policy, we hope the U.S. Fish and Wildlife Service will think long and hard before assigning power without oversight to another endangered-species program. The cost in money, time, and human effort for each step forward in the black-footed ferret program has been far greater than necessary.

Active federal attention and a solid Endangered Species Act will be necessary in a coordinated effort to protect diversity. Although attempts to weaken the legislation could have tragic consequences, a trend is apparent toward diminishing the effectiveness of both the Act and federal authority. Perhaps the weak role played by Region 6 in black-footed ferret recovery can provide an example of what could happen in other conservation efforts if federal oversight is further diluted by state or local interests.

In conclusion, a quick survey of the conservation landscape reveals that the black-footed ferret saga is not unique, and the continuing decline of diversity on the prairie dog ecosystem indicates that the recovery effort should encompass more than the ferret. We do not know what the future holds for black-footed ferrets and other members of the prairie dog ecosystem. We only hope that this account of the ferret and the obstacles to its recovery will stimulate thought about our present course, and in some small way help prevent other species from passing "gentle into that good night."

EPILOGUE

Much has happened since the manuscript for this book was completed in fall 1994. That year black-footed ferrets were reintroduced into Wyoming, South Dakota, and Montana. Pre-release conditioning resulted in short-term survival rates roughly three times higher than those of cage-raised animals released without conditioning (and the difference was highly significant, $P < 0.001$; D. Biggins pers. com.). Long-term survival—the percentage of animals that lived to produce a litter the following spring—was also significantly higher. Fewer than 2% of the unconditioned cage-raised animals but 20% of the pre-release conditioned animals lived to reproduce ($P < 0.01$; D. Biggins pers. com.).

The U.S. Fish and Wildlife Service declared in a memo that in 1995 all reintroduced animals should be pre-release conditioned (P. Gertler, U.S. Fish and Wildlife Service memo, 18 August 1995), which represents a potential change of direction for the recovery program. Until this time, the emphasis was on producing animals in captivity, and the reintroduction phase essentially had to work with the cards it was dealt. Indeed, the previous recommendation to counter low survival of cage-raised animals after release was to construct new captive facilities to produce more animals. This approach would be expensive because, compared with conditioned ferrets, at least three times as many unconditioned ferrets would need to be raised and released to result in the same number of survivors. Building new facilities would also delay reintroductions, and behaviors necessary for survival in the wild would be likely to erode with each additional generation in captivity. Now perhaps the program is moving toward a focus on quality, not just quantity, of animals produced. That is, researchers pinpoint the traits necessary for ferrets to survive in the wild, and captive-breeding schemes are then adjusted to best facilitate the acquisition of those traits.

211

Black-footed ferret production in captivity was relatively low again in 1995, with only 189 kits living as of 18 August (P. Gertler, U.S. Fish and Wildlife Service memo, 18 August 1995). In 1995 black-footed ferrets were released only in Montana and South Dakota because plague had diminished the prairie dog population at the Wyoming reintroduction site. Ferrets had been released in Wyoming for four years with little success, but they are adjusting very well to the wild in Montana. The U.S. Fish and Wildlife Service visited Chihuahua, Mexico, to investigate the largest remaining black-tailed prairie dog complex in North America, and the two countries are discussing a cooperative reintroduction on that complex. The Arizona reintroduction site is also ready.

As for policy, in fall 1995 the Service began to cooperate with the American Zoo and Aquarium Association Conservation Office to evaluate the black-footed ferret recovery program. The review will be performed by a team of species-recovery specialists. The U.S. Fish and Wildlife Service also planned to take over the Wyoming captive-breeding facility in November 1995 (a move facilitated by Wyoming's desire to pull out of the program after the collapse of its reintroduction site). In addition, there is renewed discussion of implementing a version of the 1992 "7-Point Plan" and replacing the Species Survival Plan chair with a joint chair held by representatives of the U.S. Fish and Wildlife Service and the zoo community. Federal funding for ferret recovery has declined, but private donations, notably from PIC Technologies, have kept the program afloat.

Overall, the black-footed ferret recovery program is beginning to turn in the right direction. It is our fervent hope that the species can survive the learning process, and once again run through the wild prairie night.

APPENDIX: TAXONOMIC LIST OF WILDLIFE MENTIONED IN THE TEXT

MAMMALS

Carnivora

Ursidae
> *Ursus arctos*—grizzly bear

Procyonidae
> *Procyon lotor*—raccoon
> *Nasua narica*—coati

Mustelidae
> *Mustela nigripes*—black-footed ferret
> *Mustela vison*—American mink
> *Mustela eversmanni*—Siberian ferret
> *Mustela putorius*—European ferret
> *Mustela erminea*—ermine
> *Mustela frenata*—long-tailed weasel
> *Mustela stromeri*—Stromer's polecat
> *Mustela nivalis*—least weasel
> *Mustela lutreola*—European mink
> *Taxidea taxus*—American badger
> *Martes pennanti*—fisher
> *Martes americana*—pine marten
> *Martes zibellina*—sable
> *Mephitis mephitis*—striped skunk
> *Spilogale putorius*—spotted skunk
> *Gulo gulo*—wolverine
> *Lutra canadensis*—river otter

Canidae
> *Canis latrans*—coyote
> *Canis familiaris*—domestic dog
> *Canis rufus*—red wolf
> *Canis lupus*—gray (timber) wolf
> *Vulpes velox*—swift fox

Felidae
> *Lynx rufus*—bobcat
> *Felis cattus*—domestic cat
> *Felis concolor*—puma (or panther)
> *Acinonyx jubatus*—cheetah

Rodentia

Sciuridae
> *Cynomys ludovicianus*—black-tailed prairie dog
> *Cynomys mexicanus*—Mexican prairie dog
> *Cynomys leucurus*—white-tailed prairie dog
> *Cynomys gunnisoni*—Gunnison's prairie dog
> *Cynomys parvidens*—Utah prairie dog
> *Spermophilus armatus*—Uinta ground squirrel

Muridae
> *Lagurus curtatus*—sagebrush vole
> *Microtus montanus*—montane vole
> *Neotoma* spp.—woodrats
> *Peromyscus maniculatus*—deer mouse
> *Rattus norvegicus*—Norway rat

Erethizontidae
> *Erithizon dorsatum*—porcupine

Lagomorpha
> *Sylvilagus nuttalli*—Nuttall's cottontail

213

Artiodactyla
Cervidae
    Cervus elaphus—elk
Antilocapridae
    Antilocapra americana—pronghorn
    antelope
Bovidae
    Bison bison—bison
    Capra ibex—ibex
    Oryx leucoryx—Arabian oryx
    Oryx gazella—fringe-eared oryx

Primates
Callitrichidae
    Leontopithecus rosalia—golden lion
    tamarin
Pongidae
    Gorilla gorilla—gorilla

Perissodactyla
Rhinocerotidae
    Diceros bicornis—black rhinoceros

Proboscidea
Elephantidae
    Loxodonta africana—African elephant

BIRDS

Struthioniformes
Struthionidae
    Struthio camelus—ostrich

Anseriformes
Anatidae
    Anas platyrhynchos—mallard
    Cygnus buccinator—trumpeter swan

Gruiformes
Gruidae
    Grus americana—whooping crane

Charadriiformes
Charadriidae
    Charadrius montanus—mountain
    plover

Falconiformes
Cathartidae
    Gymnogyps californianus—California
    condor
Accipitridae
    Aquila chrysaetos—golden eagle
    Buteo regalis—ferruginous hawk
    Parabuteo unicinctus—Harris' hawk
Falconidae
    Falco mexicanus—prairie falcon

Galliformes
Phasianidae
    Colinus virginianus—masked bobwhite

Strigiformes
Strigidae
    Bubo virginianus—great horned owl
    Strix occidentalis—spotted owl
    Athene cunicularia—burrowing owl

Piciformes
Picidae
    Picoides borealis—red-cockaded
    woodpecker

Passeriformes
Muscicapidae
    Turdus grayi—clay-colored robin
Emberizidae
    Calamospiza melanocorys—lark
    bunting
    Aimophila cassinii—Cassin's sparrow
    Junco phaeonotus—yellow-eyed junco
Fringillidae
    Loxioides bailleui—pallila

REPTILES

Testudines
Testudinidae
    Gopherus flavomarginatus—Bolson
    tortoise

Squamata
Iguanidae
    Uma inornata—Coachella Valley
    fringe-toed lizard

NOTES

1. THE BLACK-FOOTED FERRET

1. In the field, we noticed an immediate response to zipper or Velcro noises at a distance of 9–12 meters.
2. During our winter searches at Meeteetse, we saw instances where wild black-footed ferrets were able to locate prairie dog burrows under a 25-centimeter blanket of snow. Because white-tailed prairie dogs were hibernating at the time and prairie dog mounds were not visible under the heavy snow, the burrows were presumably located by smell alone.
3. Herter (1939, as cited in C. M. King 1989) reported that weasels could distinguish between different letters for a food reward.
4. That specimen no longer exists (see E. Anderson et al. 1986). This early description of the species was controversial until 1877, when Elliot Coues, then curator of the Smithsonian Institution, obtained several new black-footed ferret specimens (Coues 1877).

3. REPRODUCTION AND DEVELOPMENT OF THE YOUNG

1. Homeothermy and hair probably evolved together in early mammals as an adaptation to nocturnal life and cooler climates; keeping the coat clean is an essential task if the fur is to retain its insulative value (Eisenberg 1981).
2. C. M. King (1989) has suggested an additional advantage of delayed implantation for ermine. Juvenile ermine are sexually precocious before they leave the maternal nest, so the mother and her daughters are all ready for breeding at the same time. Any male

that finds a den can copulate with all the females in the family. Normally, a male would have to cover a wide area to find a similar number of mates. By finding a nest, the male ermine can maximize his genetic contribution to the next generation with much less travel. Not only that, but only the adult female will resist. The juveniles then carry the blastocyst, which takes very little energy away from their own growth, and they are assured of a litter in their first year.

3. This homogenous food base and dependence on the thermal stability of deep burrows also explain why black-footed ferrets scheduled for reintroduction should not be imprinted on other prey, such as rabbits, as some have suggested. Rabbits in North America are widely dispersed and often live in shallow scrapes under bushes. They are not like the burrow-dwelling rabbits of Europe that reside in the close proximity of a warren. North American ground squirrels excavate deep burrows, but they are generally much smaller than the ground squirrels used by Siberian ferrets. The black-footed ferret, therefore, would have to spend a considerable amount of time and energy enlarging a ground squirrel tunnel in order to simply move through it.

4. ESTABLISHING A HOME ON THE RANGE

1. The bound is the most common gait for black-footed ferrets, and they employ the quadruped, alternating cross-step for about 2% of the distance traveled, usually when they are near a burrow entrance (Clark, Richardson, et al. 1986).

2. Tinbergen (1968) defined aggression as an approach toward an opponent that inflicted damage of some kind. He divided intraspecific aggression into two categories, defensive and offensive. Many of the black-footed ferret agonistic reactions we saw in captivity appeared to be defensive, probably because of caging limitations. Offensive and defensive actions can blend, however, because of retaliation to discourage further attack.

5. FINDING FOOD WHILE AVOIDING BEING EATEN

1. Our experiments with Siberian ferrets showed that they could detect meat in a burrow behind plugs of dirt that were two-thirds of a meter in length (Miller, Biggins, et al. 1990a).

2. It perhaps goes without saying that the two diet studies were both of black-footed ferrets living on prairie dog towns, introducing some bias into the results. However, although not unexpected, the results emphasize the linkage between ferrets and prairie dogs not observed in the food habits of some other carnivores associated with the prairie dog ecosystem.

6. ASSESSING POPULATION ECOLOGY OF BLACK-FOOTED FERRETS

1. During routine animal checks in the 1991 reintroduction, two ferrets were found with clay accumulated on their collars and those collars, which had no Teflon coating, were removed (Biggins, Miller, and Hanebury 1992). During 1992, the added Teflon coating prevented clay accumulation problems (Biggins, Godbey, and Vargas 1993).
2. Siberian ferrets have larger litters than black-footed ferrets, so perhaps a study comparing habitat stability between colonial rodents in Siberia and prairie dogs in North America would be an interesting test of this hypothesis.
3. Similarly, young pine marten males occupying poorer quality habitat have home ranges significantly larger than adult males. In this species, the limiting factor is access to high-quality subnivean resting sites, which are rare on poorer quality habitat. Younger martens spend significantly more time traversing their habitat in search of such sites. Thus they are not only exposed to higher bioenergetic and thermoregulatory demands but are also more likely to be exposed to other factors such as predators and trapping, explaining relatively high juvenile mortality.

7. EXTINCTION IN THE WILD: THE LIGHT DIMS

1. For example, a 1943 *Wyoming Wild Life* article stated that a proposed bill to grant federal control of wildlife on federally owned lands was "an unlawful appropriation of the property of a state," and the Wyoming Game and Fish Commission echoed that sentiment by passing a resolution stating the bill was a "transgression upon the rights of the State and its citizens, and is a direct violation of the State Constitution" (Bagley 1943).
2. In 1977 the U.S. Fish and Wildlife Service had asked states to review the status of bobcats for listing under Appendix II of the Convention on International Trade in Endangered Species (CITES). The Service speculated that the species may become threatened without trade regulations. The states "deeply resented" the federal interference and diversion of resources, and they ultimately opposed participation in CITES because it threatened state control (Tober 1989).

8. CAPTIVE BREEDING

1. Black-footed ferrets at Sybille were kept in elevated cages with welded wire sides and top and a plywood floor. The cages were either 1.22 × 2.44 × 0.61 meters or 0.81 × 1.52 × 0.61 meters. Animals had access to both internal and external nest boxes. One external nest box was attached to the back of the cage and the other was placed on the

floor but connected to the elevated cage through tubing that simulated a tunnel. The diet was a mixture of ground prairie dog mixed with commercial mink chow. When a female entered estrus, she was moved at night to the male's cage via her nest box, and the process was viewed from the next room by means of a video camera. The next morning, and sometimes earlier, she was returned to her cage. At the Conservation and Research Center in Front Royal, Virginia, black-footed ferrets were kept in larger pens, approximately 3×4 meters, that had a dirt floor. Those pens included nest boxes and tubing for tunnels. When a female entered estrus, a slide was opened between her pen and the male's pen for the night.

9. BACK TO THE WILD

1. In answer to Dave Barry's speculation, we did not fight over who ran the badger—we took turns.

11. CONSERVING THE PRAIRIE DOG ECOSYSTEM

1. However, as a result of a lawsuit from the Fund for Animals and others, the U.S. Fish and Wildlife Service has agreed to decide the fate of candidates no later than 1995.

13. LEGAL DIMENSIONS OF BLACK-FOOTED FERRET RECOVERY

1. Endangered Species Act of 1973 (ESA), 16 U.S.C. § 1531 et seq. (1994).
2. National Forest Management Act of 1976 (NFMA), 16 U.S.C. §§ 1600–1614 (1994).
3. Only the NFMA is explicit in mandating protection of biological diversity. The ESA diversity mandate is implied from its policy objectives; *see, e.g.,* S. Rept. No. 93-307, 93d Cong., 1st sess., 300, *reprinted in* 1973 U.S. Code Cong. & Admin. News 2989–2990.
4. *Tenn. Valley Auth. v. Hill,* 437 U.S. 153, 177 (1978).
5. 16 U.S.C. § 1533(b)(3)(A).
6. 50 C.F.R. ch. 2 § 222.23(a) (1995).
7. 56 Fed. Reg. 58804 (1991).
8. 16 U.S.C. § 1533(b)(3)(C)(iii). Citizen enforcement of all nondiscretionary Section 4 obligations is allowed under Section 11, 16 U.S.C. § 1540(g)(1)(C), so this provision extends enforcement protection to a number of candidate species.
9. 16 U.S.C. § 1533(b)(3)(C)(iii).

10. *See, e.g.,* 12-Month Finding for a Petition to List the Swift Fox as Endangered 60 Fed. Reg. 31663 (1995).
11. *Northern Spotted Owl v. Hodel,* 716 F. Supp. 479, 483 (W.D. Wash. 1988).
12. 16 U.S.C. § 1536(a)(2).
13. *Carson-Truckee Water Conservancy Dist. v. Watt,* 741 F.2d 257 (9th Cir. 1984).
14. 16 U.S.C.A. § 1533(a), (b).
15. 16 U.S.C.A. § 1539(j)(2)(A).
16. 41 Fed. Reg. 790 (1982).
17. 56 Fed. Reg. 23830 (1991).
18. Letter from D. Dobel, assistant director, Region 6, to U.S. Fish and Wildlife Service field supervisors, 23 August 1991.
19. 50 C.F.R. § 17.80(b) (1995); 16 U.S.C. § 1539(j)(2)(B).
20. 16 U.S.C. § 1539(j)(2)(C)(i).
21. However, 1988 amendments to Section 4 may have reinstated some protection if there is a "significant risk" to the species. 16 U.S.C. § 1533(b)(3)(C)(iii).
22. H.R. Conf. Rept. No. 835, 97th Cong., 2d sess., 34 (1982).
23. 58 Fed. Reg. 29179 (1993).
24. U.S. Congress, Office of Technology Assessment, OTA-F-330, *Technologies to Maintain Biological Diversity* at 224 (1987).
25. 16 U.S.C. § 1533(a)(3)(A).
26. 16 U.S.C. § 1533(b)(2).
27. 16 U.S.C. § 1532(19) defines "take" as "harass, harm, pursue, hunt, shoot, wound, kill, trap, capture, or collect, or attempt to engage in any such conduct."
28. 50 C.F.R. § 17.3.
29. *Sierra Club v. Lyng,* 694 F. Supp. 1260, 1271–1272 (E.D. Tex. 1988).
30. *Palila v. Haw. Dept. of Land & Natural Resources,* 649 F. Supp. 1070 (D. Haw. 1986), *aff'd,* 852 F.2d 1106 (9th Cir. 1988).
31. *Babbitt v. Sweet Home Chapter of Communities for a Greater Oregon,* 132 L. Ed. 2d 597 (1995).
32. H.R. Rept. No. 93-412, 93d Cong., 1st sess., 4–5 (1973).
33. *Sierra Club v. Clark,* 577 F. Supp. 783 (D. Minn. 1984).
34. Presumably, lack of good-faith efforts to implement recovery plans could be actionable. See, e.g., *Greenpeace Int'l, Inc. v. Baldridge,* No. 86-0129 (D. Haw. 1988), *cited in* Rohlf 1988 (p. 89 n.15).
35. 16 U.S.C. § 1604(g)(3)(B).
36. 16 U.S.C. § 1609(a) and the Bankhead–Jones Act of 1937, 7 U.S.C. § 1010 et seq. (1994).
37. 36 C.F.R. § 213.3 (1995).
38. 36 C.F.R. § 219, § 219.20 (1995).
39. 36 C.F.R. § 219.27(g).
40. 36 C.F.R. § 219.3.
41. 36 C.F.R. § 219.19.
42. 36 C.F.R. § 219.19.

43. 60 Fed. Reg. 18895 (1995).

44. 36 C.F.R. § 219.19(a)(1).

45. *Seattle Audubon Society v. Evans,* 771 F. Supp. 1081 (W.D. Wash. 1991).

46. 36 C.F.R. § 219.19(a)(7).

47. 36 C.F.R. § 219.19(a)(7).

48. 60 Fed. Reg. 18886 (1995).

49. 60 Fed. Reg. 18894 (1995).

50. 60 Fed. Reg. 18895.

51. The National Environmental Policy Act of 1969 (NEPA), 42 U.S.C. §§ 4331–4370, § 4331(a), (b) (1994).

52. 42 U.S.C. § 4332(2).

53. See, e.g., *Natural Resource Defense Council, Inc. v. Hodel,* 865 F.2d 288, 294 (D.C. Cir. 1988).

54. The Federal Lands Policy Management Act of 1976 (FLPMA), 43 U.S.C. §§ 1701–1734, § 1701(a)(8) (1994).

55. 43 U.S.C. § 1701(a)(11).

56. *See, e.g.,* U.S. Congress, Office of Technology Assessment, OTA-F-330, *Technologies to Maintain Biological Diversity* at 55 (1987).

57. *See, e.g.,* 16 U.S.C. § 1531(a)(3).

58. *See* H.R. Rept. No. 93-412, 93d Cong., 1st sess., 4–5 (1973), which states that genetic variations are "potential resources."

59. Hearings on H.R. 4335 before the Subcomm. on Natural Resources, Agricultural Research, and Environment, of the House Comm. on Science, Space, and Technology, 100th Cong., 2d sess. (9 June 1988), *cited in* Carlson 1988 (p. 34).

60. 40 C.F.R. § 1508.25(a) (1995).

61. *Hodel,* 865 F.2d 298–300.

62. *Hodel,* 865 F.2d 300.

63. *North Dakota v. United States,* 460 U.S. 300 (1983).

64. C. Wright, A. Miller, and E. Cooper, *Federal Practice and Procedure* vol. 13B, § 3566 at 1102 (1984), cited with approval in *Guaranty Nat'l Ins. Co. v. Gates,* 916 F.2d 508, 512 (9th Cir. 1990).

65. The Migratory Bird Treaty Act of 1918, 16 U.S.C. §§ 703–711 (1994).

66. Remarks of Senator Tunney, Senate Consideration and Passage of S. 1983, with Amendments, Cong. Rec., 24 July 1973, *reprinted in* Committee on Environment and Public Works, Ser. No. 97-6, *A Legislative History of the Endangered Species Act of 1973* at 385 (1982).

67. *See* Remarks of Mrs. Sullivan, House Agreement to the Conference Report on S. 1981 Endangered Species Act of 1973, Cong. Rec., 20 December 1973, reprinted in *A Legislative History of the ESA* at 476.

68. Authorization of Section 6 of the Endangered Species Act of 1973, H.R. Rept. No. 95-333, 95th Cong., 1st sess. (16 May 1977), reprinted in *A Legislative History of the ESA* at 608–609.2.

REFERENCES CITED

Agnew, W., D. W. Uresk, and R. M. Hansen. 1986. Flora and fauna associated with prairie dog colonies and adjacent ungrazed mixed-grass prairie in western South Dakota. Journal of Range Management 39:135–39.

Alcock, J. 1984. Animal Behavior: An Evolutionary Approach. Sunderland, Mass.: Sinauer Associates.

Allen, C. H. 1990. Give headstarting a chance. Marine Turtle Newsletter 51:16–21.

Altmann, S. A. 1958. Avian mobbing behavior and predator recognition. Condor 58:241–53.

Alvarez, K. 1993. Twilight of the Panther: Biology, Bureaucracy and Failure in an Endangered Species Program. Sarasota, Fla.: Myakka River Publishing.

Anderson, E. 1977. Pleistocene Mustelidae (Mammalia, Carnivora) from Fairbanks, Alaska. Bulletin of the Museum of Comparative Zoology 148:1–21.

———. 1989. The phylogeny of mustelids and the systematics of ferrets. Pp. 10–20 *in* Conservation Biology of the Black-Footed Ferret. Edited by U. S. Seal, E. T. Thorne, S. H. Anderson, and M. A. Bogan. New Haven, Conn.: Yale University Press.

Anderson, E., S. C. Forrest, T. W. Clark, and L. Richardson. 1986. Paleobiology, biogeography, and systematics of the black-footed ferret, *Mustela nigripes* (Audubon and Bachman, 1851). Great Basin Naturalist Memoirs 8:11–62.

Anderson, J. L. 1986. Restoring a wilderness: The reintroduction of wildlife to an African national park. International Zoo Yearbook 24–25:192–99.

Anderson, S. 1972. Mammals of Chihuahua: Taxonomy and distribution. Bulletin of the American Museum of Natural History 148.

Anderson, S. H., and D. B. Inkley, editors. 1985. Black-Footed Ferret Workshop Proceedings, 18–19 September 1984 (Laramie, Wyo.). Cheyenne: Wyoming Game and Fish Department.

Apfelbach, R. 1978. A sensitive phase for the development of olfactory preference in ferrets (*Mustela putorius* F. furo L.). Zeitschrift für Säugetierkunde 43:289–95.

———. 1986. Imprinting on prey odours in ferrets (*Mustela putorius* F. furo L.) and its neural correlates. Behavioural Processes 12:363–81.

Arthur, L. M., R. L. Gunn, E. H. Carpenter, and W. W. Shaw. 1977. Predator control: The public view. Transactions of the North American Wildlife and Natural Resources Conference 42:137–45.

Audubon, J. J., and J. Bachman. 1851. The Viviparous Quadrupeds of North America. New York: V. G. Audubon Press.

Ballou, J. D., and B. Oakleaf. 1989. Demographic and genetic captive-breeding recommendations for black-footed ferrets. Pp. 247–67 *in* Conservation Biology of the Black-Footed Ferret. Edited by U. S. Seal, E. T. Thorne, S. H. Anderson, and M. A. Bogan. New Haven, Conn.: Yale University Press.

Barnes, A. M. 1993. A review of plague *(Yersinia pestis)* infection and its relevance to prairie dog populations and the black-footed ferret. Pp. 28–37 *in* Management of Prairie Dog Complexes for Black-Footed Ferret Reintroduction Sites. Edited by J. Oldemeyer, D. Biggins, B. Miller, and R. Crete. U.S. Fish and Wildlife Service Biological Report no. 13. Denver: U.S. Fish and Wildlife Service.

Bath, A. J. 1989. The public and wolf restoration in Yellowstone National Park. Society and Natural Resources 2:297–306.

Baum, M. J., and M. S. Erskine. 1984. Effect of neonatal gonadectomy and administration of testosterone on coital masculinization in the ferret. Endocrinology 115:2440–44.

Baum, M. J., and S. A. Tobert. 1986. Effect of prenatal exposure to aramatase inhibitor, testosterone, or antiandrogen on the development of feminine sexual behavior in both sexes. Physiology and Behavior 37:111–18.

Bean, M. J. 1983. The Evolution of National Wildlife Law. New York: Praeger Publishers.

———. 1992. Issues and controversies in the forthcoming reauthorization battle. Endangered Species Update 9:1–4.

Beck, B. B., D. G. Kleiman, J. M. Dietz, I. Castro, C. Carvalho, A. Martins, and B. Rettberg-Beck. 1991. Losses and reproduction in the reintroduced golden lion tamarins *(Leontopithecus rosalia)*. Dodo, Journal of the Jersey Wildlife Preservation Trust 27:50–61.

Beck, B. B., L. G. Rapaport, M. R. Stanley Price, and A. C. Wilson. 1993. Reintroduction of captive-raised animals. Pp. 265–86 *in* Creative Conservation: Interactive Management of Wild and Captive Animals. Edited by P. J. S. Olney, G. M. Mace, and A. T. C. Feistner. London: Chapman and Hall.

Bekoff, M. J. 1972. The development of social interaction, play, and metacommunication in mammals: An ethological perspective. Quarterly Review of Biology 47:412–29.

Bekoff, M. 1979. Social play behavior. Bioscience 34:228–33.

Bell, W. R. 1918. Cooperative campaigns for the control of ground squirrels, prairie dogs, and jack rabbits. U.S. Department of Agriculture Yearbook 1917:225–33.

———. 1921. Death to the rodents. U.S. Department of Agriculture Yearbook 1920:421–38.

Berg, W. E. 1982. Reintroduction of fisher, pine marten, and river otter. Pp. 159–73 *in* Midwest Furbearer Management. Edited by G. C. Sanderson. Urbana-Champaign: Office of Printing Services, University of Illinois at Urbana-Champaign.

Berger, J. 1994. Black-rhino conservation. Science 264:757.

Berger, J., and C. Cunningham. 1994. Active interaction and conservation: Africa's pachyderm problem. Science 263:1241–42.

Bertram, B. C. R. 1980. Vigilance and group sizes in ostriches. Animal Behaviour 28:278–86.

Bertram, B. C. R., and D. P. Moltu. 1986. Reintroducing red squirrels into Regent's Park. Mammal Review 16:81–88.

Biggins, D. E., and K. A. Fagerstone. 1984. Movements and activity of black-footed ferrets *(Mustela nigripes)* [abstract]. Sixty-fourth annual meeting of the American Society of Mammalogists.

Biggins, D. E., J. Godbey, and A. Vargas. 1993. Influence of pre-release experience on reintroduced black-footed ferrets *(Mustela nigripes)*. Internal report, 27 May 1993, U.S. Fish and Wildlife Service, Fort Collins, Colo.

Biggins, D. E., L. H. Hanebury, B. J. Miller, and R. A. Powell. 1990. Release of Siberian polecats *(M. eversmanni)* on a prairie dog colony [abstract]. Seventieth annual meeting of the American Society of Mammalogists.

Biggins, D. E., L. H. Hanebury, B. J. Miller, R. A. Powell, and C. Wemmer. 1991. Release of Siberian ferrets *(Mustela eversmanni)* to facilitate reintroduction of black-footed ferrets. Internal report, U.S. Fish and Wildlife Service, Fort Collins, Colo.

Biggins, D. E., B. J. Miller, and L. H. Hanebury. 1992. First reintroduction of the black-footed ferret. Internal report, U.S. Fish and Wildlife Service, Fort Collins, Colo.

Biggins, D., B. Miller, L. Hanebury, B. Oakleaf, A. Farmer, R. Crete, and A. Dood. 1993. A system for evaluating black-footed ferret habitat. Pp. 73–92 *in* Management of Prairie Dog Complexes for Black-Footed Ferret Reintroduction Sites. Edited by J. Oldemeyer, D. Biggins, B. Miller, and R. Crete. U.S. Fish and Wildlife Service Biological Report no. 13. Denver: U.S. Fish and Wildlife Service.

Biggins, D. E., M. H. Schroeder, S. C. Forrest, and L. Richardson. 1985. Movements and habitat relationships of radio-tagged black-footed ferrets. Pp. 11.1–11.17 *in* Black-Footed Ferret Workshop Proceedings, 18–19 September 1984 (Laramie, Wyo.). Edited by S. H. Anderson and D. B. Inkley. Cheyenne: Wyoming Game and Fish Department.

———. 1986. Activity of radio-tagged black-footed ferrets. Great Basin Naturalist Memoirs 8:135–40.

Bishop, N. G., and J. L. Culbertson. 1976. Decline of prairie dog towns in southwestern North Dakota. Journal of Range Management 29:217–20.

Boggess, E. K. 1982. The public and the furbearer resource. Pp. 93–106 *in* Midwest Furbearer Management. Edited by G. C. Sanderson. Urbana-Champaign: Office of Printing Services, University of Illinois at Urbana-Champaign.

Bolles, R. C. 1970. Species specific defense reactions and avoidance learning. Psychological Review 77:32–48.

Booth, W. 1988. Reintroducing a political animal. Science 241:156–58.

Boyle, R. H. 1993. The killing fields. Sports Illustrated 78(12): 61–69.

Brewer, G. D., and P. deLeon. 1983. The Foundations of Policy Analysis. Homewood, Ill.: Dorsey Press.

Bronikowski, J., B. Beck, and M. Power. 1989. Innovation, exhibition and conservation: Free-ranging tamarins at the National Zoological Park. Pp. 540–46 in AAZPA (American Association of Zoological Parks and Aquariums) Annual Proceedings. Wheeling, W.Va.: AAZPA.

Bronson, G. W. 1968. The fear of novelty. Psychological Bulletin 69:350–58.

Brown, J. 1971. Mammals on mountaintops: Nonequilibrium insular biogeography. American Naturalist 105:467–78.

Brown, J. H., and R. C. Lasiewski. 1972. Metabolism of weasels: The costs of being long and thin. Ecology 53:939–43.

Brown, P. J., and M. J. Manfredo. 1987. Social values defined. Pp. 12–23 in Valuing Wildlife: Economic and Social Perspectives. Edited by B. J. Decker and G. R. Goff. Boulder, Colo.: Westview Press.

Brussard, P. F. 1994. Science and conservation agencies: Still an uneasy partnership [President's Column]. Conservation Biology Newsletter 1(2): 1.

Budd, J. 1981. Distemper. Pp. 31–44 in Infectious Diseases of Wild Mammals. Edited by J. W. Davis, E. H. Karstad, and D. O. Trainer. Ames: Iowa State University Press.

Burger, J., and M. Gochfeld. 1992. Effect of group size on vigilance while drinking in the coati, Nasua narica, in Costa Rica. Animal Behaviour 44:1053–57.

Butler, P. J. 1992. Parrots, pressures, people, and pride. Pp. 25–46 in New World Parrots in Crisis: Solutions from Conservation Biology. Edited by S. R. Beissinger and N. F. R. Snyder. Washington: Smithsonian Institution Press.

Cade, T. J. 1986. Reintroduction as a method of conservation. Raptor Research Reports 5:72–84.

———. 1988. Using science and technology to reestablish species lost in nature. Pp. 279–88 in Biodiversity. Edited by E. O. Wilson. Washington: National Academy Press.

Cade, T. J., P. T. Redig, and H. B. Tordoff. 1989. Peregrine falcon restoration: Expectation versus reality. The Loon 61:160–62.

Cain, S. A. 1978. Predator and pest control. Pp. 379–95 in Wildlife in America: Contributions to an Understanding of American Wildlife and Its Conservation. Edited by H. P. Brokaw. Washington: CEO, U.S. Fish and Wildlife Service, U.S. Department of Agriculture Forest Service, and National Oceanic and Atmospheric Administration.

Calahane, V. H. 1954. Status of the black-footed ferret. Journal of Mammalogy 35:418–24.

Calder, W. A. 1984. Size, Function, and Life History. Cambridge: Harvard University Press.

Campbell, T. M., D. Biggins, S. Forrest, and T. W. Clark. 1985. Spotlighting as a method to locate and study black-footed ferrets. Pp. 24.1–24.7 in Black-Footed Ferret Workshop Proceedings, 18–19 September 1984 (Laramie, Wyo.). Edited by S. H. Anderson and D. B. Inkley. Cheyenne: Wyoming Game and Fish Department.

Campbell, T. M., T. W. Clark, L. Richardson, S. C. Forrest, and B. Houston. 1987. Food habits of Wyoming black-footed ferrets. American Midland Naturalist 117:208–10.

Captive Breeding Specialist Group. 1992. Black-footed ferret recovery plan review. Internal report, CBSG, Apple Valley, Minn.

Caraco, T., S. Martindale, and H. R. Pulliam. 1980. Flocking: Advantages and disadvantages. Nature 285:400–401.

Carlson, C. 1988. NEPA and the conservation of biodiversity. Environmental Law 19: 15–36.

Caro, T. M. 1979. Relations of kitten behaviour and adult predation. Zeitschrift für Tierpsychologie 51:158–68.

———. 1980a. Effects of the mother, object play, and adult experience on predation in cats. Behavioral and Neurological Biology 29:29–51.

———. 1980b. Predatory behaviour and social play in kittens. Behaviour 76:1–24.

Caro, T. 1989. Missing links in predator and anti-predator behavior. Trends in Ecology and Evolution 4:333–34.

Carpenter, J. W. 1985. Captive breeding and management of black-footed ferrets. Pp. 12.1–12.13 *in* Black-Footed Ferret Workshop Proceedings, 18–19 September 1984 (Laramie, Wyo.). Edited by S. H. Anderson and D. B. Inkley. Cheyenne: Wyoming Game and Fish Department.

Carpenter, J. W., M. J. G. Appel, R. C. Erickson, and M. N. Novilla. 1976. Fatal vaccine-induced canine distemper virus infection in black-footed ferrets. Journal of the American Veterinary Medical Association 169:961–64.

Carpenter, J. W., and C. N. Hillman. 1978. Husbandry, reproduction, and veterinary care of captive ferrets. American Association of Zoo Veterinarians Annual Proceedings 1977:36–47.

Carr, A. 1986. Introduction. Great Basin Naturalist Memoirs 8:1–7.

Carroll, R. S., M. S. Erskine, P. C. Doherty, L. A. Lundell, and M. J. Baum. 1985. Coital stimuli controlling luteinizing hormone secretion and ovulation in the female ferret. Biology of Reproduction 32:925–33.

Ceballos, G., E. Mellink, and L. R. Hanebury. 1993. Distribution and conservation status of prairie dogs *Cynomys mexicanus* and *Cynomys ludovicianus* in Mexico. Biological Conservation 63:105–12.

Chaiken, S., and C. Stangor. 1987. Attitudes and attitude change. Annual Review of Psychology 38:575–630.

Chang, M. C. 1965. Fertilizing life of ferret sperm in the female tract. Journal of Experimental Zoology 158:87–100.

Chang, M. C., and R. Yanagamachi. 1963. Fertilization of ferret ova by deposition of episisymal sperm into the ovarian capsule with special reference to fertilizable life of ova and the capacitation of sperm. Journal of Experimental Zoology 154:175–87.

Clark, T. W. 1977. Ecology and Ethology of the White-Tailed Prairie Dog *(Cynomys leucurus)*. Milwaukee Public Museum Publications in Biology and Geology, no. 3.

———. 1984. Strategies in endangered species conservation: A research review of the ongoing black-footed ferret program. Pp. 145–54 *in* Symposium on Issues in Technology and Management of Impacted Western Wildlife, [proceedings], 13–15 November 1982 (Steamboat Springs, Colo.). Edited by R. D. Coemer, J. M. Mario, J. W. Monarch, C. Pustmueller, M. Stalmaster, R. Stoecker, J. Todd, and W. Wright. Boulder, Colo.: Thorne Ecological Institute.

———. 1986. Professional excellence in wildlife and natural resource organizations. Renewable Resources Journal 4:8–13.

———. 1989. Conservation biology of the black-footed ferret, *Mustela nigripes*. Wildlife Preservation Trust Special Scientific Report no. 3. Philadelphia: Wildlife Preservation Trust International.

———. n.d. Averting Extinction: Restructuring the Endangered Species Recovery Process. New Haven, Conn.: Yale University Press. Forthcoming.

Clark, T. W., E. D. Amato, D. G. Whitemore, and A. H. Harvey. 1991. Policy and programs for ecosystem management in the greater Yellowstone ecosystem: An analysis. Conservation Biology 5:412–22.

Clark, T. W., T. M. Campbell, M. H. Schroeder, and L. Richardson. 1984. Handbook of methods for locating black-footed ferrets. Wyoming Bureau of Land Management Technical Bulletin no. 1. Cheyenne, Wyo.: U.S. Bureau of Land Management.

Clark, T. W., T. M. Campbell, D. G. Socha, and D. Casey. 1982. Prairie dog colony attributes and associated vertebrate species. Great Basin Naturalist 42:572–82.

Clark, T. W., and J. R. Cragun. 1991. Organization and management of endangered species programs. Endangered Species Update 8:1–4.

Clark, T. W., R. Crete, and J. Cada. 1989. Designing and managing successful endangered species recovery programs. Environmental Management 13:159–70.

Clark, T. W., L. Forrest, S. Forrest, and T. M. Campbell (Biota Consulting, Inc., Jackson, Wyo.). 1985. Some recommendations concerning the current plague outbreak at Meeteetse. Report to Wyoming Game and Fish Department and U.S. Fish and Wildlife Service, 6 August 1985, Cheyenne, Wyo.

Clark, T. W., and A. H. Harvey. 1988. Implementing endangered species recovery policy: Learning as we go? Endangered Species Update 5:35–42.

Clark, T. W., and S. R. Kellert. 1988. Toward a policy paradigm of the wildlife sciences. Renewable Resources Journal 6:7–16.

Clark, T. W., L. Richardson, D. Casey, T. M. Campbell, and S. C. Forrest. 1984. Seasonality of black-footed ferret diggings and prairie dog burrow plugging. Journal of Wildlife Management 48:1441–44.

Clark, T. W., L. Richardson, S. C. Forrest, D. E. Casey, and T. M. Campbell. 1986. Descriptive ethology and activity patterns of black-footed ferrets. Great Basin Naturalist Memoirs 8:115–34.

Clark, T. W., P. Schuyler, T. Donnay, P. Curlee, T. Sullivan, P. Cymerys, L. Sheeline, R. Reading, R. Wallace, A. Marcer-Batlle, Y. DeFretes, and T. Kennedy, Jr. 1992. Conserving biodiversity in the real world: Professional practice using a policy orientation. Endangered Species Update 9:5–8.

Cloudsley-Thompson, J. L. 1988. Desertification or sustainable yields from arid environments. Environmental Conservation 15:197–204.

Cohn, J. P. 1993. Defenders of biodiversity. Government Executive National Journal (April): 18–22.

Collins, A. R., J. P. Workman, and D. W. Uresk. 1984. An economic analysis of black-tailed prairie dog *(Cynomys ludovicianus)* control. Journal of Range Management 37:358–61.

Conner, M. C., R. F. Labisky, and D. R. Progulske. 1983. Scent-station indices as measures of population abundance for bobcats, raccoons, gray foxes, and opossums. Wildlife Society Bulletin 11:146–52.

Conway, C. (U.S. Fish and Wildlife Service Cooperative Research Unit, Laramie, Wyo.). 1989. Evaluation of potential black-footed ferret reintroduction sites in Wyoming. Report to Wyoming Game and Fish Department, October 1989, Cheyenne.

Conway, W. G. 1988. Can technology aid species preservation? Pp. 263–68 *in* Biodiversity. Edited by E. O. Wilson. Washington: National Academy Press.

Coppock, D. L., J. K. Detling, J. E. Ellis, and M. I. Dyer. 1983. Plant–herbivore interactions in a mixed-grass prairie: I. Effects of black-tailed prairie dogs on intraseasonal aboveground plant biomass and nutrient dynamics and plant species diversity. Oecologia 56:1–9.

Coss, R. G., and D. H. Owings. 1985. Restraints on ground squirrel anti-predator behavior: Adjustment over multiple time scales. Pp. 167–200 *in* Issues in the Ecological Study of Learning. Edited by T. D. Johnston and A. T. Pietrewicz. Hillsdale, N.J.: Lawrence Erlbaum Associates.

Cox, C. R., and B. J. LeBoeuf. 1977. Female incitation of male competition: A mechanism of sexual selection. American Naturalist 111:317–35.

Craighead, J. J., and F. C. Craighead. 1956. Hawks, Owls, and Wildlife. New York: Dover Publications.

Crews, D. 1975. Psychobiology of reptilian reproduction. Science 189:1059–65.

Culbert, R., and R. Blair. 1989. Recovery planning and endangered species. Endangered Species Update 6:2–8.

Culley, J. F. 1993. Plague, prairie dogs, and black-footed ferrets. Pp. 38–49 *in* Management of Prairie Dog Complexes for Black-Footed Ferret Reintroduction Sites. Edited by J. Oldemeyer, D. Biggins, B. Miller, and R. Crete. U.S. Fish and Wildlife Service Biological Report no. 13. Denver: U.S. Fish and Wildlife Service.

Cutlip, S. M., and A. H. Center. 1964. Effective public relations. 3d edition. Englewood Cliffs, N.J.: Prentice-Hall.

David, B. 1990. Apache trout culture: An aid to restoration. Endangered Species Update 8:76–78.

Day, A. M., and A. P. Nelson. 1929. Wildlife conservation and control in Wyoming under the leadership of the United States Biological Survey. Internal report, U.S. Biological Survey, Wyoming Game and Fish Department, and Wyoming Department of Agriculture, Cheyenne, Wyo.

DeBlieu, J. 1991. Meant To Be Wild: The Struggle to Save Endangered Species through Captive Breeding. Golden, Colo.: Fulcrum Publications.

Derrickson, S. R., and N. F. R. Snyder. 1992. Potentials and limits of captive breeding in parrot conservation. Pp. 133–63 *in* New World Parrots in Crisis: Solutions from Conservation Biology. Edited by S. R. Beissinger and N. F. R. Snyder. Washington: Smithsonian Institution Press.

Detling, J. K., and A. D. Whicker. 1988. A control of ecosystem processes by prairie dogs and other grassland herbivores. Pp. 23–29 *in* Eighth Great Plains Wildlife Damage Control Workshop Proceedings, 28–30 April 1987 (Rapid City, S.Dak.). U.S. Forest Service General Technical Report RM-154. Washington: U.S. Forest Service.

Dewsbury, D. A. 1972. Patterns of copulatory behavior in male mammals. Quarterly Review of Biology 57:135–59.

———. 1982. Dominance rank, copulatory behavior, and differential reproduction. Quarterly Review of Biology 57:135–59.

Diamond, J. M. 1975. The island dilemma: Lessons of modern biogeographic studies for the design of nature reserves. Biological Conservation 45:129–46.

Dietz, L. A., and E. Nagagata. 1986. Community conservation education program for the golden lion tamarin. Pp. 8–16 *in* Building Support for Conservation in Rural Areas: Workshop Proceedings. Volume 1. Edited by J. Atkinson. Ipswich, Md.: QLF Atlantic Center for the Environment.

DiSilvestro, R. L. 1985. The federal animal damage control program. Pp. 130–48 *in* Audubon Wildlife Report 1985. Edited by R. L. DiSilvestro. New York: National Audubon Society.

Dittmer, H. J. 1951. Vegetation in the Southwest—past and present. Texas Journal of Science 3:350–55.

DonCarlos, M. W., B. Miller, and E. T. Thorne. 1989. Observations of the 1986 black-footed ferret *(Mustela nigripes)* captive breeding program. Pp. 235–46 *in* Conservation Biology of the Black-Footed Ferret. Edited by U. S. Seal, E. T. Thorne, S. H. Anderson, and M. A. Bogan. New Haven, Conn.: Yale University Press.

Dunlap, T. R. 1988. Saving America's Wildlife. Princeton, N.J.: Princeton University Press.

Durning, A. B. 1989. Action at the grassroots: Fighting poverty and environmental decline. Worldwatch Institute Paper no. 88. Washington: Worldwatch Institute.

Durrant, S. D. 1952. Mammals of Utah. Lawrence: University of Kansas Publications.

East, K., and J. D. Lockie. 1964. Observations on a family of weasels *(Mustela nivalis)* bred in captivity. Proceedings of the Zoological Society of London 143:359–63.

Eibl-Eibesfeldt, I. 1956. Inborn and acquired in the technique of killing prey (experiments with the polecat, *Putorius putorius*). Zeitschrift für Säugetierkunde 21:135–37.

Eisenberg, J. E. 1981. The Mammalian Radiations. Chicago: University of Chicago Press.

Eisenberg, J. E., and P. Leyhausen. 1972. The phylogenesis of predatory behavior in mammals. Zeitschrift für Tierpsychologie 30:59–72.

Ellis, D. H., S. J. Dobrott, and J. G. Goodwin, Jr. 1977. Reintroduction techniques for masked bob-whites. Pp. 345–54 *in* Endangered Birds: Management Techniques for Preserving Endangered Species. Edited by S. A. Temple. Madison: University of Wisconsin Press.

Erickson, R. C. 1973. Some black-footed ferret research needs. Pp. 153–64 *in* Proceedings of the Black-Footed Ferret and Prairie Dog Workshop. Edited by R. L. Linder and C. N. Hillman. Brookings: South Dakota State University.

Erlinge, S. 1974. Distribution, territoriality and numbers of weasel *Mustela nivalis* in relation to prey abundance. Oikos 25:308–14.

Erlinge, S., and M. Sandell. 1986. Seasonal changes in social organization of male stoats, *Mustela erminea:* An effect of shifts between two decisive resources. Oikos 47:57–62.

Erlinge, S., M. Sandell, and C. Brinck. 1982. Scent-marking and its territorial significance in stoats, *Mustela erminea.* Animal Behaviour 30:811–18.

Ewer, R. F. 1973. The Carnivores. Ithaca, N.Y.: Cornell University Press.

Ezcurra, E., and G. Halffter. 1990. Conservation problems on the Mexican side of the border. Pp. 295–304 *in* Environmental Hazards and Bioresource Management in the United States–Mexico Borderlands. Edited by P. Ganster and H. Walter. UCLA (University of California, Los Angeles) Latin American Center Publications. Los Angeles: UCLA.

Faneslow, M. S., and L. S. Lester. 1988. A functional behavioristic approach to aversively motivated behavior: Predatory imminence as a determinant of the topography of defensive behavior. Pp. 185–212 *in* Evolution and Learning. Edited by R. C. Bolles and M. D. Beecher. Hillsdale, N.J.: Lawrence Erlbaum Associates.

Ferguson, D., and N. Ferguson. 1983. Sacred Cows at the Public Trough. Bend, Ore.: Maverick Publications.

Findley, J. S., and W. Caire. 1977. The status of mammals in the northern region of the Chihuahuan Desert. Pp. 127–40 *in* Transactions of the Symposium on the Biological Resources of the Chihuahuan Desert Region, United States and Mexico. Edited by R. H. Wauer and D. H. Riskind. U.S. National Park Service Transactions and Proceedings Series, no. 3. Washington: U.S. National Park Service.

Fisher, R. A. 1930. The Genetical Theory of Natural Selection. Oxford, U.K.: Clarendon.

Fitzgerald, B. M. 1977. Weasel predation on a cyclic population of the montane vole *(Microtus montanus)* in California. Journal of Animal Ecology 46:67–97.

Fitzgerald, J. P. 1993. Plague ecology in Gunnison's prairie dogs and some management suggestions regarding black-footed ferret recovery efforts. Pp. 50–79 *in* Management of Prairie Dog Complexes for Black-Footed Ferret Reintroduction Sites. Edited by J. Oldemeyer, D. Biggins, B. Miller, and R. Crete. U.S. Fish and Wildlife Service Biological Report no. 13. Denver: U.S. Fish and Wildlife Service.

Foose, T. J., R. Lande, N. R. Flesness, G. Rabb, and B. Read. 1986. Propagation plans. Zoo Biology 5:139–46.

Forrest, S. C., D. E. Biggins, L. Richardson, T. W. Clark, T. M. Campbell, K. A. Fagerstone, and E. T. Thorne. 1988. Black-footed ferret *(Mustela nigripes)* attributes at Meeteetse, Wyoming, 1981 to 1985. Journal of Mammalogy 69:261–73.

Forrest, S. C., T. W. Clark, L. Forrest, and T. M. Campbell. 1985b. Black-footed ferret population status at Meeteetse, Wyoming, July–October 1985. Final report to Wyoming Game and Fish Department, Cheyenne.

Forrest, S. C., T. W. Clark, L. Richardson, and T. M. Campbell. 1985a. Black-footed ferret habitat: Some management and reintroduction considerations. Wyoming Bureau of Land Management Wildlife Technical Bulletin no. 2. Cheyenne, Wyo.: U.S. Bureau of Land Management.

Foster, N. S., and S. E. Hygnstrom. 1990. Prairie Dogs and Their Ecosystem. Denver: U.S. Fish and Wildlife Service.

Frankel, O. H., and M. E. Soulé. 1981. Conservation and Evolution. Cambridge: Cambridge University Press.

Frazier, J. 1990. International resource conservation: Thoughts on a challenge. Transactions of the North American Wildlife and Natural Resources Conference 55:384–95.

———. 1993. Conserving sea turtles and other natural resources: What Ferdinand Marcos and Manual Noriega can teach us. Pp. 60–63 in Thirteenth Annual Symposium on Biology and Conservation of Sea Turtles, [proceedings]. B. A. Schroeder and B. C. Witherington. U.S. National Oceanic and Atmospheric Administration National Marine Fisheries Service Technical Memorandum no. NMFS-SEFSC-341. Washington: U.S. National Oceanic and Atmospheric Administration.

Galbraith, J. R. 1977. Organizational Design. Reading, Mass.: Addison-Wesley.

Garret, M. G., and W. L. Franklin. 1988. Behavioral ecology of dispersal in the black-tailed prairie dog. Journal of Mammalogy 69:236–50.

Garret, M. G., W. L. Franklin, and J. L. Hoogland. 1982. Demographic differences between an old and a new colony of black-tailed prairie dogs (Cynomys ludovicianus). American Midland Naturalist 108:51–59.

Gilbert, B. 1980. Missing and presumed dead. Sports Illustrated 53(16): 103–14.

Gilpin, M. E. 1987. Spatial structure and population vulnerability. Pp. 125–39 in Viable Populations for Conservation. Edited by M. E. Soulé. Cambridge: Cambridge University Press.

———. 1991. The genetic effective population size of a metapopulation. Biological Journal of the Linnean Society 42:165–75.

Gilpin, M. E., and J. M. Diamond. 1980. Subdivision of nature reserves and the maintenance of species diversity. Nature 285:567–68.

Gilpin, M., and M. E. Soulé. 1986. Minimum viable populations: Processes of species extinctions. Pp. 19–34 in Conservation Biology. Edited by M. E. Soulé. Sunderland, Mass.: Sinauer Associates.

Godbey, J., and D. Biggins. 1994. Recovery of the black-footed ferret: Looking back, looking forward. Endangered Species Technical Bulletin 19:10–13.

Goldstein, B. D. 1992. Science at EPA. Science 255:1336.

Golightly, R. T., and R. D. Ohmart. 1984. Water economy of two desert canids: Coyote and kit fox. Journal of Mammalogy 65:51–58.

Gorham, J. 1966. Epizootiology of distemper. Journal of American Veterinary Medical Association 149:610–22.

Gossow, H. 1970. Vergleichende verhaltensstudien an Marderartigen. I. Uber LautauBerungen und zum Beuteurhalten. Zeitschrift für Tierpsychologie 27:405–80.

Greenough, W. T., and J. M. Juraska. 1979. Experience induced changes in brain fine structure: Their behavioral implications. Pp. 263–94 *in* Development and Evolution of Brain Size: Behavioral Implications. Edited by M. E. Hahn, C. Jensen, and B. C. Dudek. New York: Academic Press.

Greenspan, B. N. 1980. Male size and reproductive success in the communal courtship system of the fiddler crab *(Uca rapax)*. Animal Behaviour 28:387–92.

Greenwalt, L. 1988. Reflections on the power and potential of the Endangered Species Act. Endangered Species Update 5:7–9.

Grieg, J. C. 1979. Principles of genetic conservation in relation to wildlife management in southern Africa. South African Journal of Wildlife Research 9:57–78.

Griffith, B., J. M. Scott, J. W. Carpenter, and C. Reed. 1989. Translocation as a species conservation tool: Status and strategy. Science 345:447–80.

Griffiths, D. 1975. Prey availability and the food of predators. Ecology 56:1209–14.

Hahn, E. W., and R. C. Webster. 1969. The Biomedical Use of Ferrets in Research. North Rose, N.Y.: Marshall Research Farms.

Hall, E. R. 1981. The Mammals of North America. New York: John Wiley and Sons.

Hamilton, D. P. 1992. Better science at EPA? Science 255:147.

Hamilton, W. D. 1964. The genetic evolution of social behavior. Journal of Theoretical Biology 7:1–52.

Hanebury, L. R., B. J. Miller, and D. E. Biggins. n.d. Structure of black-tailed prairie dog burrow systems. 25 manuscript pages. In preparation.

Hansen, R. M., and I. K. Gold. 1977. Black-tailed prairie dogs, desert cottontails, and cattle trophic relations on shortgrass range. Journal of Range Management 30:210–14.

Hanson, R. 1988. A chronology of prairie dog control operations and related developments in South Dakota. Pp. 121–22 *in* Eighth Great Plains Wildlife Damage Control Workshop Proceedings, 28–30 April 1987 (Rapid City, S.Dak.). U.S. Forest Service General Technical Report RM-154. Washington: U.S. Forest Service.

Harlow, H. J., and G. E. Menkens. 1986. A comparison of hibernation in the black-tailed prairie dog, white-tailed prairie dog, and Wyoming ground squirrel. Canadian Journal of Zoology 64:793–96.

Harlow, H., B. Miller, T. Ryder, and L. Ryder. 1985. Energy requirements for gestation and lactation, and the effect of food deprivation on a delayed implanter, the American badger. Journal of Comparative Biochemistry and Physiology 82A:885–89.

Harris, A. H. 1977. Wisconsin age environments in the northern Chihuahuan Desert: Evidence from higher vertebrates. Pp. 23–52 *in* Transactions of the Symposium on the Biological Resources of the Chihuahuan Desert Region, United States and Mexico. Edited by R. H. Wauer and D. H. Riskind. U.S. National Park Service Transactions and Proceedings Series, no. 3. Washington: U.S. National Park Service.

Harris, R. B., T. W. Clark, and M. L. Shaffer. 1989. Extinction probabilities for isolated black-footed ferret populations. Pp. 69–82 *in* Conservation Biology of the Black-Footed Ferret. Edited by U. S. Seal, E. T. Thorne, S. H. Anderson, and M. A. Bogan. New Haven, Conn.: Yale University Press.

Harrison, R. 1972. Understanding your organization's character. Harvard Business Review (May–June): 119–28.

Hartman, L. 1964. The behaviour and breeding of captive weasels (*Mustela nivalis* L.). New Zealand Journal of Science 7:147–56.

Hasler, A. D. 1966. Underwater Guideposts: Homing of Salmon. Madison: University of Wisconsin Press.

Heidt, G. A., M. K. Peterson, and G. L. Kirkland. 1968. Mating behavior and development of least weasels *(Mustela nivalis)* in captivity. Journal of Mammalogy 49: 413–19.

Heisey, D. M., and T. K. Fuller. 1985. Evaluation of survival and cause-specific mortality rates using radio-telemetry data. Journal of Wildlife Management 49:668–74.

Henderson, F. R. 1980. The status of prairie dogs in the Great Plains. Pp. 101–9 *in* Fourth Great Plains Wildlife Damage Control Workshop Proceedings, 4–6 December 1979 (Manhattan, Kans.). Washington: U.S. Forest Service.

Henderson, F. R., P. F. Springer, and R. Adrian. 1974. The black-footed ferret in South Dakota. South Dakota Department of Game, Fish, and Parks Technical Bulletin 4:1–37.

Henderson, N. D. 1970. Genetic influences on the behavior of mice can be obscured by laboratory rearing. Journal of Comparative and Physiological Psychology 72:505–11.

Hess, H. H. 1972. The natural history of imprinting. Annals of the New York Academy of Science 193:124–36.

Hillman, C. N. 1968. Field observations of black-footed ferrets in South Dakota. Transactions of the North American Wildlife and Natural Resources Conference 33:433–43.

Hillman, C. N., and J. W. Carpenter. 1983. Breeding biology and behavior of captive black-footed ferrets. International Zoo Yearbook 23:186–91.

Hillman, C. N., and R. L. Linder, editors. 1973. Proceedings of the Black-Footed Ferret and Prairie Dog Workshop. Brookings: South Dakota State University.

Hillman, C. N., R. L. Linder, and R. B. Dahlgren. 1979. Prairie dog distributions in areas inhabited by black-footed ferrets. American Midland Naturalist 102:185–87.

Hirshleifer, J. 1982. Evolutionary models in economics and law: Cooperation versus conflict strategies. Research in Law and Economics 4:1–60.

Holloway, C. W., and H. Jungius. 1973. Reintroduction of certain mammal and bird species into the Gran Paradiso National Park. Zoologica Anzeiger 191:1–44.

Homer-Dixon, T. F., J. H. Boutwell, and G. W. Rathjens. 1993. Environmental change and violent conflict. Scientific American (February): 38–45.

Homulka, C. L. 1964. Our rarest mammal? Audubon 66:244–46.

Honacki, J. H., K. E. Kurman, and J. W. Koeppl. 1982. Mammal Species of the World. Lawrence, Kans.: Allen Press.

Hoogland, J. L. 1979. Aggression, ectoparasitism, and other possible costs of prairie dog (Sciuridae, *Cynomys* spp.) coloniality. Behaviour 69:1–35.

———. 1981. The evolution of coloniality in white-tailed and black-tailed prairie dogs (Sciuridae: *Cynomys leucurus* and *Cynomys ludovicianus*). Ecology 62:252–72.

———. 1982. Prairie dogs avoid extreme inbreeding. Science 215:1639–41.

———. 1983. Black-tailed prairie dog coteries are cooperatively breeding units. American Naturalist 121:275–80.

———. 1988. Demography and population dynamics of prairie dogs. Pp. 18–22 *in* Eighth Great Plains Wildlife Damage Control Workshop Proceedings, 28–30 April 1987 (Rapid City, S.Dak.). U.S. Forest Service General Technical Report RM-154. Washington: U.S. Forest Service.

Hornocker, M. 1982. [Letter to the editor.] The Wildlifer (November–December): 51–52.

Houck, O. A. 1993. The Endangered Species Act and its implementation by the U.S. Departments of Interior and Commerce. Colorado Law Review 64: 361, 386.

Humphreys, W. F., and D. J. Kitchener. 1982. The effect of habitat utilization on species area curves: Implications for optimal reserve area. Journal of Biogeography 9: 391–96.

Immelmann, K. 1975. Ecological significance of imprinting and early learning. Annual Review of Ecology and Systematics 6:15–37.

Jackson, J. A. 1986. Biopolitics, management of federal lands, and the conservation of the red-cockaded woodpecker. American Birds 40:1162–68.

Jackson, J. A., P. Ramey, and B. J. Schardien. 1977. The red-cockaded woodpecker in north Mississippi. Mississippi Kite 7:14–17.

Janis, I. L. 1972. Victims of group think: A psychological study of foreign-policy decisions and fiascoes. Boston: Houghton Mifflin.

Johnson, D. 1969. Returns of the American Fur Company 1835–1839. Journal of Mammalogy 50:836–39.

Joyce, S. 1988. Feeding behavior and water requirements of black-footed ferrets *(Mustela nigripes)*. Master's thesis, University of Wyoming, Laramie.

Kellert, S. R. 1976. Perceptions of animals in American society. Transactions of the North American Wildlife and Natural Resources Conference 41:534–37.

———. 1979. Public Attitudes toward Critical Wildlife and Natural Habitat Issues. Superintendent of Documents. Washington: U.S. Government Printing Office.

———. 1990. Public Attitudes and Beliefs about the Wolf and Its Restoration in Michigan. Internal report, Yale University School of Forestry and Environmental Studies, New Haven, Conn.

Kellert, S. R., and J. K. Berry. 1987. Attitudes, knowledge, and behaviors toward wildlife as affected by gender. Wildlife Society Bulletin 15:363–71.

Kelly, G. M. 1977. Fisher *(Martes pennanti)* biology in the White Mountain National Forest and adjacent areas. Ph.D. dissertation, University of Massachusetts, Amherst.

King, C. M. 1975. The home range of the weasel *(Mustela nivalis)* in an English woodland. Journal of Animal Ecology 44:639–68.

———. 1983. Factors regulating mustelid populations. Acta Zoologica Fennica 174:217–20.

———. 1989. The Natural History of Weasels and Stoats. Ithaca, N.Y.: Comstock Publishing Associates and Cornell University Press.

King, C. M., and C. D. McMillan. 1982. Population structure and dispersal of peak-year cohorts of stoats *(Mustela erminea)* in two New Zealand forests, with special reference to control. New Zealand Journal of Ecology 5:59–66.

King, J. 1955. Social Behavior, Social Organization, and Population Dynamics in a Black-Tailed Prairie Dog Town in the Black Hills of South Dakota. Contributions from the Laboratory of Vertebrate Zoology of the University of Michigan, no. 67. Ann Arbor: University of Michigan.

King, W. B., J. A. Jackson, H. W. Kale II, H. F. Mayfield, R. L. Plunkett, Jr., J. M. Scott, P. F. Springer, S. A. Temple, and S. R. Wilbur. 1977. Report of the Committee on Conservation, 1976–77. The recovery team–recovery plan approach to conservation of endangered species: A status summary and appraisal. Auk 94(4, suppl.): 1DD–19DD.

Kitchener, D. J., A. Chapman, B. G. Muir, and M. Palmer. 1980. The conservation value for mammals of reserves in the western Australian wheatbelt. Biological Conservation 18:179–207.

Klatt, L. E., and D. Hein. 1978. Vegetative differences among active and abandoned towns of black-tailed prairie dogs *(Cynomys ludovicianus)*. Journal of Range Management 31:315–17.

Klebanoff, A., S. Minta, A. Hastings, and T. W. Clark. 1991. Age-dependent predation model of black-footed ferrets and prairie dogs. SIAM (Society for Industrial and Applied Mathematics) Journal of Applied Mathematics 51:1053–73.

Kleiman, D. G. 1972. Social behavior of the maned wolf *(Chrysolyon brachyurus)* and the bush dog *(Speothos venaticus):* A study in contrast. Journal of Mammalogy 53: 791–806.

———. 1989. Reintroduction of captive mammals for conservation. Bioscience 39: 152–61.

Kleiman, D. G., B. B. Beck, J. M. Dietz, L. A. Dietz, J. D. Ballou, and A. F. Coimbra-Filho. 1986. Conservation program for the golden lion tamarin: Captive research and management, ecological studies, educational strategies, and reintroduction. Pp. 959–79 *in* Primates: The Road to Self-Sustaining Populations. Edited by K. Benirschke. New York: Springer-Verlag.

Kleiman, D. G., M. R. Stanley Price, and B. B. Beck. 1993. Criteria for reintroductions. Pp. 287–303 *in* Creative Conservation: Interactive Management of Wild and Captive Animals. Edited by P. J. S. Olney, G. M. Mace, and A. T. C. Feistner. London: Chapman and Hall.

Knopf, F. L. 1993. Avian assemblages on altered grasslands. Studies in Avian Biology 15:247–57.

Knowles, C. J. 1982. Habitat affinity, populations, and control of black-tailed prairie dog populations on the Charles M. Russell National Wildlife Refuge. Ph.D. dissertation, University of Montana, Missoula.

———. 1987. Reproductive ecology of black-tailed prairie dogs in Montana. Great Basin Naturalist 47:202–6.

———. 1993. An evaluation of 0.5% permethrin dust for control of fleas in black-tailed prairie dog burrows on the UL Bend National Wildlife Refuge. Internal report, C. M. Russell National Wildlife Refuge, Lewistown, Mont.

Koford, C. B. 1958. Prairie Dogs, Whitefaces, and Blue Gramma. Wildlife Monographs, no. 3. Bethesda, Md.: Wildlife Society.

Kohm, K. A., 1991. Balancing on the Brink of Extinction: The Endangered Species Act and Lessons for the Future. Washington: Island Press.

Krebs, J. R. 1973. Behavioral aspects of predation. Pp. 73–111 *in* Perspectives in Ethology. Edited by P. P. G. Bateson and P. H. Klopfer. New York: Plenum Press.

Krueger, K. 1986. Feeding relationships among bison, pronghorn, and prairie dogs: An experimental analysis. Ecology 67:760–70.

————. 1988. Prairie dog overpopulation: Value judgment or ecological reality? Pp. 39–45 *in* Eighth Great Plains Wildlife Damage Control Workshop Proceedings, 28–30 April 1987 (Rapid City, S.Dak.). U.S. Forest Service General Technical Report RM-154. Washington: U.S. Forest Service.

Kundera, M. 1981. The Book of Laughter and Forgetting. New York: Penguin Books.

Lacy, R. C., and T. W. Clark. 1989. Genetic variability in black-footed ferret populations: Past, present, and future. Pp. 83–103 *in* Conservation Biology of the Black-Footed Ferret. Edited by U. S. Seal, E. T. Thorne, S. H. Anderson, and M. A. Bogan. New Haven, Conn.: Yale University Press.

Lande, R. 1988. Genetics and demography in biological conservation. Science 241:1455–60.

Lande, R., and G. F. Barrowclough. 1987. Effective population size, genetic variation, and their use in population management. Pp. 87–123 *in* Viable Populations for Conservation. Edited by M. E. Soulé. Cambridge: Cambridge University Press.

Lantz, D. E. 1909. Use of poisons for destroying noxious animals. U.S. Department of Agriculture Yearbook 1908:421–32.

————. 1917. Destroying rodent pests on the farm. U.S. Department of Agriculture Yearbook 1916:381–98.

Lavers, R. B. 1973. Aspects of biology of the ferret (*M. putorius* forma furo) at Pukepuke Lagoon. Proceedings of the New Zealand Ecological Society 20:7–12.

Lawrence, E. S., and J. A. Allen. 1983. On the search image. Oikos 40:313–14.

Leader-Williams, N. 1990. Black rhinos and African elephants: Lessons for conservation funding. Oryx 24:23–29.

Leopold, A. S. 1964. Predator and rodent control in the United States. Transactions of the North American Wildlife and Natural Resources Conference 29:27–49.

Leyhausen, P. 1979. Cat Behavior: Predatory and Social Behavior of Domestic and Wild Cats. Translated by B. A. Tonkin. New York: Garland Press.

Ligon, J. D., P. B. Stacey, R. N. Conner, C. E. Bock, and C. S. Adkisson. 1986. Report of the American Ornithologists' Union Committee for the Conservation of the Red-Cockaded Woodpecker. Auk 103:848–55.

Linder, D. O. 1988. "Are all species created equal?" and other questions shaping wildlife law. Harvard Environmental Law Review 12:157–98.

Linder, R. L., R. B. Dahlgren, and C. N. Hillman. 1972. Black-footed ferret–prairie dog interrelationships. Pp. 22–37 *in* Proceedings of the Symposium on Rare and Endangered Wildlife of the Southwestern United States, 22–23 September 1972 (Albuquerque, N.Mex.). Santa Fe: New Mexico Department of Game and Fish.

Linscombe, G., N. Kinler, and R. J. Auelerich. 1982. Mink. Pp. 629–43 *in* Wild Mammals of North America. Edited by J. A. Chapman and G. A. Feldhamer. Baltimore: Johns Hopkins University Press.

Longhurst, W. 1944. Observations on the ecology of the Gunnison prairie dog in Colorado. Journal of Mammalogy 25:24–36.

Loucks, O. L. 1992. Forest response research in NAPAP: Potentially successful linkage of policy and science. Ecological Applications 2:117–23.

Loughry, W. J. 1988. Population differences in how black-tailed prairie dogs deal with snakes. Behavioral Ecology and Sociobiology 22:61–67.

Lovejoy, T. E. 1986. Species leave the ark one by one. Pp. 13–27 *in* The Preservation Species. Edited by B. G. Norton. Princeton, N.J.: Princeton University Press.

MacArthur, R. H., and E. O. Wilson. 1967. The theory of island biogeography. Princeton, N.J.: Princeton University Press.

Magurran, A. E. 1989. Acquired recognition of predator odour in the European minnow *(Phoxinus phoxinus)*. Ethology 82:216–23.

Mares, M. A. 1991. How scientists can impede the development of their discipline: Egocentrism, small pool size, and evolution of sapismo. Pp. 57–75 *in* Latin American Mammalogy: History, Biodiversity, and Conservation. Edited by M. A. Mares and D. J. Schmidley. Norman: Oklahoma Museum of Natural History.

Marsh, R. E. 1984. Ground squirrels, prairie dogs, and marmots as pests on rangeland. Pp. 195–208 *in* Proceedings of the Conference for Organization and Practice of Vertebrate Pest Control, 30 August–3 September 1982 (Hampshire, U.K.). Fernherst, U.K.: ICI Plant Protection Division.

Marshall, E. 1992. Science and science advice in favor at EPA. Science 255:1504.

May, R. M. 1986. The cautionary tale of the black-footed ferret. Nature 320:13–14.

May, R. 1991. The role of ecological theory in planning the reintroduction of endangered species. Symposia of the Zoological Society of London 62:145–63.

Maynard Smith, J., and G. A. Parker. 1976. The logic of asymmetric contests. Animal Behaviour 24:159–75.

McFarlane, R. W. 1992. A Stillness in the Pines: The Ecology of the Red-Cockaded Woodpecker. New York: W. W. Norton and Co.

McNeely, J. 1988. Economics and Biological Diversity. Gland, Switzerland: International Union for the Conservation of Nature and Natural Resources.

McNulty, F. 1971. Must They Die? New York: Doubleday and Co.

Mellen, J. D. 1991. Factors influencing reproductive success in small exotic felids *(Felis* spp.): A multiple regression analysis. Zoo Biology 10:95–110.

Menkens, G. E., and S. H. Anderson. 1991. Population of white-tailed prairie dogs during an epizootic of sylvatic plague. Journal of Mammalogy 72:328–31.

Menkens, G. E., B. J. Miller, and S. H. Anderson. 1988. White-tailed prairie dog ecology in Wyoming. Pp. 34–38 *in* Eighth Great Plains Wildlife Damage Control Workshop Proceedings, 28–30 April 1987 (Rapid City, S.Dak.). U.S. Forest Service General Technical Report RM-154. Washington: U.S. Forest Service.

Merriam, C. H. 1902. The prairie dog of the Great Plains. U.S. Department of Agriculture Yearbook 1901:257–70.

Messing, J. H. 1986. A late Pleistocene–Holocene fauna from Chihuahua, Mexico. Southwestern Naturalist 31:277–88.

Miller, B. J. 1988. Conservation and behavior of the endangered black-footed ferret *(Mustela nigripes)* with a comparative analysis of reproductive behavior between the black-footed ferret and the congeneric domestic ferret *(Mustela putorius furo)*. Ph.D. dissertation, University of Wyoming, Laramie.

Miller, B. J., and S. H. Anderson. 1989. Failure of fertilization following abbreviated copulation in the domestic ferret. Journal of Experimental Zoology 249:85–89.

———. 1990a. A comparison between black-footed ferrets *(Mustela nigripes),* domestic ferrets *(M. putorius furo),* and Siberian polecats *(M. eversmanni).* Zoo Biology 9:201–10.

———. 1990b. A behavioural comparison between induced oestrus and natural oestrus domestic ferrets *(Mustela putorius furo).* Journal of Ethology 7:65–73.

———. 1993. Descriptive Ethology of the Endangered Black-Footed Ferret. Advances in Behavior [series]. Berlin, Germany: Paul Parey Press.

Miller, B. J., S. H. Anderson, M. DonCarlos, and E. T. Thorne. 1988. Biology of the endangered black-footed ferret *(Mustela nigripes)* and the role of captive propagation in its conservation. Canadian Journal of Zoology 66:765–73.

Miller, B., D. Biggins, L. Hanebury, C. Conway, and C. Wemmer. 1992. Rehabilitation of a species: The black-footed ferret *(Mustela nigripes).* Wildlife Rehabilitation 9:183–92.

Miller, B., D. Biggins, L. Hanebury, and A. Vargas. 1993. Reintroduction of the black-footed ferret. Pp. 455–63 *in* Creative Conservation: Interactive Management of Wild and Captive Animals. Edited by P. J. S. Olney, G. M. Mace, and A. T. C. Feister. London: Chapman and Hall.

Miller, B., D. Biggins, A. Vargas, M. Hutchins, L. Hanebury, J. Godbey, S. Anderson, J. Oldemeier, and C. Wemmer. 1997. The captive environment and reintroduction: The black-footed ferret as a case study. *In* Environmental Enrichment for Captive Animals. Edited by D. J. Shepherdson, J. D. Mellen, and M. Hutchins. Washington: Smithsonian Institution Press. Forthcoming.

Miller, B., D. Biggins, C. Wemmer, R. Powell, L. Calvo, L. Hanebury, and T. Wharton. 1990b. Development of survival skills in captive-raised Siberian polecats *(Mustela eversmanni):* II. Predator avoidance. Journal of Ethology 8:95–104.

Miller, B., D. Biggins, C. Wemmer, R. Powell, L. Hanebury, D. Horn, and A. Vargas. 1990a. Development of survival skills in captive-raised Siberian polecats *(Mustela eversmanni):* I. Locating prey. Journal of Ethology 8:89–94.

Miller, B., G. Ceballos, and R. Reading. 1994. Prairie dogs, poison, and biotic diversity. Conservation Biology 8:677–81.

Miller, B., R. Reading, C. Conway, J. A. Jackson, M. Hutchins, N. Snyder, S. Forrest, J. Frazier, and S. Derrickson. 1994. Improving endangered species programs: Avoiding organizational pitfalls, tapping the resources, and adding accountability. Environmental Management 18:637–45.

Miller, B., C. Wemmer, D. Biggins, and R. Reading. 1990. A proposal to conserve black-footed ferrets and the prairie dog ecosystem. Environmental Management 14:763–69.

Miller, J. A. 1991. Research updates. Bioscience 41:750–53.

Mishra, H. R., C. Wemmer, and J. L. D. Smith. 1987. Tigers in Nepal: Management conflicts with human interests. Pp. 449–63 *in* Tigers of the World: The Biology, Biopolitics, Management, and Conservation of an Endangered Species. Edited by R. L. Tilson and U. S. Seal. Park Ridge, N.J.: Noyes Publications.

Montgomery, P. 1990. Science friction. Common Cause (November–December):24–29.

Moors, P. J., and R. B. Lavers. 1981. Movements and home range of ferrets *(Mustela furo)* at Puke Puke Lagoon, New Zealand. New Zealand Journal of Zoology 8:413–22.

Morafka, D. J., and C. J. McCoy, editors. 1988. The Ecogeography of the Mexican Bolson Tortoise *(Gopherus flavomarginatus):* Derivation of Its Endangered Status and Recommendations for Its Conservation. Animals of the Carnegie Museum of Natural History [series]. Pittsburgh: Carnegie Museum of Natural History.

Morse, D. H. 1980. Behavioral Mechanisms in Ecology. Cambridge: Harvard University Press.

Morton, E. S. 1971. Nest predation effecting the breeding season of the clay-colored robin, a tropical songbird. Science 171:920–21.

Myers, N. 1979. The Sinking Ark: A New Look at Disappearing Species. New York: Pergamon Press.

Nabhan, G. 1990. Genetic resources of the US–Mexican borderlands: Wild relatives of crops, their uses and conservation. Pp. 345–60 *in* Environmental Hazards and Bioresource Management in the United States–Mexico Borderlands. Edited by P. Ganster and H. Walter. UCLA (University of California, Los Angeles) Latin American Center Publications. Los Angeles: UCLA.

Nash, J. M. 1992. The $25,000,000 bird. Time (27 January): 56–57.

Nei, M., T. Maruyama, and R. Chakraborty. 1975. The bottleneck effect of genetic variability in populations. Evolution 29:1–10.

Nice, J. 1982. Endangered species: A Wyoming town becomes ferret capital. Audubon 84:106–8.

Noss, R. F. 1983. A regional landscape approach to maintain diversity. Bioscience 33:700–706.

O'Brien, S. J., and J. F. Evermann. 1988. Interactive influences of infectious disease and genetic diversity in natural populations. Trends in Ecology and Evolution 3:254–59.

O'Brien, S. J., J. S. Martenson, M. A. Eichelberger, E. T. Thorne, and F. Wright. 1989. Genetic variation and molecular systematics of the black-footed ferret. Pp. 21–33 *in* Conservation Biology of the Black-Footed Ferret. Edited by U. S. Seal, E. T. Thorne, S. H. Anderson, and M. A. Bogan. New Haven, Conn.: Yale University Press.

O'Brien, S. J., M. E. Roelke, L. Marker, A. Newman, C. A. Winkler, D. Meltzner, L. Colly, J. F. Evermann, H. Bush, and D. E. Wildt. 1985. Genetic basis for species vulnerability in the cheetah. Science 227:1428–34.

O'Connell, M. 1992. Response to "Six biological reasons why the Endangered Species Act doesn't work—and what to do about it." Conservation Biology 6:140–43.

O'Meilia, M. E., F. L. Knopf, and J. C. Lewis. 1982. Some consequences of competition between prairie dogs and beef cattle. Journal of Range Management 35:580–85.

Paunovich, R., and S. C. Forrest. 1987. Activity of a wild black-footed ferret litter. Prairie Naturalist 19:159–62.

Peterson, L. A., and E. D. Berg. 1954. Black-footed ferrets used as ceremonial objects by Montana Indians. Journal of Mammalogy 35:593–94.

Phenicie, C. K., and J. R. Lyons. 1973. Tactical Planning in Fish and Wildlife Management and Research. U.S. Fish and Wildlife Service Research Publication no. 123. Washington: U.S. Fish and Wildlife Service.

Pizzimenti, J. L., and G. D. Collier. 1973. *Cynomys parvidens.* Mammalian Species 52:1–3.

Polderboer, E. B., L. W. Kuhn, and G. O. Hendrickson. 1941. Winter and spring habits of weasels in central Iowa. Journal of Wildlife Management 5:115–19.

Polsky, R. H. 1975. Hunger, prey feeding, and predatory aggression. Behavioral Biology 13:81–93.

Poole, T. B. 1966. Aggressive play in polecats. Symposia of the Zoological Society of London 18:23–44.

Poole, T. 1972. Some behavioral differences between the European polecat, *M. putorius,* the ferret, *M. furo,* and their hybrids. Journal of Zoology (London) 166:25–35.

———. 1974. Detailed analysis of fighting in polecats Mustelidae using Ciné film. Journal of Zoology (London) 173:369–93.

Powell, R. A. 1973. A model for raptor predation on weasels. Journal of Mammalogy 54:259–63.

———. 1978. A comparison of fisher and weasel hunting behavior. Carnivore 1:28–34.

———. 1979. Mustelid spacing patterns: Variations on a theme by *Mustela.* Zeitschrift für Tierpsychologie 50:153–65.

———. 1982. The Fisher: Life History, Ecology, and Behavior. Minneapolis: University of Minnesota Press.

Powell, R. A., T. W. Clark, L. Richardson, and S. C. Forrest. 1985. Black-footed ferret *(Mustela nigripes)* energy expenditure and prey requirements. Biological Conservation 34:1–15.

Powell, R. A., and R. D. Leonard. 1983. Sexual dimorphism and energetic requirements for reproduction of female fishers *(Martes pennanti).* Oikos 40:166–74.

Prendergast, A. 1986. The last of a breed. Frontier (August): 34.

Prescott, J., and M. Hutchins. 1991. Joining efforts for preservation of biodiversity. Transactions of the North American Wildlife and Natural Resources Conference 56:227–32.

Price, E. O. 1972. Novelty-induced self-food deprivation in wild and semi-domestic deer mice *(Peromyscus maniculatus bairdii).* Behaviour 41:91–104.

Quick, H. F. 1951. Notes on the ecology of weasels in Gunnison County, Colorado. Journal of Mammalogy 32:281–90.

Raitt, R. J., and S. L. Pimm. 1977. Temporal changes in northern Chihuahuan Desert bird communities. Pp. 579–90 *in* Transactions of the Symposium on the Biological Resources of the Chihuahuan Desert Region, United States and Mexico. Edited by R. H. Wauer and D. H. Riskind. U.S. National Park Service Transactions and Proceedings Series, no. 3. Washington: U.S. National Park Service.

Randall, D. 1986. Survival crisis at Meeteetse. Defenders Special Report, Defenders of Wildlife (January–February): 4–10.

Ratcliffe, D. A. 1986. Selection of important areas for conservation in Great Britain: The Nature Conservancy Council's approach. Pp. 136–59 in Wildlife Conservation Evaluation. Edited by M. B. Usher. London: Chapman and Hall.

Reading, R. P. 1991. Biological considerations for designing the north-central Montana prairie dog complex, an experimental population area for black-footed ferrets. Internal report, U.S. Bureau of Land Management, Malta, Mont.

———. 1993. Toward an endangered species reintroduction paradigm: A case study of the black-footed ferret. Ph.D. dissertation, Yale University, New Haven, Conn.

Reading, R. P., T. W. Clark, and S. R. Kellert. 1991. Towards an endangered species reintroduction paradigm. Endangered Species Update 8:1–4.

Reading, R. P., J. J. Grensten, S. R. Beissinger, and T. W. Clark. 1989. Attributes of black-tailed prairie dog colonies in north-central Montana, with management recommendations for the conservation of biodiversity. Pp. 13–28 in The Prairie Dog Ecosystem: Managing for Biodiversity. Edited by T. W. Clark, D. Hinckley, and T. Rich. Montana Bureau of Land Management Wildlife Technical Bulletin no. 2. Billings, Mont.: U.S. Bureau of Land Management.

Reading, R. P., and S. R. Kellert. 1993. Attitudes of Montanans toward a proposed black-footed ferret (Mustela nigripes) reintroduction, with special reference to ranchers. Conservation Biology 7:569–80.

Reading, R., and B. Miller. 1994. The black-footed ferret recovery program. Pp. 73–100 in Endangered Species Recovery: Finding the Lessons, Improving the Process. Edited by T. W. Clark, A. Clarke, and R. Reading. Covelo, Calif.: Island Press.

Reed, C. A. 1946. The copulatory behavior of small mammals. Journal of Comparative Psychology 39:185–206.

Renner, M. J. 1988. Learning during exploration: The role of behavioral topography during exploration in determining subsequent adaptive behavior. International Journal of Comparative Psychology 2:43–56.

Richardson, L., T. C. Clark, S. C. Forrest, and T. M. Campbell. 1986. Black-footed ferret recovery: A general discussion of some options and considerations. Great Basin Naturalist Memoirs 8:169–84.

———. 1987. Winter ecology of the black-footed ferrets at Meeteetse, Wyoming. American Midland Naturalist 117:225–39.

Ricklefs, R. E. 1979. Ecology. New York: Chiron Press.

Robina, M. A. 1960. Some features of the weasel (Mustela nivalis) ecology based on observations in the Moscow region. Bjulleten Otbel Biology 65:27–34.

Rogers, W. H. 1983. Energy and Natural Resources Law. 2d edition. St. Paul, Minn.: West Publishing.

Rohlf, D. J. 1988. The Endangered Species Act: A Guide to Its Protection and Implementation. Stanford, Calif.: Stanford Environmental Law Society.

———. 1991. Six biological reasons why the Endangered Species Act doesn't work—and what to do about it. Conservation Biology 5:273–82.

Rokeach, M. 1972. Beliefs, Attitudes, and Values: A Theory of Organization and Change. San Francisco: Josey-Bass.

Rosenweig, M. L. 1973. Evolution of the predator isocline. Evolution 27:81–87.

Rosenzweigh, M. R. 1979. Responsiveness of brain size to individual experience: Behavioral and evolutionary implications. Pp. 263–94 *in* Development and Evolution of Brain Size: Behavioral Implications. Edited by M. E. Hahn, C. Jensen, and B. C. Dudek. New York: Academic Press.

Russell, W. C., E. T. Thorne, R. Oakleaf, and J. D. Ballou. 1994. The genetic basis of black-footed ferret reintroduction. Conservation Biology 8:263–66.

Ryan, K. D. 1984. Hormonal correlates of photoperiod-induced puberty in a reflexive ovulator, the female ferret *(Mustela furo)*. Biology of Reproduction 31:925–35.

Ryder, O. A. 1988. Przewalski's horse—putting the wild horse back in the wild. Oryx 22:154–57.

Sagoff, M. 1980. On the preservation of species. Columbia Journal of Environmental Law 7:33.

Salwasser, H. 1990. Sustainability as a conservation paradigm. Conservation Biology 4:213–16.

Sampson, F. B., and F. L. Knopf. 1982. In search of a diversity ethic for wildlife management. Transactions of the North American Wildlife and Natural Resources Conference 47:421–31.

Sandell, M. 1984. To have or not to have delayed implantation: The example of the weasel and the stoat. Oikos 42:123–26.

———. 1986. Movement patterns of male stoats *Mustela erminea* during the mating season: Differences in relation to social status. Oikos 47:63–70.

Schaller, G. B. 1993. The Last Panda. Chicago: University of Chicago Press.

Schaller, G. B., and J. T. Emlen. 1962. The ontogeny of avoidance behaviour in some precocial birds. Animal Behaviour 10:370–81.

Schladweiler, J. L., and J. R. Tester. 1972. Survival and behaviour of hand-reared mallards released into the wild. Journal of Wildlife Management 36:1118–27.

Schmidt-Nielsen, K. 1979. Animal Physiology: Adaptation and Environment. Cambridge: Cambridge University Press.

Schon, D. A. 1983. The Reflective Practitioner. New York: Basic Books.

Scott, J. M., and J. W. Carpenter. 1987. Release of captive-reared or translocated endangered birds: What do we need to know? Auk 104:540–45.

Scott, J. M., B. Csuti, J. D. Jacobi, and J. Estes. 1987. Species richness: A geographical approach to protecting future biodiversity. Bioscience 37:782–88.

Scott, J. P., and J. L. Fuller. 1965. Genetics and Social Behavior of the Dog. Chicago: University of Chicago Press.

Seal, U. S. 1978. The Noah's Ark problem: Multigenerational management of wild species in captivity. Pp. 303–14 *in* Endangered Birds: Management Techniques for Preserving Endangered Species. Edited by S. A. Temple. Madison: University of Wisconsin Press.

Seber, G. F. 1982. The Estimation of Animal Abundance. New York: Macmillan Publishing Co.

Segal, A. N. 1975. Post-natal growth, metabolism, and thermoregulation in the stoat. Soviet Journal of Ecology 6:28–32.

Shalter, M. D. 1984. Predator–prey behavior and habituation. Pp. 349–91 *in* Habituation, Sensitization, and Behavior. Edited by H. V. S. Peeke and L. Petrinovich. New York: Academic Press.

Sheets, R. G., R. L. Linder, and R. B. Dahlgren. 1971. Burrow systems of prairie dogs in South Dakota. Journal of Mammalogy 52:451–53.

———. 1972. Food habits of two litters of black-footed ferrets in South Dakota. American Midland Naturalist 87:249–51.

Shepherdson, D. 1993. The role of environmental enrichment in captive breeding and reintroduction of endangered species. Pp. 167–77 *in* Creative Conservation: Interactive Management of Wild and Captive Animals. Edited by P. J. S. Olney, G. M. Mace, and A. T. C. Feistner. London: Chapman and Hall.

Sieg, C. H. 1988. Small mammals: Pests or vital components of the ecosystem? Pp. 123–24 *in* Eighth Great Plains Wildlife Damage Control Workshop Proceedings, 28–30 April 1987 (Rapid City, S.Dak.). U.S. Forest Service General Technical Report RM-154. Washington: U.S. Forest Service.

Siford, T. D. 1982. Mink *(Mustela vison)* attacks trumpeter swan *(Cygnus buccinator)* cygnet. Canadian Field Naturalist 96:357–58.

Silver, R. 1978. The parental behavior of ring doves. American Scientist 66:209–15.

Sims, D. A. 1979. North American weasels: Resource utilization and distribution. Canadian Journal of Zoology 57:504–20.

Skinner, S. 1985. Black-footed ferrets "plagued" by columnists. Wyoming Wildlife (November): 36–37.

Smith, E. M. 1984. The Endangered Species Act and biological conservation. Southern California Law Review 57:361–413.

Smith, R. H. 1972. Wildness and domestication in *Mus musculus:* A behavioral analysis. Journal of Comparative and Physiological Psychology 79:22–29.

Smith, S. M. 1975. Innate recognition of coral snake pattern by a possible avian predator. Science 187:759–60.

Snyder, N. R. F., and H. A. Snyder. 1989. Biology and conservation of the California condor. Current Ornithology 6:175–267.

Soulé, M. E. 1983. What do we really know about extinction? Pp. 11–24 *in* Genetics and Conservation. Edited by C. M. Schonewald-Cox, S. M. Chambers, B. MacBryde, and L. Thomas. Menlo Park, Calif.: Benjamin Cummings.

Soulé, M. E., M. Gilpin, W. Conway, and T. Foose. 1986. The millennium ark: How long a voyage, how many staterooms, how many passengers. Zoo Biology 5:101–13.

Stanley Price, M. R. 1986. The reintroduction of the Arabian oryx *(Oryx leucoryx)* into Oman. International Zoo Yearbook 24–25:179–88.

———. 1989. Animal Reintroduction: The Arabian Oryx in Oman. Cambridge: Cambridge University Press.

———. 1991. A review of mammal reintroductions, and the role of the Reintroduction

Specialist Group of IUCN/SSC. Pp. 9–25 *in* Beyond Captive Breeding: Re-introducing Endangered Mammals to the Wild. Edited by J. H. W. Gipps. Oxford: Clarendon Press.

Strickland, D. 1983. Ferret update. Wyoming Wildlife (March): 4–6.

Strickland, M. A., C. W. Douglas, M. Novak, and N. P. Hunziger. 1982. Marten. Pp. 599–612 *in* Wild Mammals of North America. Edited by J. A. Chapman and G. A. Feldhamer. Baltimore: Johns Hopkins University Press.

Stroganov, S. U. 1962. Carnivorous Mammals of Siberia. Moscow: Academy of Science of the USSR. Jerusalem: Israeli Program Scientific Translations, Siberian Branch.

Stromberg, M. R., R. L. Rayburn, and T. W. Clark. 1983. Black-footed ferret energy requirements: An energy balance estimate. Journal of Wildlife Management 47:67–73.

Summers, C. A., and R. L. Linder. 1978. Food habits of the blacktailed prairie dog in western South Dakota. Journal of Range Management 31:134–36.

Symons, D. 1978. Play and Aggression: A Study of Rhesus Monkeys. New York: Columbia University Press.

Tan, P. L., and J. J. Counsilman. 1985. The influence of weaning on prey-catching behavior in kittens. Zeitschrift für Tierpsychologie 70:148–64.

Tanner, W. W. 1985. Snakes of western Chihuahua. Great Basin Naturalist 45:615–75.

Tear, T. H., and D. Forester. 1992. Role of social theory in reintroduction planning: A case study of the Arabian oryx in Oman. Society and Natural Resources 5:359–74.

Templeton, A. R. 1986. Coadaptation and outbreeding depression. Pp. 105–16 *in* Conservation Biology. Edited by M. E. Soulé. Sunderland, Mass.: Sinauer Associates.

———. 1990. The role of genetics in captive breeding and reintroduction for species conservation. Endangered Species Update 8:14–17.

Terborgh, J., and B. Winter. 1980. Some causes of extinction. Pp. 119–33 *in* Conservation Biology: An Evolutionary Perspective. Edited by M. E. Soulé and B. A. Wilcox. Sunderland, Mass.: Sinauer Associates.

Tessler, A., and D. R. Shaffer. 1990. Attitudes and attitude change. Annual Review of Psychology 41:479–523.

Thorne, E. T. 1987. Captive propagation of the black-footed ferret in Wyoming. Pp. 419–24 *in* AAZPA (American Association of Zoological Parks and Aquariums) Regional Conference Proceedings. Syracuse, N.Y.: AAZPA Publications.

Thorne, E. T., and B. Oakleaf. 1991. Species rescue for captive breeding: Black-footed ferret as an example. Pp. 241–61 *in* Beyond Captive Breeding: Re-introducing Endangered Mammals to the Wild. Edited by J. H. W. Gipps. Oxford: Clarendon Press.

Thorne, E. T., and E. S. Williams. 1988. Disease and endangered species: The black-footed ferret as a recent example. Conservation Biology 2:66–74.

Thornhill, R. 1984. Fighting and assessment in *Harpobitticus* scorpionflies. Evolution 38:204–14.

Tileston, J. V., and R. R. Lechleitner. 1966. Some comparisons of the black-tailed and white-tailed prairie dogs in north central Colorado. American Midland Naturalist 75:292–316.

Tinbergen, N. 1968. On war and peace in animals and man. Science 160:1411–18.

Tober, J. A. 1989. Wildlife and the Public Interest: Nonprofit Organizations and Federal Wildlife Policy. New York: Praeger Publishers.

Tschetter, B. J. 1988. Estimates of South Dakota prairie dog acreages, 1987. South Dakota Department of Game, Fish, and Parks Report no. 88.01. Pierre: South Dakota Department of Game, Fish, and Parks.

Turnell, J. 1985. The private landowner perspective. Pp. 6.1–6.3 *in* Black-Footed Ferret Workshop Proceedings, 18–19 September 1984 (Laramie, Wyo.). Edited by S. H. Anderson and D. B. Inkley. Cheyenne: Wyoming Game and Fish Department.

Ubico, S. R., G. O. Maupin, K. A. Fagerstone, and R. G. McLean. 1988. A plague epizootic in white-tailed prairie dogs *(Cynomys leucurus)* of Meeteetse, Wyoming. Journal of Wildlife Diseases 24:399–406.

Uresk, D. W. 1987. Relation of black-tailed prairie dogs and control programs to vegetation, livestock, and wildlife. Pp. 312–23 *in* Integrated Pest Management on Rangeland. Edited by J. L. Capinera. Boulder, Colo.: Westview Press.

Uresk, D. W., and A. J. Bjugstad. 1983. Prairie dogs as ecosystem regulators on the northern high plains. Pp. 91–94 *in* Proceedings of the Seventh North American Prairie Conference, 4–6 August 1980 (Southwest Missouri State University, Springfield).

Uresk, D. W., and D. B. Paulson. 1989. Estimated carrying capacity for cattle competing with prairie dogs and forage utilization in western South Dakota. Pp. 387–90 *in* Symposium on Management of Amphibians, Reptiles, and Small Mammals in North America, 19–21 July 1988 (Flagstaff, Ariz.). U.S. Forest Service General Technical Report RM-166. Washington: U.S. Forest Service.

U.S. Fish and Wildlife Service. 1985. Red-Cockaded Woodpecker Recovery Plan. Atlanta: U.S. Fish and Wildlife Service.

———. 1988. Black-Footed Ferret Recovery Plan. Denver: U.S. Fish and Wildlife Service.

———. 1990. Strategy for block clearance of prairie dog colonies and complexes. Internal report, 1 December 1990, U.S. Fish and Wildlife Service, Denver.

———. 1992. Federal and State Endangered Species Expenditures: Fiscal Year 1991. Washington: U.S. Fish and Wildlife Service.

U.S. General Accounting Office. 1988a. More Emphasis Needed on Declining and Overstocked Grazing Allotments. GAO/RCED-88-80. Washington: U.S. General Accounting Office.

———. 1988b. Endangered Species: Management Improvements Could Enhance Recovery Program. GAO/RCED-89-5. Washington: U.S. General Accounting Office.

———. 1989. Spotted Owl Petition Evaluation Beset by Problems. GAO/RCED-89-79. Washington: U.S. General Accounting Office.

———. 1992. Endangered Species Act: Types and Number of Implementing Actions. GAO/RCED-92-131BR. Washington: U.S. General Accounting Office.

Vale, T. R. 1975. Report to the Bureau of Land Management on range conditions and grazing in Nevada. Biological Conservation 8:257–60.

Van Horne, B. 1983. Density as a misleading indicator of habitat quality. Journal of Wildlife Management 47:893–901.

Vargas, A. 1994. Ontogeny of the endangered black-footed ferret *(Mustela nigripes)* and effects of captive upbringing on predatory behavior and post-release survival for reintroduction. Ph.D. dissertation, University of Wyoming, Laramie.

Vaughan, T. A. 1978. Mammalogy. Philadelphia: W. B. Saunders Press.

Verbeek, N. A. M. 1985. Behavioral interactions between avian predators and their avian prey: Play behavior or robbing? Zeitschrift für Tierpsychologie 67:204–14.

Vermeij, G. J. 1982. Unsuccessful predation and evolution. American Naturalist 120: 701–20.

Vogel, S., C. P. Ellington, and D. L. Kilgore. 1973. Wind induced ventilation of the burrows of the prairie dog *(Cynomys ludovicianus)*. Journal of Comparative Physiology 85:1–14.

Volchanetskii, I. 1931. Gefangenschtsbeobachtungen am Steppeniltis *(Putorius eversmanni* Less). Zoologische Garten, Leipzig 7:262–73.

Volkman, J. M. 1992. Making room in the Ark: The Endangered Species Act and the Columbia River basin. Environment 34:18.

Wallace, M. 1990. The California condor: Current efforts for its recovery. Endangered Species Update 8:32–35.

Wallace, M. P., and S. A. Temple. 1987. Releasing captive-reared Andean condors to the wild. Journal of Wildlife Management 51:541–50.

Walters, J. R. 1991. Application of ecological principles to the management of endangered species: The case of the red-cockaded woodpecker. Annual Review of Ecology and Systematics 22:505–23.

Warnock, B. H. 1977. Impressions of Chihuahua plant life. Pp. xv–xvii *in* Transactions of the Symposium on the Biological Resources of the Chihuahuan Desert Region, United States and Mexico. Edited by R. H. Wauer and D. H. Riskind. U.S. National Park Service Transactions and Proceedings Series, no. 3. Washington: U.S. National Park Service.

Warwick, D. 1975. A Theory of Public Bureaucracy: Politics, Personality, and Organization in the State Department. Cambridge: Harvard University Press.

Waser, P. M., and W. T. Jones. 1983. Natal philopatry among solitary mammals. Quarterly Review of Biology 58:355–90.

Wauer, R. H., and D. H. Riskind, editors. 1977. Transactions of the Symposium on the Biological Resources of the Chihuahuan Desert Region, United States and Mexico. U.S. National Park Service Transactions and Proceedings Series, no. 3. Washington: U.S. National Park Service.

Weinberg, D. 1986. Decline and fall of the black-footed ferret. Natural History (February): 63–69.

Welbergen, P., F. R. Van Dijken, and W. Scharloo. 1987. Collation of the courtship behaviour of the sympatric species *Drosophila melanogaster* and *Drosophila simulans*. Behaviour 101:253–74.

Wemmer, C. 1985. Black-footed ferret management and research: Views of a zoo biologist. Pp. 31.1–31.10 *in* Black-Footed Ferret Workshop Proceedings, 18–19 September

1984 (Laramie, Wyo.). Edited by S. H. Anderson and D. B. Inkley. Cheyenne: Wyoming Game and Fish Department.

Wemmer, C., and S. Derrickson. 1987. Reintroduction: The zoologist's dream. Pp. 48–65 in AAZPA (American Association of Zoological Parks and Aquariums) Annual Proceedings. Wheeling, W.Va.: AAZPA.

Western, D. 1989. Conservation without parks: Wildlife in the rural landscape. Pp. 158–65 in Conservation for the Twenty-First Century. Edited by D. Western and M. Pearl. New York: Oxford University Press.

Wilcox, B. A. 1980. Insular ecology and conservation. Pp. 95–117 in Conservation Biology: An Evolutionary Perspective. Edited by M. E. Soulé and B. A. Wilcox. Sunderland, Mass.: Sinauer Associates.

Wilcox, B. A., and D. D. Murphy. 1985. Conservation strategy: The effects of fragmentation on extinction. American Naturalist 125:879–87.

Wildt, D. E., and K. Goodrowe. 1989. The potential of applying embryo technology to the black-footed ferret. Pp. 160–76 in Conservation Biology of the Black-Footed Ferret. Edited by U. S. Seal, E. T. Thorne, S. H. Anderson, and M. A. Bogan. New Haven, Conn.: Yale University Press.

Wiley, J. W., N. F. R. Snyder, and R. S. Gnam. 1992. Reintroduction as a conservation strategy for parrots. Pp. 165–200 in New World Parrots in Crisis: Solutions from Conservation Biology. Edited by S. R. Beissinger and N. R. F. Snyder. Washington: Smithsonian Institution Press.

Wiley, R. H. 1973. The strut display of male sage grouse: A fixed action pattern. Behaviour 47:129–52.

Wilkinson, C. F., and H. M. Anderson. 1985. Land and resource planning in the national forests. Oregon Law Review 64: 114, 171–73, 296.

Williams, C. F. 1976. Practical Guide to Laboratory Animals. St. Louis: C. V. Mosby Co.

Williams, E. S. 1982. Canine distemper. Pp. 10–13 in Diseases of Wildlife in Wyoming. Edited by E. T. Thorne, N. Kingston, W. R. Jolley, and R. C. Bergstrom. Cheyenne: Wyoming Game and Fish Department.

———. 1987. Disease survey of carnivores near Meeteetse. Pp. 93–106 in Endangered and Nongame Bird and Mammal Investigations: Nongame Annual Completion Report. Cheyenne: Wyoming Game and Fish Department.

———. 1990. Proposed survey for diseases of carnivores in the Conata/Badlands, South Dakota. Internal proposal, Wyoming State Veterinary Laboratory, University of Wyoming, Laramie.

Williams, E. S., E. T. Thorne, M. J. G. Appel, and D. W. Belitsky. 1988. Canine distemper in black-footed ferrets (Mustela nigripes) in Wyoming. Journal of Wildlife Diseases 24:385–98.

Wilson, E. O., editor. 1988. Biodiversity. Washington: National Academy Press.

Witteman, G. L., R. E. Beck, S. L. Pimm, and S. R. Derrickson. 1990. The decline and restoration of the Guam rail, Rallus ownstoni. Endangered Species Update 8:36–39.

Wustehuße, C. 1960. Beiträge zur Kenntnis besonders des Spiel und Beutefangverhaltens einheimischer Musteliden. Zeitschrift für Tierpsychologie 17:579–613.

Wyoming Game and Fish Department. 1986. Recommendations for the capture of black-footed ferrets to enhance the captive breeding program. Internal report, Wyoming Game and Fish Department, Cheyenne.

———. 1987. A strategic plan for the management of black-footed ferrets in Wyoming. Internal report, Wyoming Game and Fish Department, Cheyenne.

Yaffee, S. L. 1982. Prohibitive Policy: Implementing the Endangered Species Act. Cambridge: MIT Press.

Youngman, P. M. 1982. Distribution and systematics of the European mink, *Mustela lutreola* Linnaeus 1761. Acta Zoologica Fennica 166:1–48.

INDEX

Page numbers followed by *f* indicate a figure; *t* after a page number indicates a table.